PROTECTOR OF THE FAITH

PROTECTOR
OF THE
FAITH

**CARDINAL JOHANNES DE TURRECREMATA
AND THE DEFENSE OF THE
INSTITUTIONAL CHURCH**

**by
Thomas M. Izbicki**

The Catholic University of America Press
Washington, D.C.

Library of Congress Cataloging in Publication Data

Izbicki, Thomas M.
    Protector of the faith.

    Bibliography: p.
    Includes index.
    1. Torquemada, Juan de, 1388-1468. 2. Catholic
Church—Government—History. 3. Church—History of doc-
trines—Middle Ages, 600-1500. I. Title.
BX4705.T69I93   282′.092′4   81-1400
ISBN 0-8132-0558-1   AACR2.

To my parents, who first fostered my interest in history.

CONTENTS

PREFACE

Catholic historians have often described the conciliar era (1413–50) in melodramatic terms. The Council of Constance (1414–18) healed one schism but opened the way for another. The Council of Basel (1431–49) was the villain of the piece; it tried, unsuccessfully, to usurp papal prerogatives. Heroic roles have been assigned to defenders of the Roman primacy: Nicholas of Cusa was called "the Hercules of the Eugenians"; the sobriquets "defender of the faith" or "protector of the faith" have been assigned to the Dominican cardinal Johannes de Turrecremata.[1] In fact, papalist historians have produced a distorted picture of Turrecremata's career, dissolving the outlines of his personality and intellect into the image of a single-minded champion of papal absolutism. Such an approach leaves open only one question: to what extent was Turrecremata a precursor of the First Vatican Council?[2]

Recent scholarship has raised serious questions about this portrait. One notable challenge has been the demonstration that Turrecremata's papalism did not spring full grown from his forehead. Born into the Great Schism, and a participant in the Council of Constance, Turrecremata initially shared many conciliarist ideas common in his day. He arrived at his highly influential refutation of them only after years of struggle and hard labor.[3] Moreover, new light has been cast on Turrecremata's entire career, highlighting the breadth of his interests; the Dominican cardinal was an active reformer, an opponent of heresy, and a patron of the arts, as well as a papal apologist.[4]

In certain respects, none of these recent works does justice to Turrecremata's ecclesiology, his doctrine of the nature and government of the Church. Certainly, no one work explores all the riches of cardinal's thought.[5] The best and most comprehensive recent studies, those of Karl Binder, tend to summarize the *Summa de ecclesia* and to treat the cardinal's doctrines as agreeing always with modern Roman Catholicism.[6] A different problem appears in the works of Antony Black, who has discussed Turrecremata's thought in almost purely political terms. Such an analysis omits a crucial dimension of Turrecremata's ecclesiology, namely, his lively concern with the Church's saving mission; no study that ignores this basically religious aspect can be deemed nearly accurate.[7] The present book attempts to steer between these two poles, presenting a balanced assessment of Turrecremata's ecclesiology within a chronological framework. Primarily institutional questions will be raised, those concerned with the defense of the visible Church and of papal power. However, each answer will consider the spiritual dimension of the problems treated, even when purely spiritual matters are allocated less space in the text. Only thus can we hope to comprehend the doctrines of one of the papacy's greatest apologists, a figure whose authority has been invoked in discussions of the Roman primacy to the present day. Indeed, an accurate understanding of Turrecremata's ecclesiology, with its matching concern for the right order of the institutional Church and the right discipline of clergy and laity, sheds light on the formation of the Catholic position that came to dominate the Counter-Reformation.[8]

The author accepts blame for any blunders he may have made, but he wishes to thank teachers, colleagues, and friends for their indispensable aid and support. Foremost among these is Professor Brian Tierney of Cornell University, who directed the doctoral thesis from which this volume derives. Subsequent drafts were written in Berkeley, where the author was a Robbins Fellow in the University of California Law School, and were retyped with patience and skill by María Elena Romo. Both at the Robbins Collection and in the Institute of Medieval Canon Law, Professor Stephan Kuttner created the atmosphere conducive to research and scholarly writing. Drafts of the book have been read by Mr. John Kenney, formerly of the Institute staff, Father John Hilary Martin, O.P., and, for the last go-around, Helen Rand Parish. Finally, the author particularly thanks Mrs. Leonardo Olschki and Professor Walter Ullmann. To the latter, despite disagreements, he owes a large intellectual debt.

Notre Dame, Indiana
December 1, 1980

ABBREVIATIONS

AFP   *Archivum Fratrum Praedicatorum*

Aquinas   *Sancti Thomae Aquinatis Doctoris Angelici opera omnia, iussu impensaque Leonis XIII P.M. Edita,* ed. Fratres Praedicatores (Rome, 1882–)

CSD   Johannes de Turrecremata, *Commentaria super Decreto,* 5 vols. (Venice, 1579)

DRta   *Deutsche Reichstagsakten,* vol. 13, ed. Gustave Beckmann (Stuttgart, 1925); vol. 14, ed. Helmut Weigel (Stuttgart, 1933)

Friedberg   *Corpus iuris canonici,* ed. Aemilius Friedberg, 2 vols. (Leipzig, 1879). References indicate volume, column, and alphabetical subdivision.

Haller   *Concilium Basiliense,* ed. Johannes Haller et al., 8 vols. (Basel, 1896–1936)

Mansi   Johannes Dominicus Mansi, ed., *Sacrorum conciliorum nova et amplissima collectio,* 53 vols. (Paris, 1901–27). References indicate volume and column.

MC   Antony Black, *Monarchy and Community* (Cambridge, 1970)

Rocaberti   Johannes Thomas Rocaberti de Pereleda, ed., *Bibliotheca maxima pontificia*, 21 vols. (Graz, 1969–70)

SE   Johannes de Turrecremata, *Summa de ecclesia una cum eiusdem Apparatu super decreto Papae Eugenii IV in Concilio Florentino de unione Graecorum emanato* (Venice, 1561). References indicate book, chapter, and folio.

WE   Karl Binder, *Wesen und Eigenschaften der Kirche bei Kardinal Juan de Torquemada O.P.* (Innsbruck, 1954)

Names are given in their best known form. Vatican manuscripts are cited by *fondo* and shelfmark, the name of the library being well understood.

Et primum offero Cardinalem Turrecremata, quem pontifex hoc epitheto honoravit, ut protector fidei diceretur propter illius librem catholicam doctrinam, quem edidit de poteste papae.

—Ambrosius Catharinus Politus

1
LIFE
AND
WORKS

At Three Councils: Serving Eugenius IV

A fortunate appointment in his twenty-eighth year thrust a young man who would become famous as Johannes de Turrecremata into the tug-of-war between councils and popes that was to dominate his era, his life, and his writings.

In October of 1416 Catherine of Lancaster, regent of Castile during the minority of her son Juan II, dispatched an embassy to the Council of Constance. Her decision to send envoys was the fruit of personal diplomacy by Sigismund of Luxemburg, king of the Romans, who persuaded her to renounce allegiance to Benedict XIII, Avignon claimant to the papal throne. Among the members of this embassy was Luis de Valladolid, Dominican provincial of Castile and Juan II's confessor.[1] Fray Luis's travelling companion was a young friar named Juan de Torquemada, son of Alvaro de Torquemada, a Castilian nobleman in royal service; henceforth we shall call this friar, according to tradition, by the Latin version of his name. Born in Valladolid in 1388 at the height of the Schism, Johannes de Turrecremata had entered the Dominican convent of San Pablo de Valladolid while still an adolescent. And there, fortunately, Turrecremata's exemplary conduct and keen mind came to the attention of his superiors, including Luis de Valladolid.[2]

The ambassadors of Castile, including this young Dominican, reached Constance on March 30, 1417, and presented their credentials four days later. After prolonged negotiations, a Spanish nation was formed on equal footing with the others in the council, the French, German, English, and Italian nations. In June of 1417 Turrecremata was incorporated into the council as a junior member of the new Spanish nation and as such participated in the conclusion of its historic work.[3] By that time the council was far advanced in its appointed tasks of reunification, reform, and defense of the faith. The fathers had already issued the decree *Haec sancta* with its claim that the council's powers were given to it by Christ, had deposed the Pisan pope, John XXIII, and had accepted the resignation of the Roman claimant, Gregory XII. The assembly had also issued a posthumous condemnation of John Wyclyf and sent John Hus to the stake.[4] And on July 26, 1417, the council, now composed of representatives of all three obediences in the Schism, deposed Benedict XIII. Prolonged negotiations between the nations now produced an agreement that some reforms should be enacted before, and some after, the election of a new pope. Accordingly, on October 5, 1417, the assembly enacted five reform decrees, the most important of which, *Frequens,* provided for a regular series of general councils to oversee the government of the Church. A conclave composed of cardinals and representatives of the nations then elected Odo Colonna pope to reign over a reunited Christendom as Martin V. On March 20, 1418, a second series of reform decrees was enacted. In a closing session, on April 22, 1418, Pope Martin affirmed his acceptance of all decrees enacted *conciliariter* at Constance, without indicating explicitly whether this affirmation included *Haec sancta* and *Frequens.*[5]

After the council adjourned, Turrecremata's superiors sent him to the Dominican convent in Paris to study theology, a fitting preparation for his future career. At that time the University of Paris was the intellectual center of the conciliar movement. Among its masters and students were such future leaders of the Council of Basel as Thomas de Courcelles and the Dominican John of Ragusa. At the same university, Turrecremata acquired the erudition he would later use in opposition to that council. Turrecremata received his licentiate in theology on March 3, 1424, and became a master on February 16, 1425. He then returned to Castile, where he served as prior of San Pablo de Valladolid and San Pedro Martir in Toledo; in this interval, he may also have been engaged in the teaching of theology.[6]

Turrecremata served as prior until he was drawn once again, in a more important role, into the theater of great ecclesiastical events. In 1431 he represented the Castilian Dominicans at the order's general chapter in Lyons, where he helped the reforming party retain Master General Texier. Texier promptly named Turrecremata and the provincial of the observant Lombard congregation Johannes de Montenegro, along with John of Ragusa and four other friars, to represent the order at a forthcoming council.[7]

The Council of Basel was the second ecclesiastical assembly called by Martin V on the timetable established in the decree *Frequens*. Despite grumbling about the failure of the preceding Council of Pavia-Siena to reform the Church, the momentous Council of Basel had an inauspicious beginning. It became viable only through a combination of circumstances: the decision of its president, Cardinal Cesarini, to open negotiations with the Hussites; an attempt by Martin V's successor, Eugenius IV, to transfer the assembly to Bologna for a later meeting with the Greeks; and the new pope's political misfortunes in Italy. Clerics of all ranks and representatives of princes frequented Basel in increasing numbers, discussing reform of the Church in head and members.[8] France was one of the European powers quickest to fish these troubled waters; where France led, Castile followed. Juan II took advantage of Turrecremata's impending departure for Basel to name the friar his official observer at the council, a gesture that implied but a limited degree of approval. Thus, Turrecremata was primarily a royal envoy when he was incorporated into the Council of Basel on August 30, 1432. As we shall see, however, he never lost sight of his order's interests and soon recalled its traditional loyalty to the pope. Turrecremata began his residence in Basel by offering the fathers, on behalf of Juan II, a word of caution, unheeded by an assembly bent on forcing the pope to recognize its legitimate existence.[9]

In the autumn of 1432 the council girded itself for action, assigning its chief work, not to the member nations, who were subject to control by the princes, but to four deputations. These organs of the council, composed of members of each nation, were concerned with faith, peace, reform, and other matters. Membership in these deputations was open to all clerics, which delivered control into the hands of the lower clergy. The Council of Basel was the one exception in ecclesiastical history to the rule that prelates were the chief members of a general council, whatever the role of popes, princes, or clerics. Indeed, these lesser clergy would carry the Council of Basel to extremes that eventually disgraced the conciliar movement.

Under this novel regime, Turrecremata became a Spanish member of the reform deputation.[10] In that role he took a hard line against corruption, even as he opposed council excesses. Turrecremata spoke for the deputation concerning the execution of reform decrees; he also served on special commissions on simony, liturgy, reunion with the Greeks, and the proposed canonization of Peter of Luxemburg.[11] These actions reveal his complex attitude toward the council. As a royal agent, Turrecremata was supposed to discourage confrontation between council and pope, a duty consonant with a mendicant friar's interest in the privileges the pope had given the Dominicans and similar orders. Yet, his work on the reform deputation reveals a sincere interest in rooting abuses out of the ecclesiastical institution. At first Turrecremata hoped to balance out these interests. Such was the import of a sermon he delivered to the fathers on the feast of Saint Ambrose (December 7, 1432), exhorting them to combine zeal for reform with loyalty to Rome.[12]

Turrecremata's preaching seems to have fallen on deaf ears. The council was already committed, with grudging papal approval, to a series of theological debates against the Hussites on their chief points of disagreement with Roman orthodoxy. The Bohemian delegation, including representatives of all factions in the Hussite movement, reached Basel on January 4, 1433. These delegates refused to take the oath of incorporation, which would have bound them to accept the council's decisions. Moreover, they stood their ground in debates with such Catholic champions as John of Ragusa and Juan Polemar. This failure of orthodoxy to vanquish heresy moved Turrecremata to intervene with more zeal than tact. On February 6, 1433, John of

Ragusa entered the hall of the Basel Dominican convent to answer the arguments on the eucharist put forward by John Rockycana, the Utraquist archbishop of Prague—and found there a table of reference works for the defense of orthodoxy, which Turrecremata had set up. Although the Catholic spokesman angrily ordered the table removed—it was a reminder of Ragusa's own failures—this act established Turrecremata as a zealous defender of orthodoxy on whom the fathers might depend in difficult theological controversies.[13] Failing to win over the Hussites by debating with them, the council entrusted the Bohemian question to skilled negotiators like Polemar, who might reach an accommodation with the moderate among the heretics.

The council then turned its attention to reform, in May of 1433 the reform deputation drafting a decree to curtail the role of the papacy in the selection of bishops and abbots. This was done in response to persistent criticism that the papacy had virtually abolished the ancient practice of electing the church's prelates. The fathers decided that so important a measure required public discussion. On June 6, 1433, the reform deputation selected Turrecremata to attack the decree and one Dionysius Parisiensis to defend it.[14] While the two prepared to debate, however, the decree was modified to win wider acceptance and the debate cancelled. Undaunted, Turrecremata produced a pamphlet in which he asserted that the council could reform the Church but not meddle with papal prerogatives, which would cause scandal. This attempt to moderate the council's actions failed entirely; on July 13, 1433, the fathers enacted the proposed reform decree.[15]

Meanwhile, Pope Eugenius had fallen on evil days. His unsuccessful war against the Colonna family, the kin of his predecessor, had cost him control of the papal states; Rome itself became unsafe for him. The weakened pope was forced to temporize with the growing power of the council, and as early as February of 1433, Eugenius offered the fathers limited powers to negotiate with the Hussites. He tried next to bribe King Sigismund, who once more wished to direct a general council, by crowning him emperor. Then, in the spring of 1433, Eugenius tried to take control of the council by replacing its president, Cesarini, with a committee led by the canonists Juan de Mella and Panormitanus. But the fathers refused to let these legates share the presidency and, instead, threatened to depose the pope. Another legation, which was led by the archbishop of Taranto, was treated similarly. Eugenius found this combination of conciliar threats and local reverses too powerful to resist; in the bull *Dudum* (August 1, 1433) he conditionally approved the council's continuation and past acts. This did not satisfy the fathers, whom Cesarini barely restrained from further threats of deposition. Finally, Eugenius gave way entirely, issuing on December 14, 1433, a new version of *Dudum* that gave an unqualified approval to the acts of the council. (Eugenius was later to maintain that this was an invalid concession made under duress, and that he had mentally reserved his own rights from being affected by this concession.)[16]

Eugenius then nominated a new committee of presidents for the council, including Cardinals Cesarini, Albergati, and Cervantes, as well as the archbishop of Taranto. Wary of this change of papal policy, the fathers decided that the presidents should take the oath of incorporation into the council: they expected the committee to bind itself, and the pope by implication, to obey the decrees of both the assembly and the Council of Constance; nor would they allow it to direct the council's proceedings in a manner favorable to the pope. In a speech delivered on February 18, 1434, Turrecremata denied that the legates' oath could bind the pope, whereas John of Segovia, a Salamancan theologian, defended the proposal. Segovia's arguments carried the day, and the presidents took the oath, raising the council's prestige to a new height. Turrecremata's policy of moderation was ruined; thereafter, he spoke out as a conscious apologist for the papacy.[17] Eugenius rewarded Turrecremata by taking him into his service. In April of 1434 Turrecremata became master of the Sacred Palace, a post traditionally reserved for a Dominican, which involved oversight of preaching and studies at the papal court.[18]

In his new capacity, Turrecremata still worked zealously within the council for the defense of the faith. First, an internal dispute in the Bridgetine order was appealed to pope and council. During the hearing, one faction charged the monks of Vadstena, the chief house of the order, with ascribing near-Scriptural authority to the revelations of

their foundress, Saint Bridget of Sweden. In 1434, on behalf of the deputation for faith, Cardinal Cervantes asked
Turrecremata to study those revelations. The Dominican
decided that they were orthodox and worthy of devout
reading. The council concurred but warned the Vadstena
monks against valuing too highly a corpus of esoteric vi-
sions.[19] Then, in June of 1435, the council took up the case
of Agostino Favaroni, a leading light of the Augustinian
order, who had been accused of falling into Hussite errors
he had set out to refute. On behalf of the faith deputation,
Cardinal d'Aleman asked Turrecremata to examine Favaroni's works. While Turrecremata worked on these materials, the Italian nation asked for, and received, sole right
to hear the case. Accordingly, Turrecremata delivered to
the Italians a treatise in which he attacked Favaroni's errors:
on October 15, 1435, the Italian nation censured the Augustinian. Favaroni appealed this decision to Eugenius
who, for once in harmony with the council, ignored his
appeal.[20]

Turrecremata was drawn also into the long-standing debate on the doctrine of the Immaculate Conception. Opposition to this doctrine had long been common among
Dominicans, which often left them vulnerable to criticism
by the Franciscans and the secular clergy. On December
8, 1435, the feast of the Immaculate Conception was celebrated at Basel; a theological controversy at once ensued,
and on March 23, 1436, Cardinal d'Aleman found it necessary to launch a formal inquiry. Johannes de Romeyo,
a secular cleric, and Petrus de Porqueri, a Franciscan, were
appointed to defend the doctrine, with Johannes de Montenegro and Turrecremata as their opponents. In April the
defense of the doctrine passed into the abler hands of John
of Segovia, who vanquished Montenegro in open debate.
Proceedings were then adjourned because Turrecremata
had not completed his thorough study of the doctrine. In
March of 1437, while the council was deeply involved in
negotiations with the Hussites and the Greeks, Turrecremata finally announced that he was prepared to debate the
Marian question. The presidents replied that the council
was now too occupied with other business; so Turrecremata
set aside the materials he had gathered. When the council
defined the doctrine of the Immaculate Conception on

September 17, 1439, however, Turrecremata issued his
tract as a counterblast. (John of Segovia later charged in
his history of the council that his old opponent had attacked
the doctrine of the Church; nevertheless, the Basel definition, issued while the council was already at war with the
pope, was never accepted by theologians.)[21]

A constant background to these events was the council's
continued negotiations with the Hussities. Juan Polemar
and his colleagues discovered that the moderates were willing to concede many points if the council would permit
communion under both species. These negotiations exacerbated divisions within the Hussite movement: extremists
rejected all talk of compromise, while moderates responded
vigorously. The end result was the battle of Lipany (May
30, 1434), in which the extremists, led by Prokop the Bald,
were crushed. This victory allowed the moderates to negotiate more confidently with the Basel assembly. An agreement was finally reached at Iglau in Moravia (1436) that
made the Utraquists an autonomous body within the Catholic Church. The laity was allowed the chalice, but other
Hussite demands were watered down to the point of the
innocuous. These compacts allowed Emperor Sigismund,
whose reign had spanned the entire Hussite crisis, to regain
the Bohemian throne for the last months of his life.[22]
Nevertheless, the compacts did not solve all outstanding
problems between Hussites and Catholics (nor were they
solved by the eve of the Reformation), and negotiations
between Utraquists and Basel continued.

Some of the council fathers, particularly the Dominicans,
were unhappy with the concessions already made. They
asked Turrecremata to refute the Utraquists' errors concerning the eucharist. Turrecremata's tract (completed in
December of 1436) denied that it was necessary for the
laity to receive communion under both species and foreshadowed the reaction of the papacy to the compacts: an
unswerving resistance to making any concessions to heretics. The papacy always sought to persuade the rulers of
Bohemia to become orthodox and compel their subjects to
do likewise.[23] On January 4, 1437, Turrecremata joined
Juan Polemar in a formal condemnation of the errors of
Peter Payne.[24]

New friction had developed in 1435 between pope and

council over reform and over negotiations with the Greeks for reunion of the universal Church. At first, reform dominated the assembly's proceedings. On January 22, 1435, regulations concerning clerical celibacy and judicial procedures were enacted; on June 9 liturgical abuses were censured. These decrees were consonant with Turrecremata's idea of reform. In June of 1435, however, the council abolished—without compensation—the elaborate system of fees which financed the Roman curia.[25] Tension between pope and council mounted; factions began to form in Basel supporting or opposing the curtailment of papal power. Thus, in November of 1435, and again in March of 1436, Turrecremata persuaded the reform deputation to reject proposals which would have prevented appeals to Rome from decisions of councils. This was Turrecremata's one significant victory over the more radical element in the council.[26] Yet, the main thrust of the proceedings remained antipapal. Thus, on March 25, 1436, the assembly enacted a thorough reorganization of the curia and papal elections. Turrecremata protested in vain the provision that required a pope-elect to swear that he would obey conciliar decrees. Turrecremata's tracts in this period had a querulous tone; for the first time he questioned the validity of the decree *Haec sancta*, in which he came to see the seeds of an ecclesiastical revolution.[27]

The proceedings of the council became heated. Turrecremata's defense of the Roman see drew much criticism upon him and his order. This was one factor behind the secular clergy's renewal, in 1436, of the old demand that the friars be stripped of their privileges. Johannes de Montenegro was the chief spokesman of the friars in the ensuing debates; Turrecremata also spoke for the Dominicans *tamquam vicarius generalis*. One secular cleric, the Paris master John Beaupere, took the occasion to criticize Turrecremata personally. Such arguments made inevitable an irreconcilable rift in the Basel assembly.[28]

The fatal rift was caused by negotiations with the Greeks over the site of a council of reunion. A majority of the fathers, led by Cardinal d'Aleman, wanted the Greeks to travel beyond the Alps; the minority, led by Cardinals Cesarini and Cervantes, was willing to go to Italy. Turrecremata became a member of the latter party, whose ideas were agreeable to both the pope and the Greeks. The minority made its first unsuccessful proposal of an Italian site on December 5, 1436.[29] The two factions began to quarrel openly, leading to a rupture on May 7, 1437, when each approved a decree approving contradictory sites for a council with the Greeks. When the Greeks reached agreement with Pope Eugenius on an Italian site, Cesarini and his supporters began to leave Basel to participate in the new council.[30] Cesarini's decision to leave Basel appears to have been based upon two concerns: his desire to promote Christian unity and his dislike of the growing radicalism of the assembly over which he was presiding. This concern caused the cardinal to turn for advice to Turrecremata, who produced for him a collection of excerpts from the works of Aquinas that supported papal power against conciliar pretensions. Cesarini's receptiveness to papalist doctrines in this crucial period also points toward the revival of pro-papal ecclesiological doctrines in the mid-quattrocento, a revival whose chief figure would be Johannes de Turrecremata.[31]

When the Greeks left Constantinople on November 27, 1437, on gallies chartered by the pope, Turrecremata had already left Basel to help Eugenius IV prepare for the new council. Turrecremata and Giovanni Aurispa, the papal secretary, were sent to Castile in an attempt to win the support of Juan II. Caught between the arguments of the pope's representatives and pressure from France, Juan II temporized, instructing his envoy at Basel, Rodrigo Sánchez de Arévalo, to work for peace between pope and council but refusing to send an official representative to the Council of Ferrara.[32] When Turrecremata and Aurispa reached Ferrara to report to the pope, the new council had already opened in defiance of a prohibition issued at Basel. Turrecremata, never loath to defend Roman orthodoxy, joined Cesarini in the earliest debate of the council in defending the doctrine of Purgatory.[33]

While the Greeks and Latins discussed doctrine at Ferrara, the Council of Basel discussed the deposition of Eugenius IV. Although the princes of Europe were displeased with the possibility of another schism, some of them, most notably Charles VII of France, chose neutrality in the struggle between pope and council in order to barter potential adherence to either party for concessions of increased control of their local clergy. The result was a diplomatic struggle in which papal and conciliar legations argued their respective cases before assemblies of princes and notables at the same time that they conducted negotiations on the details of possible concordats. One of the first of these diplomatic battles took place before a meeting of the imperial Diet at Nuremburg in 1438. Eugenius sent Cardinal Albergati to Germany with a suite that included Turrecremata and Nicholas of Cusa. The Germans listened politely to speeches for both parties but refused to support either one.[34] A meeting of the German princes was scheduled to be held at Frankfurt in March of 1439 in order to hold further discussions on the struggle between pope and council. Albergati, who was returning to Italy, left behind the archbishop of Taranto, Turrecremata, and the legist Giovanni Francesco di Capodalista to attend the meeting in Frankfurt. Turrecremata spent the winter in Nuremberg, turning a draft of an undelivered address into a pamphlet that foreshadowed the attack on conciliarism contained in his later works.[35]

Plague broke out in Frankfurt, forcing the princes' meeting to move to Mainz. There it opened on March 21, 1439, without the presence of the papal legates, who remained at Nuremberg due to a dispute over their letters of safe conduct. Nicholas of Cusa represented the pope unofficially, replying to Basel's representative, John of Segovia. The ambassadors of France and Castile urged that the electors help organize a council at a neutral site, which would absorb the rival assemblies and resolve their differences. The princes issued the Acceptatio of Mainz, which, like the French Pragmatic Sanction of Bourges, accepted Basel's reform decrees without taking its part against the pope. By April, when the papal legates finally reached Mainz, most of the dignitaries had departed. In a public audience for those who remained, first Turrecremata, and then Capodalista pleaded the Eugenian cause. Turrecremata's brief speech described himself and his colleagues as representatives of the infallible pope. This was the first time that Turrecremata ever made this claim for the Roman pontiff; nor was such a papalist concept dear to his German listeners. Turrecremata's speech at Mainz therefore won

Eugenius no friends in that time of crisis. Disappointed, the legates returned to Italy.[36]

When in the spring of 1439 Turrecremata reached Florence, the new site of the council, negotiations for union had reached a critical stage. Debates over the doctrine of the Trinity had convinced Bessarion of Nicaea and Isidore of Kiev that the Greek and Latin Fathers were in substantial agreement on the doctrine of the Trinity. This resolved, as far as they were concerned, the old debate over the relationship of the Spirit with the Father and Son (the *filioque* controversy). Moreover, John VIII was eager to bring these negotiations to a successful conclusion; he needed Western aid to protect Constantinople from the Turks.[37] A last set of debates on other issues was due to begin. Johannes de Montenegro, who had been the chief Dominican spokesman during Turrecramata's absence, was selected to defend papal power. Turrecremata himself was selected to defend Latin eucharistic practices. When these debates were held on June 16 and June 18, 1439, the Latin spokesmen ably upheld the practices of the Roman Church. Finally the Greeks, with the notable exception of Mark Eugenicus, declared themselves satisfied. On June 26, 1439, a commission was selected to draw up a decree of union. Among its members were Bessarion, Isidore, Cesarini, Montenegro, and Turrecremata. Finally, on July 5, 1439, the council promulgated the decree of union *Laetantur coeli*. Although this ecclesiastical reunion proved short lived, it was a major triumph for Eugenius IV, whose works of peace stood in stark contrast with the schism being inaugurated by the Council of Basal.[38]

Even while the Council of Florence concluded its negotiations with the Greeks, the Council of Basel had decided to take definitive action against Eugenius IV, who had convoked the rival assembly. Some prelates and ambassadors present at Basel, notably the canonist Panormitanus, representing the House of Aragon, tried to prevent the assembly from deposing the pope. But d'Aleman and his supporters, most of them members of the lower clerical ranks, were adamant. On May 16, 1439, they voted to depose Eugenius, a sentence published on June 25, little more than a week before the solemn promulgation of the bull of union *Laetantur coeli*. The Council of Basel then created an electoral college, which chose as pope Duke Amadeus VIII of Savoy, who became Felix V. Once more Western Christendom was confronted with the spectacle of two contending claims to the papal throne.[39] When Pope Eugenius took notice of the decree of deposition, he did so forcefully. In the bull *Moyses* (September 5, 1439), the pope declared all past concessions null and void, since the Basel assembly had extracted them under duress. Eugenius attacked even the decree *Haec sancta,* on which the Council of Basel had based its acts. Eugenius described *Haec sancta* as a decree issued by only one obedience present at Constance, that of John XXIII. *Haec sancta* was thus not the decree of a general council and so could not be invoked to justify any act. To underline this point, Eugenius staged a debate on the problem of papal relations with councils. Turrecremata defended the pope; Cesarini, the council. Turrecremata made a frontal assault on conciliarism, using the pope's argument against the validity of *Haec sancta* to help prove that the pope, not a general council, was that agent of Christ which ruled over the Church. At the conclusion of the debate, Cesarini owned himself convinced by his opponent while Pope Eugenius hailed Turrecremata as "defender of the faith."[40] A more tangible reward was bestowed on December 18, 1439, when the pope created new cardinals. Among those promoted were the archbishop of Taranto, Bessarion, Isidore, the French bishop Guillaume d'Estoutville, and Johannes de Turrecremata, who became known, from the name of the first titular church, as the cardinal of San Sisto.[41] But the Dominican was not in Florence to receive his red hat.

Eugenius had sent Turrecremata as ambassador to Charles VII of France, with the nominal duty of making peace between England and France but the real task of winning French support for Eugenius against the Council of Basel. The Estates General was supposed to meet at Bourges to consider, among other business, the new schism. Turrecremata and his fellow legates travelled to that city, but the meeting was delayed while the king subdued the Praguerie, a revolt of nobles led by the Dauphin Louis.[42] The legates made good use of the time they spent waiting at Bourges. Basel had recently replied to the bull *Moyses* and elected a new pope, Felix V (November, 1439). This aged widower of pious repute now attempted to take control of the council, an act which produced new dissension, and even named his own college of cardinals. For his part, Turrecremata spent the winter composing a reply to the council's censure of Eugenius's bull. In his tract he pointed to the election of Felix and the other acts of the Basel assembly as acts of rebels against the legitimate authority of the true pope. This defense of legitimate authority remained the rallying cry of the Eugenians till the end of the Schism. While Turrecremata wrote, an assistant, Peter of Versailles, worked to win the good will of the bishop of Bourges. Thus, when the legation from Basel, led by John of Segovia, reached Bourges, it found its papal counterpart well entrenched.[43] And when Charles VII reached Bourges in August of 1440, the papal legates appealed to him to support the pope, a fellow monarch, against open rebellion by the Council of Basel, which was an astutely designed form of argument. The king, still shaken by the Praguerie revolt, listened readily to the papalists' arguments and to Turrecremata's reminder that Eugenius had supported the claim of the king's brother-in-law, René of Anjou, to the throne of Naples. On September 2, 1440, Charles rewarded the labors of the legates by acknowledging Eugenius IV as the true pope. Although he still talked of a third site for a council and refused to revoke the Pragmatic Sanction, Charles eventually made a choice. While French support for the Council of Basel slipped away, Juan II of Castile readily recalled Arévalo from Basel. England and Burgundy had already sided with the pope; Aragon and Milan would soon come to terms with Eugenius, leaving only the German princes as supporters of the council. Turrecremata's role in this papalist diplomatic success earned him Eugenius's utmost confidence. His mission in France accomplished, Turrecremata returned to Italy, entering Florence on November 24, 1440.[44]

Charles VII did make one last attempt to promote the idea of a neutral site for a council, an attempt blocked, however, by Turrecremata. In the winter of 1440–41, the French king sent Turrecremata's erstwhile colleague Peter of Versailles to Florence bearing a petition for the choice of a neutral site that questioned the very validity of the Council of Florence. Eugenius named Cardinals Cesarini,

Capranica, and Turrecremata commissioners to deal with this petition. The Dominican cardinal, in the name of this commission, delivered a crushing response to the French proposal, which was never revived by the king or his agents.[45] Turrecremata then composed a gloss on *Laetantur coeli* that demonstrated the validity of the Council of Florence while it underlined its most important achievement.[46]

Meanwhile the Council of Florence, with Turrecremata's participation, was making further progress toward reunion with the Eastern churches. Turrecremata played a key role in successful negotiations with the Coptic Church.[47] Eugenius tried to send aid to the Greeks and, on March 1, 1442, named Cesarini legate for a crusade against the Turks in the Balkans. The pope hoped to secure the support of Bohemia for this project and at the same time convert the Hussites to Roman orthodoxy. Accordingly, Turrecremata composed a tract intended to promote this twofold policy by refuting Hussite errors. The Bohemians, however, ignored both this essay in religious propaganda and the crusade itself. Without Bohemian assistance Cesarini and the king of Poland led an army into the Balkans, but, after some initial success, their force was routed by the Turks at Varna (1444), where Cesarini perished.[48]

Meanwhile Turrecremata resumed work for the reform of the Church. The cardinal's experiences at Basel had forced him to shift his attention from general reform, which had come to smack of revolution, to the reordering of local religious communities.[49] Turrecremata set these communities an example by himself adhering to the Dominican rule. Even after promotion to the cardinalate, he continued to wear the habit and read the office of his order.[50] Only in 1442, after his mission to France, did Turrecremata find time to concentrate on local reforms. In that year the monk Arsenius, a leader of the Santa Justina congregation of reformed Benedictines, appealed to Turrecremata for aid and advice. The cardinal responded by composing a commentary on the Benedictine rule to guide Arsenius's work of reform.[51]

Orthodoxy also concerned Turrecremata in these years. By 1443 conditions were ripe for Eugenius to move southward from Florence. In June, while at Siena, the pope took cognizance of charges of heresy against the Salamancan

theologian Alfonso Tostado de Madrigal, whose loyalty to
Eugenius was as suspect as his doctrines were. Tostado was
forced to expound his doctrines before Cardinals John of
Taranto, Turrecremata, and Capranica. Turrecremata
took a deep interest in the affair, producing a tract which
censured Tostado on several points, particularly his doctrine of the forgiveness of sins. For the time being, the
accused submitted to this judgment. On his return to Castile, however, Tostado denounced the proceedings at Siena
as unjust and won the support of Juan II of Castile; the
pope therefore let the matter rest. Three years later Tostado became bishop of Avila, a post in which he served
well.[52]

Afterwards, in September of 1443, Eugenius IV returned in triumph to Rome, the city he had fled almost a
decade before. Eugenius could well afford to celebrate his
return from exile. The Council of Basel was weak and
divided; it seemed only a matter of time before the Germans, too, must abandon that now enfeebled assembly and
come to terms with the pope.[53] Under these circumstances
Turrecremata was able to retire from the field of diplomacy, and in 1446 Eugenius rewarded him with a new
titular church, the basilica of Santa Maria in Trastevere.[54]

In the meantime, those younger diplomats—Nicholas of
Cusa, Thomas of Sarzana, and Juan Carvajal—labored long
and arduously to win the German princes to the Eugenian
cause. At times their efforts were impeded by the pope's
own actions, such as his attempt to depose certain hostile
ecclesiastics from their sees. But on February 14, 1446,
Frederick III, king of the Romans, agreed to support Pope
Eugenius on the condition that German grievances were
redressed. Carvajal and Thomas of Sarzana, accompanied
by Aeneas Silvius Piccolomini (a former supporter of the
Council of Basel who had entered Frederick's service), travelled to Rome to win papal support for this agreement,
whereupon Eugenius appointed a commission of cardinals
to scrutinize its terms. Three of its members, Johannes de
Turrecremata, John of Taranto, and Alonso Borgia, Cardinal of Valencia, deemed excessive the concessions made
by the legates. But Eugenius IV, now mortally ill and wish-
ing to die as head of a united Church, had already guaranteed ratification in naming to the commission Cardinals

Le Jeune and Capranica, as well as Thomas of Sarzana and Carvajal, themselves new members of the Sacred College. The cause of unity at any price proved triumphant at a meeting held on January 7, 1447. On February 14 Eugenius's assent to these terms was formally given, and nine days later the ailing pontiff breathed his last.[55]

Service under Later Popes

Thomas of Sarzana, who succeeded Eugenius IV as Nicholas V (1447–55), would finally bring peace to the Church. First, the German princes made peace with Rome. King Frederick signed the Concordat of Vienna (1448), which promised him, in return for his support of the new pope, the right to fill certain lucrative benefices with his own servants. Without German support, or at least neutrality, the Council of Basel was finished. It had already dwindled to a shadow of its former self, holding its sessions in Lausanne since the city of Basel was plague-ridden. The council now decided to bow out gracefully by "electing" Thomas of Sarzana as pope and dissolving itself. Felix V, long at odds with the Council of Basel, also came to terms and abdicated in return for recognition as a cardinal. Nicholas V was likewise magnanimous with the erstwhile leaders of the council. He received d'Aleman back into the College of Cardinals and confirmed the promotions of several of Felix V's cardinals. Other conciliarists, including John of Segovia, were given benefices and allowed to retire.[56]

Although he had been a key supporter of Nicholas's election, actually casting the deciding vote, Turrecremata inevitably played a less prominent role in this pontificate than in the last; Nicholas's reign was a time of reconciliation, not of heroic struggle. But the Cardinal of San Sisto was by no means idle. One notable instance of Turrecremata's activities involved his native Castile, where the old Christians, supposedly of pure Spanish blood, hated the New Christians for their success as much as for their bloodlines. The *conversos,* or *marranos,* of Jewish blood, had risen high in the Church, the government, and the professions. Resentment towards them boiled over at Toledo in 1449, where a riot against royal taxes became a persecution of *conversos* because one of them was serving as a tax collector. Hoping to focus attention on the *conversos* and away from himself, Alvaro de Luna, Juan II's favorite, fanned the flames. He employed a propagandist named Pedro Sarmiento to accuse the *conversos*, even before the king himself, of remaining crypto-Jews. On June 5, 1449, John II deprived the Toledo *conversos* of their legal rights in that city.[57] News of this decision angered responsible churchmen, including Cardinal Turrecremata. Perhaps influenced by the cardinal, Nicholas issued the bull *Humani generis*, which quashed the offensive law. But under Castilian pressure the pope withdrew the bull—a decision that prevented neither the overthrow of Alvaro de Luna by the nobility nor Turrecremata's denunciation of Sarmiento (1450) for having propounded the heretical idea that no Jew could become a good Christian, a clear denial of the efficacy of baptism.[58] Thereafter, speculation became rife as to whether the Torquemadas were of Jewish origin. The *conversos* were eager to claim so eminent a churchman as one of their own; the Dominicans thought otherwise. Such gossip, it seems, left Turrecremata unmoved but may have influenced the future conduct of his nephew Tomás de Torquemada, the famous inquisitor.[59]

During Nicholas's reign Turrecremata, less active now, fortunately had leisure to write lengthy works. The cardinal began his most important labor, the composition of a coherent defense of the institutional Church and its head, the pope. Ecclesiological ideas adumbrated in his polemical tracts were now fully developed in a series of books. The work first begun but last completed was a commentary on Gratian's *Decretum*, a book that had provided conciliarists with many of their key proof texts, as had the most famous of the glosses on those texts. Turrecremata decided that it was incumbent upon him to correct those canonistic doctrines which conflicted with his papalist concept of the Church.[60] But this project almost failed at the outset. Turrecremata, who had always cited canon law in his polemical tracts, found the composition of a formal commentary difficult beyond expectation. Lacking a legal education, he became hopelessly entangled in Gratian's discussion of the principles of law. So, on the advice of friends, Turrecremata turned to the tracts *De consecratione* and *De poenitentia*, the most theological portions of the *Decretum,* completing his commentaries in 1449 and dedicating them to Nicholas V. The project was then halted by illness.[61]

When Turrecremata recovered his health, he began two new, but related, works. One, completed in 1451, was a reordering of the *Decretum* along the lines of the Gregorian decretals. This labor gave Turrecremata a stronger grasp of canon law, of which he later made effective use.[62] Then, in 1453, he composed his most famous work, *Summa de ecclesia.* This was by no means the first treatise on the nature and government of the Church; however, it was the most comprehensive medieval synthesis of ecclesiological doctrines acceptable to Rome. Turrecremata grounded his system on theological (particularly Thomistic) principles, which he applied to practical questions with well-chosen citations from canon law.[63] This exposition of doctrine was coupled with criticism of the enemies of the Roman Church. Turrecremata denounced conciliarism as a fruit of the antipapal writings of Marsilius of Padua and William of Ockham, a charge which has survived till the present day. Turrecremata also attacked the Hussites, whom he placed in company with the Lollards as latter-day Waldensians.[64]

During these years of residence in Rome, Turrecremata worked even more energetically for ecclesiastical reform. He tried to implant in his native Castile those ideals discussed in his commentary on the Benedictine rule. In this struggle his allies were two successive priors of San Benito de Valladolid, Garcia de Frias and Juan de Gumiel. Turrecremata used his influence with Eugenius IV and Nicholas V to force Castilian monasteries, among them San Claudio de Leon, San Salvador de Oña, and Sahagún, to join a congregation of observant Benedictines. On the practical side, Turrecremata also contributed funds for the upkeep of reformed monasteries.[65]

In 1445 Turrecremata decided to increase the endowment of his home convent, San Pablo de Valladolid. But disquieting reports reached him that its friars were ill-disciplined and its buildings in disrepair. So, in 1449 he persuaded Pope Nicholas to cancel all illegal contracts made by the friars and then began work for the reform and repair of the convent. He hoped to make San Pablo a Castilian center for the Dominican observant movement, a hope realized only after long labors lasting well into the reign of Pius II.[66] Turrecremata also took a more general interest in the affairs of his order. Although he was not its cardinal protector, he represented the Order of Preachers at the curia and worked to obtain indulgences for the friars, defend those involved in theological controversies, and procure the canonization of saintly members of the order. In return Turrecremata expected the Dominicans to follow his advice. Thus, he felt free to tell the general chapter of 1450 what qualities to look for in a possible successor to Master General Texier; likewise, he rebuked Master General Auribelli (elected in 1453) for setting a bad example in undermining the autonomy of the Lombard congregation of observants[67] (in 1462 Turrecremata was to be instrumental in Pius II's deposition of Auribelli).

Cardinal Turrecremata did serve as cardinal protector of another order. Upon the death of Cardinal Cervantes in 1453, Pope Nicholas named Turrecremata his successor as protector of the Camaldolese. The new protector embarked on a reform campaign, an effort which culminated in two sets of reform decrees. Those enacted by a general chapter at Pisa in 1457 made the order's program of studies more rigorous; those enacted at Pontebuono in 1459 imposed stricter discipline on the monks. Although not entirely successful, these efforts were a step toward the general renovation of discipline that would be accomplished by the end of the century.[68]

The last years of Nicholas V's reign were overshadowed by the Turkish menace, a threat that would ultimately bring Turrecremata back into world affairs. Despite the pope's efforts to send aid, the Ottoman sultan, Mehmed II, took Constantinople on May 29, 1453. The last Byzantine emperor, Constantine XI, died defending the city; the papal legate, Isidore of Kiev, barely escaped with his life; and the tenuous bond of East-West union, forged at Florence, was snapped. Nicholas tried to retrieve this situation by calling for a crusade, an appeal that was largely ignored. When Nicholas died on March 24, 1455, Turks were threatening Serbia, Bosnia, and Albania, three Christian strongholds in the Balkans.[69]

To continue work for a crusade the cardinals chose Al-

fonso Borgia, who, as Pope Calixtus III (1455–58), achieved
but limited success against the Turks. Calixtus also worked
toward a peace in Europe as a whole that would enable
him to mobilize its resources for a crusade. Thus, he recognized the Utraquist George Podiebrad as king of Bohemia, under the terms of an agreement drafted by Aeneas
Silvius Piccolomini, who had been made a cardinal. Piccolomini had been deeply moved by the fall of Constantinople and would spare no effort to see the Turks punished.
But owing to a misunderstanding, the agreement intended
to mobilize Bohemian resources for a crusade proved detrimental rather than helpful to the cause. The pope
thought the king had promised to revoke the Basel compacts, whereas King George thought the agreement ratified
Utraquist privileges. The resulting quarrel over religious
policy outlived both men and left Bohemia too divided to
wage war on the Turks. Aside from its failure to further
the crusade, Calixtus's reign proved largely detrimental to
the welfare of Christendom. The Borgia pope, shortly after
his election, abrogated the "capitulations" he had signed
in conclave, giving the cardinals a larger share in the powers
and revenues of the Roman see, an action resented by many
cardinals, including Domenico Capranica. The always latent tension between papal power and the pretensions of
the cardinals was thus transformed into an open and long-
lived conflict. Calixtus exacerbated the rift by filling lucrative posts with his fellow Catalans, and the angered Romans
openly took sides with the aggrieved cardinals. Further,
Calixtus proved to be a blatant nepotist, making his worldly
nephew Rodrigo Borgia, the later Alexander VI, a cardinal
and vice-chancellor of the Roman Church.[70]

In contrast to all this disharmony, slim evidence does
suggest that Calixtus and Turrecremata worked together
reasonably well.[71] On April 24, 1955, the pope named Turrecremata administrator of the cardinalatial see of Palestrina, vacated by the recent death of John of Taranto.[72] In
the same year Calixtus made Turrecremata abbot *in com-
mendam* of Subiaco. (The cardinal found the abbey in disrepair and its Benedictine monks in need of reform, defects
he remedied before placing the abbey under direct papal
supervision. Six years later Pius II would visit Subiaco at
Turrecremata's request and find it a model monastery.)[73]

Perhaps it was to escape curial squabbles that Turrecremata now resumed earnest labor on his *Decretum* commentary, turning it into a companion to the *Summa de ecclesia*. Commentary on key texts in the former was cross-referenced to expositions of fundamental doctrines in the latter, each work butressing its companion. In 1457 he completed his volume of commentary on the *Distinctions*, which he dedicated to Calixtus. [74]

Upon Calixtus's death in 1458, Cardinal Turrecremata was plunged into the drama of electing a new pope, this time on the losing side. The Romans had rioted and driven the Catalans out of the city; while the cardinals waited out this storm, speculation was rife about the identity of the next pope, for the death of the acknowledged favorite, Cardinal Capranica, had left the field wide open. Although rumors mentioned Johannes de Turrecremata, he showed no desire to occupy the see whose dignity and prerogatives he had so long defended. Nor was Turrecremata an ecclesiastical politican who would garner votes by fair means or foul.[75] He soon joined one of the two factions (both dominated by the usual political chicanery) in search of a pope able to conduct a crusade. As a contender Aeneas Silvius Piccolomini had the support of most of the Italians and of opportunists like Rodrigo Borgia. The worldly Cardinal d'Estoutville, on the other hand, had the support of the French interest, of those willing to believe his promises of preferment, and of the most ardent advocates of a crusade—Bessarion, Isidore of Kiev, and Turrecremata—who considered Piccolomini too crippled by gout to bear the burden of office. Of the two contenders Piccolomini proved the more adroit politician, winning over the more timid or greedy of d'Estoutville's faction while playing on the fears of the Italians that a French pope would remove himself to Avignon. When the election of Piccolomini began to seem inevitable, his opponents tried to disrupt the conclave: Turrecremata and Isidore stalked out of the hall on the excuse of a call of nature but returned quickly when no one followed them; Bessarion tried to gag Cardinal Colonna when he rose to cast the deciding vote. Despite such rash acts, Piccolomini ascended the papal throne as Pius II (1458–64).[76]

Nevertheless, Turrecremata's anti-Turkish policy soon

elevated him in the councils of the new pope. Pius promptly made peace with the more worthy of his recent opponents by avowing an interest in promoting a crusade, which pleased Turrecremata as well as the Greeks.[77] The pope expected to achieve his goal by gathering the princes at Mantua to settle their differences and prepare for war against the Turks. Turrecremata, whom Pius made cardinal bishop of Palestrina,[78] worked fervently for the success of this congress. In the winter of 1458–59 he wrote a tract that pilloried Moslem errors such as they were commonly understood at the time. In strong language Turrecremata repeated the hackneyed charge that Mohammed was a false prophet influenced by Nestorian errors. Other age-old charges of false doctrine and immorality were trotted out to rouse the fervor of Christians for war against the infidels.[79] Pius II, interested in arousing such sentiments, preferred Turrecremata's repetition of old charges to the more enlightened views of John of Segovia and Nicholas of Cusa, who advocated dialogue with Islam.[80]

Pius chose Turrecremata and five other cardinals to accompany him to Mantua. They reached Florence just when the saintly archbishop of the city, the Dominican observant Antoninus, was on his deathbed. In Mantua the Pope found few princes represented. Philip of Burgundy alone was eager for a crusade; other representatives straggled in and offered various excuses for their lack of crusading fervor. The pope's entourage became discouraged and discontented; among the cardinals only Turrecremata and Bessarion consistently supported Pius's crusade policy.[81] Tired of listening to excuses, Pius formally declared war on the Turks in January of 1460. He also lashed out at one of his critics, Diether von Isenberg, the archbishop-elect of Mainz. Pius had expected Diether, in return for confirmation of his election, to pay excessive fees and promise never to call for a new council; Diether flatly refused, demanding that the imperial Diet take strong measures against the pope and dismissing the crusade as an excuse for taxing the Germans. Pius replied in the bull *Execrabilis*, which condemned appeals from pope to council. Thus, this former adherent of the Council of Basel issued the strongest anticonciliar pronouncement to appear in Turrecremata's lifetime.[82]

Following the Congress of Mantua, Pius II became embroiled in European politics, which included his bitter struggle with Sigismondo Malatesta.[83] The pope never lost interest in the crusading ideal, however, and leaned heavily on Turrecremata's aid and counsel. Pius dramatized this goal in a formal reception for the relic of the head of Saint Andrew and even wrote a letter to Sultan Mehmed II (apparently it never was delivered) in which he promised to make Mehmed a true emperor if he would become a Catholic. Pius's understanding of Muslim errors, which he asked the sultan to renounce, apparently derived from Turrecremata's tract against the Turks, and not from one of the more enlightened authors like John of Segovia.[84]

Turrecremata played a more active role in church affairs in this period than he had in the last two pontificates, though he was painfully aware of his advancing years. In 1460 he expressed a desire to be freed from some of his duties; in 1462 he was too infirm to walk in the procession that conveyed the head of Saint Andrew to the Vatican.[85] In 1460, however, Pius named him to the see of León and thereby plunged him into a confrontation with the king of Castile. (Turrecremata had already held the sees of Cadiz [1440–42] and of Orense [1442–45].) But because he wanted León for a political ally, King Henry IV of Castile, the son of Juan II, favored the papal nuncio Antonio Veneris as bishop and prevented Turrecremata's agents from taking charge of the diocese. In vain the pope angrily denounced first the royal councillor Rodrigo Sánchez de Arévalo, then his own nuncio for misleading the king. Finally Turrecremata, who had kept a discrete silence throughout the whole affair, accepted a transfer back to the see of Orense (1463–66), and Veneris became bishop of León.[86]

In the meantime Turrecremata, like the pope, continued to work for a crusade against the Turks. King Stephen Thomas of Bosnia sought Pius's aid in repelling the infidels' advance. To reinforce his plea, he sent to Rome three Bogomil nobles, members of a Balkan Manichee sect, to be converted to Roman Catholicism and serve as pledges for his good faith and the good behavior of their fellow Bogomils in the coming war with the Turks. Pius asked Turrecremata to supervise the effort to convert these nobles.

The cardinal left the actual work of instruction to experts in the nobles' native tongue, Serbo-Croatian, while he composed a refutation of Manichean errors for use as a catechism. On May 9, 1461, the Bogomil nobles adjured their errors in a solemn ceremony at the Vatican. But their conversion had no impact in Bosnia. When the Turks crossed the border, the Bogomils ignored the call to arms, and, in 1463, the kingdom of Bosnia was overrun and its king beheaded.[87]

An even more sensational failure of papal diplomacy, also abetted by Turrecremata, contributed to the woes of Bohemia. Deeming that a united Bohemia might be assigned a major role in a crusade, the pope decided that the agreement he had arranged between his predecessor, Calixtus, and George Podiebrad ensured the conversion of the Utraquists to Roman orthodoxy. Accordingly he threatened to unilaterally revoke the Basel Compacts, the foundations of religious peace in Bohemia. Ambassadors of King George warned the pope in 1461 that such a step would provoke civil war in Bohemia. Pius and his cardinals received the envoys coldly; Carvajal, Cusa, Bessarion, and Turrecremata all advised them that obedience to the pope's commands was the only licit course of action. Podiebrad remained unconvinced. When the pope did revoke the compacts, the king tried to turn Europe against the Roman see, even suggesting that the princes conduct a crusade without papal authorization. One of Pius's last acts was a threat of excommunication against King George. In 1466 Paul II was to declare Podiebrad a deposed heretic, which resulted in a civil war that deepened the religious divisions of Bohemia.[88]

Contrasting with these diplomatic failures, Turrecremata's major successes at reform came during the reign of Pius II. The resistance to reform at San Pablo de Valladolid collapsed between 1459 and 1463 under pressure from Turrecremata, the cardinal's brother Pedro (a royal official), Master General Auribelli, and the pope himself. Thereafter San Pablo, together with the related college of San Gregorio, became a center for the reform of other convents. This work was speeded by a papal endowment for the convent, and Turrecremata himself funded construction and sent a gift of books. (In 1468, the year of

Turrecremata's death, Auribelli chartered a Castilian congregation of observants along the lines of the Lombard
congregation. Subsequent efforts made the Spanish Dominicans a vital religious community during an era of lax
ecclesiastical discipline, and in the sixteenth century they
would produce a Thomist revival and labor mightily in the
New World.)[89]

Contemporaneously with his work for San Pablo, Turrecremata in 1460 founded the Brotherhood of the Annunciation to dower poor girls so that they could marry
and not fall into sin. As its headquarters he chose the Dominican church of Santa Maria sopra Minerva in Rome (a
painting can still be seen there, in which Turrecremata
presents the dowered girls to the Virgin of the Annunciation).[90] Turrecremata had observed even earlier the phys-
ical decay and lax discipline in the Minerva convent, and
in 1461 Pius II authorized him to reform it without interference from Master General Auribelli. This reform project became an enthusiasm of Turrecremata's later years.
When discipline had been restored, he affiliated the convent with the observant Lombard congregation to ensure
the maintenance of order, took up residence at the Minerva,[91] and gave the church a rebuilt choir and a new
cloister ornamented with devotional paintings.[92]

Soon—through the new means of typography—these
paintings would be seen by many who had never gone to
Rome. The movable type process was diffused throughout
Europe by printers who had fled Germany during Pius II's
war against Diether von Isenberg; in 1465 Conrad von
Schweinheim and Arnold Pannartz settled at Turrecremata's own abbey of Subiaco and produced the first printing in Italy.[93] At once Turrecremata saw the value of the
medium. So, in 1466 he had printed in Germany a volume
of his *Meditationes*, devout reflections on the paintings in
the new cloister at the Minerva. And the following year he
hired another travelling German printer, Ulrich Han, to
print an illustrated copy of this work in Rome, the first
illustrated book published in Italy.[94] Parenthetically, the
Meditationes were not Turrecremata's first devotional work;
in May of 1463 he had completed a commentary on the
Psalms, a work with only slight ecclesiological overtones,
which he dedicated to Pius II. The pope returned the com-

pliment by naming Turrecremata successor to the recently deceased Isidore of Kiev as cardinal bishop of Sabina.[95]

Seriously ill by now, Pius II nevertheless made one final effort to launch a crusade. Though only Burgundy and Venice were truly interested, the pope himself took the cross and left Rome for Ancona, intending to embark there for the East. Turrecremata, too old to undertake the journey, pledged money for the support of the crusade; his enforced stay in Rome spared him the visual evidence of Pius' failure: the pope's tiny army, held together by his own will, never sailed from Ancona. On August 11, 1464, Nicholas of Cusa died while giving his last efforts to the cause, and on August 15 the pontiff breathed his last in that Adriatic port; his army dispersed, and Venice disbanded its fleet.[96]

When the conclave to name a successor opened in Rome, Turrecremata entered it in very poor health. Rumors circulated that he would be carried out either dead or pope. But the cardinals chose a younger man, Pietro Barbo, a nephew of Eugenius IV, who reigned as Paul II (1464–71).[97] Neither illness nor age had deprived Turrecremata of his wits, however. In 1464 he completed his commentary on the *Decretum*, dedicating the volumes on the *Causae* to the new pope. At last, Turrecremata had completed his systematic exposition of ecclesiological doctrines favorable to the Roman Church, a labor that well justified the title "defender of the faith" once bestowed on him by Eugenius IV.[98]

In his few remaining years, the aged cardinal was again plunged into controversy. In 1466 a report reached Paul II that Fraticelli were in central Italy, and the pope began proceedings against those extreme advocates of the Franciscan poverty ideal. Zealous churchmen began to write refutations of their errors; among them was Nicholas Palmericus, the Augustinian bishop of Orte, who went too far by casting doubt on the mendicant ideal of Christ's poverty. As a Dominican friar, Turrecremata felt called upon to reply and did so in two tracts pillorying Palmericus's ideas. To still this budding controversy between members of the curia, Paul II asked Turrecremata to write a treatise on the true relationship between poverty and perfection; after its completion, the doctrinal dispute was allowed to die out.[99]

Turrecremata's final polemical tract dealt, once more, with the affairs of Castile. Castilian nobles had rebelled against royal authority, rallying to a figurehead, Alfonso, the half-brother of King Henry IV. They claimed that they only wanted restoration of their ancient rights and that these rights were founded upon Roman law. In 1467 Henry's representative in Rome, Rodrigo Sánchez de Arévalo, replied by denying Roman law any place in the dispute. The Roman empire he insisted, had merely usurped royal rights; the empire of the present day had no power over Castile, which had stood alone against Moslem aggression; and in fact the Roman empire had only attained legitimacy by papal sanction. These arguments, touching on the ancient if fratricidal bond between emperor and pope, were controversial in the extreme; they were criticized by such authors as the curial referendary Dominicus de Dominicis. In 1468 Turrecremata, too, attacked Arévalo. The cardinal defended the legitimacy of the Roman empire, arguing that it had been founded by natural law on the consent of its subjects to its just rule. It had been valid in Christ's own day and needed no legitimization by the pope. (Turrecremata did agree with Arévalo that Castile, and France too, had won its independence by defeating the Moors.) Arévalo, for his part, refused to be drawn into a personal contest with the venerable (and irritable) Turrecremata, pretending insead that someone else had circulated specious arguments under Turrecremata's name.[100]

Despite these occasional polemical thunderings, which matched his occasional rages caused by gout, Cardinal Turrecremata began turning his mind to forms of religious thought higher than mere apologetics. After completing his work on the Psalms, he devised a series of scholastic questions on the Gospel texts in the liturgical lectionary and dedicated the work to Cardinal d'Estoutville. He then composed a mystical treatise inspired by devout reading of a feast day office, a tract which may well have been his very last work.[101] In 1468, knowing he was near death, Turrecremata donated his library to the Minerva convent. Then, virtually pen in hand, Cardinal Johannes de Turrecremata died on September 26, 1468. His body lies in a simple tomb in the Annunciation Chapel of Santa Maria sopra Minerva.[102]

Catholic historians have often eulogized this eminent churchman. What they say is largely true: Turrecremata was pious, zealous, brave, munificent, upright, no grasper for power. However, certain faults are not lost in the plaudits: Turrecremata was also stubborn, dogmatic, and harsh to the lax and erring. In old age, his gout made him irritable and hard to live with. His mind lacked the creative spark found in Cusa's works, the literary talent displayed by Pius II. Yet Turrecremata's achievement was considerable. Through hard work, carried often to excessive length, he mastered the literature of theology and canon law. No labor was too hard to undertake; no subject beneficial to the devout reader was left untouched. Turrecremata's great merit as a papal apologist consisted in never losing sight of the Church's saving mission amid the forest of authorities on whom he drew to build his doctrine of the Church. Thus, his chief works, the *Summa de ecclesia* and *Commentaria super decreto,* seem the writings of a moderate in comparison with those of preceding or subsequent generations of papal apologists.[103]

One true measure of a man is found in his dealings with his fellows. Here Turrecremata overshadows most of his contemporaries, having earned the respect of all the popes he served, even the somewhat cynical Pius II. His friends included such diverse figures as the learned Bessarion, the worldly d'Estoutville, the historian Flavio Biondo, the dedicated papal servant John of Taranto, and the holy Antoninus of Florence. Turrecremata also chose wisely and well when bestowing his patronage.[104] He readily saw the value of the new art of printing and employed its best practitioners; he gave aid to the humanist Giovanni Tortelli, the poet Juan de Mena, the painter Fra Angelico, and many lesser figures.[105]

In sum, Cardinal Turrecremata shone with a moral and intellectual light against the dark tapestry of his own times. By the later Middle Ages, the College of Cardinals had both achieved great power and earned harsh criticism. Many reformers sought to limit its size, wealth, and influence; general councils tried to keep the cardinals from controlling their own proceedings or (at Constance) the election of the one pope for all Christendom. In this conciliar epoch, however, the Sacred College recovered some prestige, numbering in its ranks such luminaries as Cesarini, Albergati, Capranica, d'Aleman, Isidore of Kiev, Bessarion, Cusa, and Turrecremata. These men did good works whenever possible and avoided the abuse of power (thus, Turrecremata limited his support of kinsmen and familiars).[106] But moral rot continued to take its toll with the promotion of papal kinsmen, royal favorites, and scions of noble Italian houses. By the reign of Pius II, who gave John Joffry the red hat solely to please Louis XI of France, even the cardinals thought they were deteriorating.[107] Matters worsened as the older generation of cardinals died out; after Turrecremata's death, only Carvajal, Bessarion, and d'Estoutville were left of the great names from past pontificates. After them, the College of Cardinals, though it boasted an occasional luminary, seemed to warrant the jibes of Erasmus and the diatribes of Luther.[108] This decline, and Turrecremata's contrasting presence, are well symbolized in one significant scene. On June 17, 1462, when Pius II celebrated Corpus Christi at Viterbo, members of the curia vied in lining the route of the solemn procession of the Host with spectacular tableaux. The most garish and displeasing was that staged by Cardinal Rodrigo Borgia, a depiction of Pope Pius as lord of the world. The most sober and reverent was that presented by Turrecremata, as described in the pope's own approving words:

> Next came [the tableau of] the Cardinal of San Sisto [Turrecremata]. As befitted his ecclesiastical dignity, he showed a representation of the Last Supper, with Christ and the disciples, and the institution of the Sacrament in memory of the Passion and the everlasting protection of mankind against the wiles of the devil to the end of time. And he had represented Saint Thomas Aquinas administering that holy and solemn Sacrament.[109]

2
THE
CHURCH AS
INSTITUTION

Membership: Congregatio Fidelium

When Johannes de Turrecremata wrote his masterpiece, the *Summa de ecclesia* (1449–53), he was confronted with two challenges: refuting the Hussites and overthrowing conciliarism.

The followers of Hus Turrecremata had first confronted directly when he intervened in John of Ragusa's debate with John Rockycana and later indirectly when he censured the opinions of Agostino Favaroni. Against the conciliarists Turrecremata had vented increasingly bitter criticism as he despaired of convincing the Council of Basel that reform could be combined with obedience to the pope. This two-fold attack upon current errors was no simple task, for conciliarism emphasized the corporate nature of the Church in direct contradiction to the Hussite emphasis on the in-visible community of saints. Turrecremata had therefore to defend the visible Church—while at the same time de-nying that the ecclesiastical institution, via a general council, should be allowed to judge the pope and limit the use of his governmental powers. Furthermore, Turrecremata had to steal orthodox thunder from the conciliarists, who in-cluded the anti-Lollard apologist Thomas Netter, and anti-Hussites, like his coreligionist John of Ragusa. Turrecre-mata did all this so effectively that his *Summa* superseded completely Ragusa's tract on the Church.[1]

A preliminary look is needed at the historico-doctrinal

31

context in which Turrecremata operated. The ferocious controversy between heretic and orthodox—whether conciliarist or papalist—over the nature of the Church stemmed partly from the fact that they drew different conclusions from the same Christians tradition. Indeed, in the Scriptures themselves one can find an unresolved ambiguity between the idea that the Church had room in its ranks for sinners and the belief that it was an elite or community of saints. The broader concept of the Church had its strongest base in gospel parables of the kingdom of heaven, where sinner and saint would remain intermixed till the Last Judgment. The elite concept of the Church rested on Pauline texts that described the Church as free of stain and wrinkle (Eph. 5:27); this inner elite of saints or elect made up the Mystical Body of Christ.[2]

The early Fathers never fully clarified the ambiguous status of sinners in the Church. Their ecclesiological doctrines were concerned with the inner elite united to Christ by charity as well as faith, rather than with the visible institution that numbered sinners among partakers in the sacraments. However, when confronted with rigorists like the Donatists, who wanted to purge the present Church of sinful members, Augustine and the other Fathers argued consistently that, at the final winnowing of souls, only God could separate the wheat from the chaff. Yet despite his response to the Donatists, Augustine thought the true "congregation of the faithful" (congregatio fidelium) was identical with the Mystical Body of Christ.[3]

This patristic emphasis on the Church's spiritual elite remained the primary doctrine down to scholastic times, when greater emphasis was placed on the membership of all baptized Christians (whatever their state of soul) in the congregation of the faithful. Confronted by Waldensian heretics who denied the visible institution any connection with the true invisible Church, scholastics began instead to emphasize that institution and equate it with the Mystical Body of Christ and the congregatio fidelium. Several currents of thought reinforced this institutional bent. A belief that the Church and its sinful members had fallen away from the primitive purity of apostolic times had always characterized reform movements. The Waldensians, who had begun as reformers within the ranks of the Church, now argued that the institution had abandoned its apostolic model for more temporal pursuits. Other dissidents, including the more radical Franciscans, took up similar ideas. Defenders of Roman orthodoxy responded by arguing that the primitive Church had actually embodied (in embryonic state) the present form of ecclesiastical institution.[4] Moreover, canonists built upon the medieval concept of the *congregatio fidelium* an entire body of doctrine on the Church's hierarchical structure and corporate nature. These juridical ideas about the Church coincided with arguments on ecclesiastical power by whole generations of publicists, who ascribed to the pope and the Church Militant perfections best ascribed to God and the Church Triumphant. Small wonder that reformers, whether orthodox or heterodox, viewed the law as the source of the Church's woes.[5]

These woes took a singularly painful form in the Schism, which, in creating two rival ecclesiastical governments, sundered the much prized unity of the visible Church. No one pope guarded both the faith and the union thought to be a mark of the true Church. Under these circumstances some theologians naturally began to question whether the true Church was not located elsewhere than in the visible institution. Both the Lollard and Hussite movements, though maintaining medieval emphasis on the sacraments, fell into heresy. Other churchmen, theologians and jurists, turned to the corporate doctrine of the Church for a solution to the Schism. They argued that the whole Church, via a general council, had power from Christ to end the Schism and begin a much-needed process of reform. Indeed, after the failure of the Council of Pisa, the Council of Constance did reunite the Church and enact some reform decrees. But the Council of Basel produced a new schism that cast doubt on the credibility of conciliarism. Into this breach stepped Turrecremata, who, having grown up during the Schism, promised to defend orthodoxy against Lollard and Hussite assaults while he guaranteed that the papacy would once more safeguard the unity of the Church.[6]

In his *Summa de ecclesia*, Turrecremata began by carefully reiterating the definition of the Church as the "congregation of the faithful." Initially he listed sixteen meanings of the term *ecclesia*, all of which could be found in theology or law. *Ecclesia* could signify things as diverse as the hierarchy, the elect, the totality of the blessed, or a gathering for prayers; each of these definitions had been employed by Aquinas or some other orthodox writer.[7] Intent on refuting Hussite heresy, however, Turrecremata affirmed the primacy of the term *congregatio fidelium*, the definition for the concept of the visible Church that had been used most often by late medieval apologists, because of its antiquity and juridical potential:

> It is the collectivity of all catholics or of the faithful . . . Or the Church is the totality of the faithful who assemble for the worship of the one true God through the profession of one faith. . . . The Church is the convocation of many for the worship of one God.[8]

Further, Turrecremata denied that there was any salvation outside this *congregatio fidelium*, the body of true believers worshiping the true God. Without faith, one could not receive the grace necessary to please God; without grace, not even the best works could save an infidel from damnation. This was a doctrine inherited from Augustine and other doctors, who had developed it as a counterweight to heresies like Pelagianism. (Boniface VIII had made a more political use of the doctrine, identifying the Roman obedience with the Church outside which there is no salvation.)[9] So Turrecremata considered salvation neither a private matter nor separable from the work of the visible Church. Since there was only one deposit of faith accepted and taught by the one Church, the believer must enter its ranks through baptism as the sign of adherence to the truth. The Christian became a member of the congregation of the faithful for his own good, communing with his brothers while worshiping the true God.[10] Baptism itself was a formal act, with a freight of grace and a load of institutional obligations, that made the Christian subject to the authority of the clergy: ministers of the sacraments, teachers of the truth, correctors of wrongful behaviour. Turrecremata accepted the reasoning of Aquinas and other Inquisition apologists that baptism legally bound the believer to remain orthodox. If he fell into heresy, the clergy could compel him, for his good and that of the community, to return to the true faith.[11] So much for faith, but what about works?

Turrecremata's "congregation of the faithful" was all-embracing, with room for sinners beside the saints. Wycliff and Hus, and orthodox reformers as well, had always pointed to discrepancies between the faith professed by members of the Church and their often sinful behavior.[12] Of course, Turrecremata knew that these criticisms were founded on fact; like John of Ragusa, he had to prove that the sinner was still a member of the holy Catholic Church. Thomas Aquinas had distinguished between "unformed faith," mere adherence to correct doctrine, and faith "formed" by charity, which is faith brought to its proper perfection. On this basis, Turrecremata argued that the baptized believer who did not pursue perfection was only nominally a member of the Church, a member "dry and dead." The living member displayed his health of soul by entering into a communion of true charity with his fellows, a union sealed by the outpouring of the Holy Spirit. Here Turrecremata followed Augustine in seeing charity as the inmost bond of the Church[13] The sacraments existed within the Church to promote this spirit or bond of charity. Like Aquinas, Turrecremata thought such union was most perfectly expressed in the sacrifice of the mass, where the faithful fed on the body and blood of Christ. Baptism was the gateway to this eucharistic feast; the other sacraments, particularly penance, promoted the sanctification of souls through absolution of sinners and special infusions of grace. So the truly penitent sinner could advance, with the aid of sacramental grace, to the communion of the saints, his faith, like theirs, being formed by true charity.[14]

Turrecremata's definition thus stressed the visible Church, to which all believers belonged whatever their state of grace, and in which all might receive the sacraments. An inner elite of souls transformed by charity was simply part of this "congregation of the faithful," not its totality or an opposing body. This doctrine contrasted sharply with Hussite doctrines of a true Church that was purely spiritual. And Turrecremata drove home the point by assimilating into his ecclesiological synthesis all the *notae ecclesiae* and the traditional biblical metaphors for the Church, including the Mystical Body of Christ—giving each a distinct institutional emphasis. (In further contradistinction to heretical groups, Turrecremata assigned to the ecclesiastical insti-

tution itself some characteristics of the true Church noted
by the Fathers in their polemics against these heretics.)
Parallel to his discussion of the *notae ecclesiae* Turrecremata
placed an Aristotelean discussion of the Church with exactly the same implications, upholding the ecclesiastical institution and assigning sinners a real place in its membership.

Turrecremata chose the classic list of *notae ecclesia* ("marks
of the Church") formulated by the First Council of Constantinople (381) and describing the Church as one, holy,
catholic, and apostolic. Although other versions existed, he
selected this list and gave it a specifically institutional point
of reference—without ignoring its other, more spiritual
implications.[15]

Both in tradition and in Turrecremata's discussion of
them, foremost among these marks of the Church was that
of unity. Cyprian had emphasized unity in order to combat
schismatic tendencies in the churches of Roman Africa.
Turrecremata saw the similar threat that the Church would
be fragmented by the errors of Hussites and Lollards and
the disobedience of conciliarists. Accordingly his discussion
of ecclesiastical unity is no dry theological argument, but
a passionate (if erudite) defense of a beloved institution by
a witness to the Schism and the Conciliar Crisis.[16] Turrecremata listed eight bonds of union among members of the
congregation of the faithful, each intertwining to create the
design of an institution divinely established as a means of
salvation for its members. Foremost of these bonds was the
role of Christ as head of all the Church. The Church expressed one faith in its divine head, a faith expressed in
the sacrament of baptism through which the believer came
to the other sacraments. All believers shared one hope of
salvation and were unified toward that end by a single,
vivifying bond of love or charity. The loving unity of this
body, called (from its true head) the Mystical Body of
Christ, was sealed by the outpouring of the Holy Spirit. So
it arrived at its one goal: eternal beaitutide.

In this unified system, a major part—often threatened
by Hussites and conciliarists—was assigned to the papacy.
Under the pope's visible presidency and unified government, the Church Militant operated on earth to achieve its
one saving goal.[17] Jesus himself had made Peter the Prince
of Apostles, arbiter of all divisive disputes among the faith-

ful, in order to safeguard the Church's unity. Without Peter's authority, handed down to his successors, the popes, the ecclesiastical institution would be wracked with schisms. Turrecremata went so far as to accuse the Greeks of an error of faith in rejecting the unifying supremacy of the bishop of Rome.[18] He also criticized others for this fault, denouncing Marsilius of Padua for describing the papacy as a superfluous human institution exalted by Constantine. (Wycliff and Hus had taken up much the same theme.) Turrecremata even thought, as we shall see, that there was a dangerous Marsilian element in conciliarism.[19] Against these critics of the papacy, Turrecremata reaffirmed the papalist doctrine defined in Boniface VIII's *Unam Sanctam* that submission to Rome is necessary for salvation: "Whoever is outside the Church of Peter, which is the Church of Christ, is not in the Church."[20]

Turrecremata's discussion of each of the other *notae ecclesiae* similarly emphasized the ecclesiastical institution and its saving work. The visible Church, with its sacraments and possession of the theological virtues, offered the means of sanctification; even the laws of this institution had a place in its saving labor, laws helping to conform the Church Militant to the image of the Church Triumpahnt.[21] Wycliff and Hus—envisioning a true Church of only the elect, living virtuous lives in grace—had objected to inclusion of any sinful believers in this holy body free of stain and wrinkle. Like the fathers at Constance, Turrecremata thought such ideas were a denial of the sanctity of the *congregatio fidelium* and a threat to the Church's saving work.[22] So he elaborated the old patristic argument, oft repeated by Catholic apologists, that the Church in its present state included sinners as well as saints. Indeed, the Church's main work in this world was to lead sinful believers to the perfection of charity, for sinners would be purged from the Church only at the Last Judgment—removing all stains and wrinkles and finally conforming the Church Militant to the image of the Church Triumphant.[24] For, as opposed to heretics and infidels, the Church had the universal (or catholic) truth, the universal remedy for human sinfulness. All men were called to the catholic community of believers and worshippers of God, cause and end of all things; the sacraments, with their ministers, were valuable everywhere for the good of souls; therefore, the Church was the universal or catholic means of salvation and sanctification.[24] The faith, doctrine, and worship of this Christian community were all of apostolic origin, founded, in particular, upon Peter and his successors. Peter's see was "the mother of sacerdotal dignity and the teacher of right understanding," the visible director of the Church's labors in this world.[25] Turrecremata's insistence on the apostolicity of the institution answered charges that the present state of the Church reflected a debasing pursuit of power and wealth.[26] Where Lollards and Hussites saw discontinuity between the primitive Church and the visible institution, Turrecremata saw continuity in the work of salvation from the days of Abel, the first man to live by faith, through Christ's saving mission and perfection of the Church, to his own day. Offices and dignities potentially present in the primitive Church had been fully developed for the work of saving souls—a labor not impeded by the continued presence of sinners in the congregation of the faithful.[27]

Turrecremata reached similar conclusions in his Aristotelean analysis of the Church, first presented in a censure of Agostino Favaroni's works and then amplified in the first book of his *Summa*. Once again, he focussed on the congregation of the faithful with its saving work and its sacraments. In this analysis, however, he placed less emphasis on the ministry of the clergy and more on the nature of the Church's mission in this world, underlining its role as a vehicle of salvation rather than as an end in itself. Thus, analyzing the Church in terms of Aristotle's four causes, Turrecremata described Christ as the efficient cause. The sacraments were secondary (or instrumental) efficient causes, enabled by virtue of Christ's Passion to promote the welfare of souls.[28] The material cause on which Christ and the sacraments worked was the body of the faithful, open to grace through belief.[29] The formal cause of the Church was the union of the faithful with their divine head, a relationship often described as the unity of the Mystical Body of Christ.[30] The Church did not exist as an end per se, having been founded for the perfection of all believers in this life that they might have eternal beatitude in the next. The clergy, led by the pope, served this end. They were not a cause in themselves, only servants of the final cause, acting in the best manner possible and without regard to the personal wishes of the faithful. This was particularly true of the chief servant, the Roman pontiff, who was not ordinarily responsibile to the Church for his conduct of office. Nonetheless, the Church's mission was the touchstone against which the pope's conduct of office could be measured objectively. Here, in the spiritual mission of the clergy, Turrecremata endeavored to establish bounds beyond which even the chief of the clergy, the pope, might not stray.[31]

In his tract against Favaroni, as in his *Summa* and other works, Turrecremata showed a medieval taste for symbolic language, elaborating on the meaning of each scriptural metaphor applicable to the Church. Like John of Ragusa, he interpreted each to portray a Church that granted membership to sinners as well as to saints. In the parable of the fishnet (Matt. 3:47–50), for example, where just and unjust in the Kingdom of Heaven would not be separated until the last day, Turrecremata saw the "kingdom" as the visible Church with its sinful and saintly members.[32]

Most noteworthy was Turrecremata's reinterpretation of the Mystical Body, a concept with a long potential history. Traditionally the major metaphor for the Church was Paul's description of the true believer as a member of Christ's body (e.g., Eph. 4:1–16). Early Fathers, including Augustine and Gregory the Great, had used the description as a metaphor for the spiritual Church rather than the institution; the same spiritual meaning was employed by medieval theologians, who did not clearly distinguish between the terms "mystical body" and "real body" (or eucharist) until the thirteenth century.[33] In that century, however, Scholastic writers—Aquinas and other Dominican doctors—began to connect the term "mystical body" with the visible Church. This more institutional idea of the Mystical Body influenced Boniface VIII's bull *Unam Sanctam*; however, the Thomist John of Paris used it to chide Boniface for forgetting that Christ (not the pope) was the true head of the Mystical Body. Then, during the Schism, this interpretation became a favorite weapon of conciliarists, like Dietrich of Niem and Pierre d'Ailly, who argued that the pope was subject to a council representing the whole Church, or Mystical Body of Christ.[34] Naturally, the institutional concept was repulsive to Wycliff and Hus, for whom the "mystical body" metaphor was one of the best Scriptural proofs of their spiritual concept of a true Church composed only of the elect, with sinners excluded. The fathers at Constance found this argument subversive, for it endangered their own claim to represent the Mystical Body and thus be able to judge the several contenders for the papal throne. Inevitably, the heresy trials held at Constance condemned both Wycliff and Hus.[35]

Turrecremata first discussed the controversial doctrine of the Mystical body in his criticism of Agostino Favaroni's works, which he felt used the term too literally. In fact, Favaroni had described the true Mystical Body as composed solely of the elect (a Hussite error that Turrecremata had already set out to refute). The Augustinian did ascribe to Christ some members only potentially saved, men without faith, hope, or charity in their present state but concluded, with extreme literalism, that Christ sinned in the misdeeds of such members.[36] In reply to Favaroni, and thus indirectly to Wycliff and Hus, Turrecremata for the first time expounded his own interpretation of the Mystical Body. He reminded his readers that the Mystical Body was a body only metaphorically. Like a human body, it had members united to one head, but in a material organism there was an identity of natures between head and members that was not present in the spiritual organism. Members of Christ's body were only similar, not identical, to their divine head, because they lived good Christian lives. Thus, sins were acts contrary to the union of the Mystical Body, separating the sinner from it; and no misdeed of a Christian could be attributed to the sinless Christ but, rather, only to the author of the deed.[37] But answering Favaroni was only a starting point.

Turrecremata wanted a definition of the Mystical Body that would include all the visible Church, so he stressed conformity rather than differences between head and members. Christ, the Incarnate Word, was head of the whole body, giving it identity and direction by virtue of his Passion and Resurrection.[38] There were several modes of conformity with Christ, in an ascending scale of perfection. First and broadest was the human nature that the god-man shared with all human beings, sinners as well as saints.[39] Second was conformity through faith, without which the soul could not receive the grace necessary for more perfect union with Christ. The third mode of conformity was charity, the bond of love uniting Christ and all true believers. The final mode, crown of all, was the outpouring of the Holy Spirit. According to Aquinas this outpouring sealed the union of head and members in the Mystical Body of Christ.[40]

In this schema Turrecremata left no place for predestination as a mode of conformity. He never denied that God knew in advance who would be saved and who would be damned, since this aspect of Paul's doctrine had been expounded by Augustine, Boethius, Aquinas, and Ockham, as well as by Wycliff and Hus.[41] But Turrecremata did hope to render the doctrine of predestination innocuous for ecclesiology. Election (known or assumed), as a criterion for measuring the present state of believers, especially that of priests, would threaten the Church with chaos.[42] Like other anti-Hussite apologists, Turrecremata drew a picture of laymen trying to guess whether their ministers were among the elect, a vain quest for knowledge possessed only by God. He saw such guesswork as conducive to turmoil and schism rather than to the salvation of souls, and in his tract against Favaroni's errors he cited the quarrels among Hussites to show the pernicious effects of such speculation.[43]

With typical insistence, Turrecremata brought his discussion of predestination back to the question of sinful members of the Church. Men unconverted, yet predestined to salvation, had only potential membership in the Church, for Christ—he was refuting Favaroni—could not have dead members.[44] But this did not excuse the sins of believers, who put themselves in danger of damnation. A present remedy was, however, at hand: a Christian's state of belief and state of grace were in the care of the visible Church. The eventual inclusion of the elect in the Church Triumphant was God's business and not man's. The ecclesiastical institution could not be thrown into chaos by heretics like Wycliff and Hus, men who asked questions answerable only by God.[45]

Structure: Congregation or Corporation?

Turrecremata's masterly defense of the institutional Church had a second major thrust: it was aimed not against

heretics but against conciliarists. A fresh analysis and synthesis of the conciliar position must be intruded here, in
order for us to understand how Turrecremata demolished
this more amorphous yet equally formidable challenge.

In the conciliar epoch, Catholic theologians like Turrecremata and John of Ragusa shared a common defense of
the visible Church against assaults by heretical Lollards and
Hussites. Initially the issue among the orthodox at the
Council of Basel was the scope of permissible reforms, not
the very nature of Church government. Even the papal
apologists present, Turrecremata included, accepted the
Constance decree *Haec sancta* as a valid statement of ecclesiological principles, although they did not believe its reference to reform included interference with the prerogatives
of the pope.[46] Gradually, though, the growing extremism
of the Basel assembly alienated more and more conservative ecclesiastics. And the council undermined its reformist
image by trying to replace the Roman curia with a similar
body of its own to judge causes, distribute benefices, and
collect taxes.[47] The council's internal rupture over the location for its meeting with the Greeks, and the attempt of
a majority faction to depose Eugenius IV, pushed revolt
towards apparent revolution. In the ensuing schism between council and pope, basic questions of ecclesiology
came to the fore, since embassies from both sides had to
debate (before meetings of princes and magnates) their
conflicting claims to rule the visible Church. Disputants
drew on a common fund of authoritative texts and ecclesiological ideas to prove rival doctrines were true expressions of Christian tradition—until Turrecremata emerged
from the conflict, determined to tear conciliarism out of
the Church by its roots.[48]

The Dominican cardinal claimed that these roots were
planted in the soil of false doctrine, in the errors of the
condemned heretics Marsilius of Padua and William of
Ockham; his accusation became a commonplace of ecclesiastical historians challenged only by John Neville Figgis,
who thought that the great general councils of the fifteenth
century were modelled on secular representative assemblies
like the English Parliament.[49] Modern research, particularly by Brian Tierney, has undermined both of these previous explanations of conciliarism. Turrecremata's thesis

failed to appreciate that conciliarists borrowed only the orthodox doctrines employed by Marsilius and Ockham. Thus, Ockham, in order to censure John XXII for tampering with the Franciscan doctrine of Christ's absolute poverty, had employed canonistic doctrines (especially from Huguccio of Pisa) that allowed removal of a heretic pope. And to prevent even a council from condemning this Franciscan ideal, Ockham had proclaimed the self-sustaining authority of truth as discerned by the remaining faithful few—a truly subversive doctrine, one that was later employed by Protestants of the Reformation. But those conciliarists who made use of Ockham's works, Henry of Langenstein, Conrad of Gelnhausen, and Jean Gerson, accepted only the more orthodox ideas of the *Venerabilis inceptor*; they rejected Ockham's novelties, since they wanted to exalt a general council that could judge claims to the papacy and prevent ecclesiastical anarchy.[50] Again, Marsilius had claimed that papal power was a human creation and that real power in the Church rested with the faithful, whose agent, the general council, could judge an erring pope. This portion of Marsilius's theory of communical sovereignty was founded on orthodox ideas, but few conciliarists cared to identify themselves with the doctrines of a condemned heretic. Even Dietrich of Niem and Nicholas of Cusa, who used arguments derived from Marsilius's *Defensor pacis*, carefully refrained from identifying the source of those arguments.[51]

Concilarism, it is now possible to show, had a far more orthodox origin, drawing as it did upon traditional theories of ecclesiological authority and reinterpreting them to suit the needs of the time. Perhaps chief of these sources was the canonistic concept of the Church as a corporation. From Gratian's time to the outbreak of the Schism, canonists generally sought to advance papal power, since centralization at the expense of local interests seemed advisable for the welfare of the Church. But the *Decretum* included patristic texts, particularly by Augustine, that emphasized the authority given by Christ to the Church; other citations suggested that the pope could be deposed for heresy and that a general council was the best judge of matters of faith. All of these texts could be used to create a theory that exalted council over pope, and the Decretalists contributed the unifying thread to such a development: a juridical concept of the Church more potent than the passive notion of all believers gathered in one fold. When canonists applied to the whole Church the corporate theories (of Hostiensis and Innocent IV) derived from studying local ecclesiastical bodies, it was but a short step to holding that the corporate Church could judge its rector, the pope, through a general council if he endangered the welfare of the whole corporation. Critics of the papacy, from Frederick II onward, often appealed to councils against adverse judgments by reigning popes. John of Paris and the younger Guilelmus Durantis, more orthodox than Marsilius or Ockham, also looked to a council to correct abuses of papal power. Finally an overwhelming scandal in the Roman Church provided the impetus that joined demands for a reforming council with the nascent conciliarism of the canonists.[52]

That catalyst was, of course, the Schism. Responsible ecclesiastics came to see a general council, representing the whole Church, as the only agency able to resolve or set aside conflicting claims to the papacy and effect much needed reforms. Various nonlegal sources—theology, philosophy, polemic (even the condemned ideas of Marsilius)—were used to justify these claims, and theologians like Henry of Langenstein, Pierre d'Ailly, and Jean Gerson employed juridical notions as well. They held that the Mystical Body, via a council representing the whole, could judge an erring pope in the name of Christ, its true head. Circumventing the legal maxim that only the pope could call a council, they appealed to equity (epikeia), superior to the letter of the law, and asserted that any responsible dignitary, prince or prelate, could convoke a council when necessary.[53] None of these arguments really came to dominate a coherent conciliar ecclesiology, however, and the conciliarists tended instead to gravitate toward a wholist view of the Church.

Their corporate idea of the Church gained preeminence, in Turrecremata's mind at least, as the most dangerously coherent statement of conciliarist principles. The potential synthesis of corporate theory and demands for a council was actually achieved by the noted canonist Franciscus de Zabarella, a leading figure at the Council of Constance.[54] Zabarella developed his conciliar theory shortly before the

Council of Pisa, for the success of which he also worked. The pope, according to Zabarella, was rector of the ecclesiastical corporation, governing the faithful in the ordinary course of events. But if the Roman pontiff fell into heresy or some other fault harmful to the welfare of the Church, he could be called to account by a general council representing the whole corporation. Ordinarily the right to call a council belonged to the pope; however, in an emergency it devolved onto the cardinals, then the emperor, and then other lay and ecclesiastical magnates.[55]

Still, at the time of the Council of Basel, there was no single conciliar ideology, only a common desire for ecclesiastical reform. The ideas of d'Ailly and Gerson were championed by John of Ragusa and a nonparticipant in the council, Alfonso Tostado.[56] Zabarella's corporate theory was advocated by the formidable Nicholas de Tudeschis, "Panormitanus," the author of widely read canonical commentaries that taught conciliarist doctrines. His polemical tracts and speeches were among the most persuasive defenses of Basel's deposition of Eugenius IV. (Yet the influence of Panormitanus was diluted, for, as ambassador of the House of Aragon, he often gave the council advice that was in conflict with his own writings.) Perhaps the most original thinker of the age was Nicholas of Cusa—lawyer, philosopher, and mystical theologian—whose *De concordantia Catholica*, composed in his early years at Basel, presented a scheme of reforms applicable to Church and State in order to bring both into harmony with the divine order of the universe. Although he held that the invisible Church was composed of angels and men (an Aquinan idea familiar to Turrecremata), Cusa, too, concentrated his greatest attention on the Church Militant, the visible institution. The pope should promote unity and concord among all believers, he wrote, bringing them into harmony with God's scheme of universal order; if he failed in this task, and especially if he fell into heresy, the pope undermined his own authority and that of the Church, and in that case he could be judged by a general council, the Church's representative. Into this scheme of government Cusa integrated an elaborate hierarchy of ecclesiastical authorities—including pope, cardinals, and local and general councils—each deriving, from Christ through the

Church, its power to promote harmony. Later, disillusioned with the Council of Basel, Cusa served Eugenius IV as a prominent member of the curia and an internal worker for ecclesiastical reform, and his ecclesiology underwent a noticeable transformation. Gone were parallels to the reform of the Holy Roman Empire, but the system continued to rest on an order of hierarchies related to the order of the universe. Now the pope was paramount as head of the ecclesiastical hierarchy, as font of jurisdiction and personification of the Church, though room was left for the powers of cardinals and of a general council.[58]

Finally, the conciliarist ecclesiology of Turrecremata's chief opponent, John of Segovia, has received close attention in recent years. Chief historian of the Council of Basel, theologian of great stature, and advocate of substituting dialogue for crusades against Islam, Segovia insisted that the whole Church had received from Christ a power superior to the pope's—a power exercised by a council. In his exposition of this common conciliarist belief, Segovia used analogies to the constitutions of Italian city-states (an argument little used since the condemnation of its chief advocate, Marsilius of Padua).[59] Segovia also saw a spiritual dimension in the struggle between the Council of Basel and Pope Eugenius IV: quoting the old idea of a Church that included angels and men, he compared the struggle between council and pope, in which all believers must choose sides, to the choice made by the angels between God and Lucifer. In the present crisis the Council of Basel, as representative of the Mystical Body, suffered pains like those of Christ's Passion.[60]

By contrast with the arguments of the conciliarists, a far greater unity marked those of the papalists. Their unity of purpose, strengthening as the conciliar movement failed, was reinforced by a common emphasis on the pope's juridical supremacy over the entire congregation of the faithful. Christ, they argued, had given Peter and his successors power superior to that of any believer or all of them together. This was the unanimous opinion of Turrecremata, Anotninus of Florence, Petrus de Monte, and Rodrigo Sánchez de Arévalo.[61] These papal apologists also emphasized the troubles that would plague the Church if supreme power rested with an assembly rather than with one person.

A monarchic papacy, they argued, could more easily prevent schisms and combat heresy.[62]

But Turrecremata's assault on conciliarism was more focussed and more broadly based than that of his fellow papalists. The Dominican cardinal went out of his way to read conciliarist tracts, in order to understand the enemy he was attacking.[63] During his research Turrecremata came to realize the importance in the conciliar polemic of key texts from Gratian's *Decretum*. Particularly significant, he felt, was the Augustinian idea that Peter had received the power of the keys as the Church's representative—a text that lent itself to conflicting interpretations. The decretist understanding of this text was propapal, arguing that Peter and his successors, the popes, most perfectly embodied the power bestowed by Christ on the Church. Augustine's authority was also cited, however, to support a contrary thesis. Zabarella, Panormitanus, and John of Segovia argued that the Church itself had received supreme power to govern the faithful; the pope was but the Church's minister, the rector of the ecclesiastical corporation, and as such accountable to this corporation (which was represented by a general council) for his conduct of office.[64] Turrecremata early decided that this Augustine-based interpretation of the Petrine role in the establishment of the Church tended to subvert the good order of the ecclesiastical institution. So in the tract he wrote at Nuremberg the cardinal warned against heeding those who described Peter as the rector of a corporation; that would make the Church Peter's ruler, instead of vice versa.[65] In his *Decretum* commentary, Turrecremata further developed the same theme, thereby underlining his view that the corporate theory of the Church was the greatest rival to the papalist doctrine he was presenting:

> *The Church excommunicates.* This is, the authority of the Church excommunicates. Therefore, if he [Peter] signified Holy Church, it was not, as some wrongly teach, that he is under the sign and name of the Church as its representative or procurator. This exposition is quite false, since many errors would follow in the name of the Church. The first is that Peter acquired no dignity or authority of his own from the grant [Matt. 16:18], but only that of the Church, whose procurator he was in receiving anything in its name. But this is quite false, since Christ said to Peter "Blessed are you etc. I

will give to you etc." Second, it would follow that the term *princeps* would properly be applied to the Church. He would have received the keys of the principate in its name. He would have received possession of the kingdom and the episcopate in its name. Not he, but that in whose name he received them, would be king and bishop. Third, it would follow that the power of the keys was given to the community, which we hold to be impossible of those keys properly called those of the kingdom of heaven.[66]

Here we have the fundamental contention of Turrecremata's polemic against the conciliar movement. He found that he had to ascribe to the papacy all key titles and powers of ecclesiastical government and deny them to the Church as a corporate whole. At the deepest level, he had to cut *Haec Sancta*'s linking of Christ with a council representing the Church, by denying that the Church could have received power to govern the faithful. If he could sever this link, then conciliar pretensions would be left with no pretense to validity.[67] Turrecremata's effort to break the link came in his discussion of plenitude of power, the supreme juridical authority in the Church. He argued, especially in *Summa de ecclesia*, book 2, chapter 71, that there were two possible definitions of "plenitude of power": one included both sacramental and governmental powers of the clergy, orders and jurisdiction; the other was limited to jurisdiction alone. In his exposition, as we shall see presently, Turrecremata found both of these concepts incompatible with conciliarism.[68]

Thus, in treating the idea of plenitude of power as involving as orders and jurisdiction, Turrecremata concentrated on the inability of the Church as a whole to receive sacerdotal ordination. Only individuals could receive holy orders, since a human soul must receive the indelible mark of grace to allow effective performance of the sacraments.[69] The Church, whether described as a corporation or as the Mystical Body, did not have a soul; hence, it could not receive sacerdotal ordination. Since the Church could not be ordained, it could not have the plenitude of power defined as both orders and jurisdiction. For, being incapable of receiving one aspect of this plenitude of power, it was consequently incapable of receiving the other.[70] Turrecremata noted further that neither Scripture nor the liturgy suggested that individual priests acted in the Church's name. Commands given to priests in the Church's name were given only figuratively, just as a bishop-elect could give commands to priests he had not ordained.[71] Nor could the whole Church be said to possess powers—particularly priestly powers—that it could not exercise. It was the duty of individual priests, not the faithful, to celebrate mass and absolve penitents. Therefore, the entire Church did not have the plenitude of power described as orders and jurisdiction.[72] Nor did the group of all priests. They could not gather together from the ends of the earth to exercise the plenitude of power, for God would not have made such a clumsy disposition of authority. Thus, neither the whole Church nor all of its clergy could hold supreme authority over the faithful. So, Turrecremata was left free to ascribe that power to the pope.[73]

In treating the idea of plenitude of power as limited to jurisdiction alone, Turrecremata was on more difficult ground. In many ecclesiastical corporations, including monasteries and cathedral chapters, the more distinguished members shared in the decision-making process. The very idea of the Church as a corporation had grown from the efforts of canonists to determine the legal status of such bodies. Turrecremata had to prove, accordingly, that the Church was a different sort of entity, not governed by the corporate regulations of the canonists.[74] His argument here turned on the fact that the Church was composed of laymen as well as clerics. The laity, the larger part of the faithful, was by definition unable to hold and exercise the power of jurisdiction. (Women in particular were unworthy to share in the plenitude of power.) Since the largest part of the membership could not exercise jurisdiction, the whole corporation was incapable of exercising it.[75] Turrecremata further argued that the Church could not possess the plenitude of power because the transaction of crucial business would require a mass meeting of the faithful, which was clearly an impossibility.[76] Then, since the whole Church could not hold or exercise the plenitude of power, it was no rival of the pope.[77] Indeed, any effort to make an ecclesiastical corporation the pope's rival would threaten the unity that was one of the marks of the true Church.[78]

Another favorite conciliarist argument, derived from a text of Cyprian, described the pope as a member of the ecclesiastical body, a part of the whole. He was superior to any other part but inferior to the Church, which was represented by a council.[79] Turrecremata replied that the papacy was head of the Church and the human agent responsible for ecclesiastical unity; without the papacy, the whole congregation of the faithful would disperse. Thus, the Church could not be superior to the papacy, its head and principle of union.[80]

Finally, as an apologist for the papacy and an opponent of the corporate theory of the Church, Turrecremata had to create an alternative interpretation of the key Augustinian text that said that Peter received the keys as the Church's representative. Turrecremata argued that this text proved the pope superior to the Church. Since Peter represented the Church in receiving the power of the keys for himself and his successors, the popes, in turn, established all ecclesiastical governments[81] To Turrecremata's mind, the only true ecclesiastical corporation (universitas) was the succession of popes and of bishops, who received powers of ecclesiastical government from them. The congregation of the faithful was dependent on the Roman see, whose supremacy was beyond question.[82] Turrecremata dismissed all other patristic metaphors for the powers of the Church. Thus, the union of charity in the Mystical Body permitted ascribing to the Church some attributes of both Christ himself and the pope, his earthly representative. But these metaphors lacked any real significance for a proper papalist doctrine on the nature and government of the Church.[83]

His doctrine was essentially monarchical, reflecting the times. Turrecremata composed his ecclesiological treatises during a period of profound political change. After serious reversals in the fourteenth century, European monarchies were recovering and consolidating their power, while local and external interests—including the local clergy and the pope—were under increasing assault. A whole polemical literature grew up around the extent of a monarch's powers and the rights of the community to resist arbitrary commands, a literature parallel and related to the polemics between conciliarists and papalists. In the sixteenth century, Huguenots would cite conciliarist doctrines, kept alive by the Gallican party at the University of Paris, to justify resistance to the Catholic regime in France.[84] And Turrecremata himself, during his career as diplomat, made common cause with the monarchist movement in France. Yet it would be a mistake to view him as a mere apologist for absolute monarchy.

For Turrecremata's chief interest was the visible Church, the sacramental and juridical body dedicated to the salvation of souls. This Church had to be defended from its heretical detractors; its internal foes, the conciliarists, had to be prevented from causing disorder and dissension. Only thus could human beings confidently become members of the congregation of the faithful, receiving the sacraments from clerics themselves subject to the just rule of the pope. Ever mindful of good order in the Church he expected the believer to join, Turrecremata succinctly and categorically proclaimed, "[It] is the flock, [and] not the shepherd."[85]

3
THE
POWERS OF
THE CLERGY

Orders and Jurisdiction

Borrowing a phrase from Hugh of St. Victor, Johannes de Turrecremata described the clergy as the more worthy side of the ecclesiastical body.[1] But Turrecremata had to vindicate such an exalted status in his own era, by demonstrating the right order of this worthier part of the Church. Lollard and Hussite movements threatened the traditional privileges of the clergy, criticized their possession of temporal goods, and denied that sinful priests could validly perform the sacraments. This last challenge was the gravest, for though it retained the medieval emphasis on sacramental grace, it created uncertainty about the availability of that grace to the faithful. Nor would these heretics accept correction by the ecclesiastical hierarchy, not even by popes and councils, but took their stand on Scriptural grounds, thereby implying a difference between the teachings of the visible Church and the Truth accepted by the invisible Church.[2] Though he shared his assault on such heresies with the conciliarists, among them John of Ragusa, Turrecremata thought conciliarists were themselves adherents of the heresies of Marsilius and Ockham. Their false doctrines, especially that of placing the Church's authority in opposition to the pope's, threatened ecclesiastical unity. Turrecremata believed that the unified work of the clergy for the salvation of souls depended on loyalty to the Roman see.[3]

In refuting such errors of his day, Turrecremata had to
discuss the two chief powers of the clergy, *orders* and *jurisdiction*, whose distinction had first been clearly developed
by the canonists. Lollard and Hussite errors, which threatened the basic sacramental structure of the medieval
Church, related to the power of orders, the ability of an
ordained priest to perform the sacraments. Conciliarist errors and the failure of the heretics to accept correction
pertained to the power of jurisdiction: the ability of the
clergy, particularly prelates, to govern the ecclesiastical institution. Though both of these God-given powers belonged to the clergy, they were distributed in different ways
for use in the Church's saving work. And it was incumbent
on Turrecremata to show that the right ordering of those
two powers entailed obedience to the pope.[4]

The Catholic doctrine of priesthood considered the benefit of sacraments to their recipients as independent of the
administering priest's sanctity of soul or state of election.
This doctrine had been firmly established by Augustine in
polemics against the Donatists; it had endured, despite opposition from heretics like the Waldensians, and became
a part of scholastic theology.[5] Turrecremata was thus re-
affirming traditional beliefs when he argued that the indelible stamp of ordination on the soul could not be blotted
out by sin. The sinful priest might be deprived of the use
of his powers but not of the powers themselves. So Turrecremata charged the Hussites with believing that human
malice could impede the workings of grace and thus denying the faith surety of salvation.[6] Further, a key role in
the sacrament of orders belonged to bishops, who had the
power of ordaining priests. Although Marsilius, Wycliff,
and Hus had all questioned the nature of bishops' superiority over priests, Turrecremata restated Hugh of St.
Victor's argument that the episcopate had the fullness of
priestly power, since its sacerdotal acts extended to the
whole Mystical Body through ordination and the consecration of new bishops. Nevertheless, Turrecremata did
not describe episcopacy as a higher *ordo* ("sacramental
grade") than simple priesthood; neither did he claim that
the bishop of Rome had a higher power of orders than
other bishops.[7] He simply had no need to assert papal supremacy in the power of orders. For proof of supremacy

in the other powers, jurisdiction—the power of ecclesiastical government—was sufficient to place the Roman pontiff above all other prelates as the visible head of the Church, its ruler and unifying force.

In the sphere of jurisdiction, Turrecremata could challenge communal or corporate conciliarist doctrines with weapons drawn from an ample legal and theological heritage. For one, he used what has come to be known as the "mendicant doctrine" of supreme papal jurisdiction. Some early canonists had suggested that the confirmation of episcopal election by higher powers, not the election itself, conferred jurisdiction upon a bishop-elect. Then, in controversies at the University of Paris, the same doctrine was adopted by many apologists for the papally granted privileges of the mendicant orders—they used it to claim that bishops were the pope's agents in all matters of ecclesiastical government, a form of argument that shocked their adversaries, the secular masters. The mendicant doctrine was first taught by such Franciscans as Thomas of York and Bonaventure. Augustinians later took up the Franciscan doctrine and carried it to extremes, but the Dominicans were slower to follow. Only in the fourteenth century did Herveus Natalis firmly establish this doctrine of jurisdiction in the thought of the Order of Preachers, setting an example that Turrecremata would follow in his papalist polemics. With his lively concern for the welfare of the Church, however, Turrecremata would not repeat the excesses of his mendicant predecessors, who often seemed to be more interested in arguments on the distribution of power in spiritual and temporal spheres than in the salvation of souls.[8]

In his *Summa* Turrecremata defined jurisdiction as the governmental power of "ruling the Christian people according to divine law."[9] Like orders, jurisdiction was derived from God rather than men and thus, he ventured, came down from God by way of the pope. Yet, unlike orders, jurisdiction was not conferred once for all time, as it allowed (although it did not automatically cause, as the Hussites contended) the deposition of prelates who abused their authority.[10] Jurisdiction, involving as it did the subjection of inferiors to superiors, naturally lent itself to an orderly, hierarchic disposition.[11] Further, jurisdiction existed to promote the salvation of souls and not just the good order of the ecclesiastical institution, which was itself a means to that higher end. In addition, Turrecremata departed from the excesses of previous mendicant papal apologists to specify that jurisdiction was subordinate to the vital sacramental power of orders—an emphasis that probably reflects his experience of the Schism that had so badly impeded the saving work of the Church.[12]

Not surprisingly, Turrecremata argued for papal supremacy in both fora of jurisdiction as distinguished by the early scholastics: the *internal* forum of penance and the *external* forum of ecclesiastical trial and censure. Aquinas and Bonaventure had already imported the canonistic idea of jurisdiction into the discussion of these fora, and Turrecremata followed their example.[13] In the internal forum of conscience Aquinas had noted a close connection of orders and jurisdiction: jurisdiction assigned to the priest the "material" over which he exercised power of absolution. To be sure, this was the original arena of jurisdictional debate between mendicants and seculars, who disputed the papally granted right of friars to hear confessions. By Turrecremata's day the main fight had moved into the external forum of causes, with conciliarists and papalists disputing the location of supreme governing authority in the visible Church.[14] Nevertheless, Turrecremata was also concerned with issues of the older controversy, as he and Johannes de Montenegro had fought an attempt in the Council of Basel to revoke the privileges of the mendicants. Turrecremata argued that the equal sacramental powers of priests must be regulated by jurisdiction in order to preserve the good order of the Church and insure its efficient work for the salvation of souls. This regulating power was given by the pope to bishops, who in turn assigned cures of souls to priests. But the pope's cure of souls covered all the earth; so, he could use his supreme power of jurisdiction in the internal forum and thereby license friars to hear confessions from the faithful whenever such exemptions would serve the welfare of the Church.[15]

The pope was also supreme in the external forum of causes, in which obdurate sinners were punished by censures, the spiritual weapons of the Church, such as excommunication.[16] Imposition and removal of censures was a power of jurisdiction reserved to bishops, who could be punished if they abused it.[17] Again, the pope was the source and overseer of this power of excommunication, able to redistribute the power of jurisdiction in the external forum to benefit the welfare of the Church.[18]

This contention of Turrecremata's—papal supremacy in both fora of jurisdiction—needed extensive supporting argumentation, for there was a solid tradition that argued that bishops, as the successors of the Apostles, received jurisdiction from Christ. The secular masters at Paris taught the episcopalist doctrine, which was often extended to making parish priests the direct successors of the Disciples; and their adherence to this proto-Gallican notion was undeterred even by papal condemnation of one of their number, Jean de Pouilly, who was prosecuted for heresy by the Dominicans Herveus Natalis and Petrus de Palude.[19] In addition, Turrecremata had to redeem papalism from the disgrace of the Schism, a task for which he found able collaborators in Nicholas of Cusa, Antoninus of Florence, Petrus de Monte, and Arévalo. But among them, it was Turrecremata who made the most effective use of the mendicant doctrine of jurisdiction.[20] He held that jurisdiction descended from the Roman pontiff in a hierarchic pattern to all prelates and pastors.[21] Just as God was the sole distributor of grace, so the supreme pontiff distributed all powers of ecclesiastical government:

> Although neither the Spirit nor grace are distributed to others by the pope, but by God alone; nevertheless, the power of jurisdiction is distributed to him by others, [that is] the motive power of direction and ecclesiastical government, to prelates and rectors; and this suffices for headship [of the Church].[22]

Ecclesiastical unity, an abiding concern in the aftermath of the Schism, required subordination of all other ecclesiastical powers to the papacy. In Turrecremata's view, therefore, any denial that prelates received jurisdiction from the pope was tantamount to an attack on the ideal of unity.[23]

In supporting this doctrine, so relevant to his age, Turrecremata had to show that it reflected conditions in the early Church. No power could be ascribed to the popes that had not first been conferred on Peter; accordingly,

Turrecremata argued that there were no references in Scripture to Christ's granting episcopal powers to the other Apostles.[24] Proof of this contention required some of his greatest dialectical efforts, including proof that all Scriptural texts concerning the powers of the other Apostles referred to orders and not to jurisdiction.

A particular problem was the "power of the keys," a term that had both sacramental and governmental implications. Matt. 18:18 recorded Christ's promise to the Twelve of the power to bind and loose—a promise made in terms similar to those in the *Tu es Petrus*, the promise of the keys to Peter (Matt. 16:18). Turrecremata reduced Matt. 18:18, along with similar texts in Luke and John, to a promise of priestly ordination.[25] But to round out this argument, Turrecremata had to reinterpret the *Tu es Petrus*, which most theologians, publicists, and canonists considered the record of Peter's institution as first bishop and first pope. Turrecremata, on the contrary, reduced it to a promise of future elevation to episcopacy and to the Vicariate of Christ. Like Herveus Natalis before him, Turrecremata argued that the Church needed no other bishop, not even the future bishop of Rome, while Christ was present on earth.[26] For Turrecremata the crucial passage in Scripture, recording Peter's institution as pope, was John 21: 15–17, the injunction "Feed my lambs. . . . Feed my sheep." Turrecremata thought this an unmistakably papalist text, which could not be confused with any other, recording Peter's episcopal consecration and conferral of the supreme power of jurisdiction in the visible Church.[27]

The Petrine pontificate therefore set a permanent pattern, for the prince of the Apostles was able to rule the Church without the consent of others, whether given individually or in council. As the number of believers increased, Peter named his fellow Apostles as bishops, with a share in his power of jurisdiction. Later still, Peter chose Paul and other worthy men to share in these labors, conferring jurisdiction even on those he had not directly ordained; Peter's successors, the popes, inherited this sole right to confer the power of jurisdiction. Such reasoning, as we have noted above, was Turrecremata's interpretation of Augustine's dictum that Peter had received the keys *in figura ecclesiae*.[28]

Besides the power of the keys, an episcopalist doctrine presented yet another obstacle to wide acceptance of Turrecremata's mendicant doctrine of papal jurisdiction: the idea that an individual bishop received both orders and jurisdiction (through a line of predecessors) from whichever Apostle had founded his see. This concept of apostolic succession was an ancient one and a cardinal point of episcopalist ecclesiology, one which suggested that a bishop had an inalienable right to rule his diocese. Mendicants like Herveus Natalis were willing to go to extreme lengths in attacking such an interpretation.[29] Turrecremata's approach to the problem, though less cavalier, was colored by these past polemics. The cardinal argued that Peter had allowed the other Apostles to transmit the power of orders to their successors (the bishops) but had retained for himself and his successors (the popes) the sole right to confer the power of jurisdiction. In jurisdiction, the only apostolic succession was that of bishops receiving from the papacy powers similar to their predecessors.[30]

Finally, Turrecremata summarized the pope's jurisdictional supremacy under the heading "plenitude of power" *(plenitudo potestatis)*. The term had been coined by Leo I to describe papal power in comparison with the power of a papal vicar *in partem sollicitudinis,* who shared in the Roman pontiff's work for the welfare of the Church. The canonists gradually turned "plenitude of power" into a description of the pope's supreme governing authority in the Church. Bernard of Clairvaux popularized the term among theologians, and the mendicants, Aquinas among them, were quick to adopt it. Moreover, Innocent III introduced the idea of plenitude of power, with all its legal and theological implications, into his decretals. It was this very supreme power of ecclesiastical government—whether understood as including or excluding any reference to the power of orders—that Turrecremata denied could be held or exercised by the whole Church.[31]

By virtue of the plenitude of power, the pope was head of the visible Church, commanding obedience from the other bishops even to the point of intervening in their work of ecclesiastical government.[32] Bishops were papal agents who received a share of jurisdiction *in partem sollicitudinis.*[33] Even the power of orders, in which bishops were the pope's equals, was affected by the plenitude of power, which regulated pastoral ministry. Bishops, metropolitans, primates, and patriarchs were all part of a hierarchy of jurisdiction whose summit was the papacy.[34] Jurisdiction was diffused through this hierarchy via confirmation of elections, made directly or through intermediaries. Each grade of the hierarchy was supposed to supervise the conduct of members in the lower grades, correcting or removing unworthy prelates. Unjust sentences could be appealed all the way to the pope, the font of all jurisdiction.[35] Since the lesser clergy received their share of jurisdiction from the bishops,[36] the pope could grant local exemptions from episcopal authority, making monks and friars directly subject to Rome. The important principle to be safeguarded in granting of exemptions was that of obedience to the Vicar of Christ.[37]

But Turrecremata reminded his readers that this governmental hierarchy, even the papacy with its plenitude of power, was no end in itself. He wrote that Christ had given the clergy the power of jurisdiction only to promote proper reception of the sacraments:

> The pope and other ministers of the Church do not seem to have ministry with this power [jurisdiction] except for the preparation of the subject for the dispensation of the sacraments.[38]

Thus, exceptions to the ordinary exercise of ecclesiastical power could be made in the interest of the salvation of souls, for example, allowing a priest to absolve the dying of excommunications usually reserved to higher powers.[39] So, even when struggling against conciliarism and Hussitism, Turrecremata never lost sight of the pastoral mission of the Church—a vision of the Church's saving labors which sets him apart from the more doctrinaire papal apologists of the Middle Ages.

Magisterium and Infallibility

In Turrecremata's day *magisterium,* the power to authoritatively teach Christian doctrine, was seen as an aspect of jurisdiction in the external forum. In tackling this aspect of jurisdiction, Turrecremata had perforce to deal with the unsettled question of infallibility and indefectibility, previously developed by canonists, Franciscans, and, in his own time, conciliarists and papalists. Although the canonists had regarded the pope's right to settle doctrinal controversies as quite incontrovertible, they seem never to have regarded the Roman pontiff as infallible. Canon law included several references to popes who had fallen into heresy and lost their immunity to judgment by lesser powers. Nor did the jurists ignore the distinction between *authority* and *learning*, arguing that official pronouncements bound the wisest doctor, even if he be more aware of the truth than an individual pope of prelate. The Roman Church, usually understood to be the whole Church or some loyal portion of it, was believed to be free of wrinkle or stain and thus never lose the true faith. Nevertheless, the canonists did not readily translate the Church's indefectibility into an unerring magisterial authority.[40]

The claim of infallibility was first put forward by the Franciscan theologian Pierre Olivi, who wanted to prove that Nicholas III's decretal *Exiit,* affirming the Minorite doctrine of Christ's poverty, was an irreformable doctrinal definition. In terms borrowed from the canonist Huguccio, Olivi argued that any pope who contradicted an infallible, irreformable decree of a predecessor fell from his see because of his errors.[41] Accordingly, John XXII's decision to turn against the Conventual Franciscans after he quashed the Spirituals forced their minister general, Michael of Cesena, to believe that the pope had fallen from his see when he tried to tamper with the provisions of *Exiit.* Michael took into exile with him the brilliant theologian William of Ockham, whose polemical works suggested that a small remnant of the Church, some small group of believers, might remain the only guardian of the truth, able to judge the errors of popes, prelates, and councils. Ockham's doctrine, dangerously close to a subjective view of Christian doctrine, would have a widespread influence on later thinkers.[42]

In the fourteenth century, the Franciscan development of a suspect theory of infallible *magisterium* was countered by arguments from other mendicant theologians, some of them involved in official inquiries into Olivi's orthodoxy. Most of these writers, including Augustinus Triumphus

and Petrus de Palude, were inclined to consider infallible
the papal office itself—pope and cardinals together—not
the Roman pontiff alone.[43] The most coherent and forth-
right papalist theory of infallibility was advanced by the
Carmelite Guido Terreni, who dismissed Gratian's examples of papal heresy and largely ignored the canonists' safeguards against the ill effects of papal error on the Church.
Terreni's argument that God would not allow the pope to
err when pronouncing judgment in matters of faith is believed to have weighed heavily in John XXII's decision not
to condemn the idea of infallibility because it was favored
by the Michaelists.[44] After the outbreak of the Schism, however, Terreni's doctrine of infallibility, which foreshadowed
the future definition by the First Vatican Council, was
largely ignored. Conciliarists, faced with the need to reunite
and reform the Church while defending orthodoxy, tended
to describe a general council as possessing supreme teaching authority, though they did not agree on whether the
Holy Spirit's guidance made a council's doctrinal decrees
infallible.[45] In their response papal apologists and champions of orthodoxy—Eugenians like Antoninus, Petrus de
Monte, and Turrecremata himself—had to prove the pope,
not a council, the most reliable guardian and teacher of the
truth.[46]

Turrecremata's papalist discussion of *magisterium,* like all
of his anticonciliar arguments, was closely tied to his concern for the welfare of the church. The Church needed a
single teaching authority to preserve its characteristic unity.
Were there no one power to decide difficult doctrinal questions, the Church would split into a multitude of bickering
sects, as the Hussite movement had done.[47] So the preaching office given to priests at ordination[48] was regulated by
prelatial authority guided by the learning of the doctors.[49]
In doctrinal disputes supreme power of decision was the
pope's, the Church's chief teacher, whose pronouncements
bound all doctors.[50] Turrecremata, combining law and polemic, argued that this papal *magisterium* was an aspect of
jurisdiction in the external forum. Since the pope was the
font of this aspect of jurisdiction as of all others, papal
decisions in matters of faith were virtually those of the
whole Church.[51]

Turrecremata had to explain how such supreme mag-

isterial authority could be properly exercised, especially
when learned doctors disagreed. Ancient church councils
had been assemblies of the wise and powerful, whose decisions had overwhelming prestige, and Turrecremata still
accepted conciliar condemnations of false doctrine issued
in his own day. But he had lost faith in the absolute reli-
ability of ecclesiastical assemblies when the Council of Basel
compounded its antipapal endeavours with another of-
fense, the attempt to define Mary's Immaculate Conception
as dogma. So he turned once more to the papacy, which
had power to end divisive theological disputes by making
pronouncements binding upon all doctors.[52] The pope's
decisions were more trustworthy than those of the multitude and unrivalled by even those of general councils,
which received their authority from the Roman see.[53] According to Turrecremata, Christ had made Peter the
Church's chief teacher when he said, "I have prayed for
you, Peter, that your faith may not fail. Strengthen your
brothers" (Luke 22:32).[53]

As guardian of the truth, the pope judged disputes over
doctrine and "edited" creeds, adding clauses that affirmed
sound doctrine or condemned heresies. It was exactly this
type of editing, the addition of the *filioque* to the Nicene
Creed, to which the Greeks at Florence had objected. Turrecremata answered that the *filioque* served as a weapon
against heresy and thus was worthy of acceptance in the
East.[55] The Roman pontiff's plenitude of power also gave
him a unique ability to canonize saints.[56] In addition, the
papacy regulated the study of theology, approving the
works of learned doctors and watching over the universities. (There is a remote echo of old disputes at Paris in
Turrecremata's claim that the pope could compel the
schools to accept friars as students or as masters.)[57]

Turrecremata's exalted conception of papal *magisterium*
forced him to confront several burning issues of late medieval theology: the relationship of Church and Scripture;
the relationship of Scripture and Tradition; the possibility
that the pope might fall into heresy.

Because of the errors of Lollards and Hussites who
thought the visible Church might embrace error while the
invisible Church held to truth grounded in Scripture, the
first of these problems—the relationship of Church and

Scripture—was the most important. Moreover, Catholic theologians had been discussing the same possibility even before Ockham attacked John XXII's orthodoxy, at least since Henry of Ghent's residence in Paris in the thirteenth century.[58] The fathers at Constance had been forced to confront this issue when John Hus demanded that his errors be refuted on Scriptural grounds, a demand implying that truth and magisterial authority did not agree.[59] Conciliarists like Gerson, d'Ailly, and Thomas Netter were forced to take up this challenge and try to prove that Scripture and Church could not be in conflict. In their argument they invoked the authority of Augustine's statement that the Church moved him to accept the authority of Scripture, which they understood as proof that the Holy Spirit had inspired the Church's recognition of the canonical books of the Bible. Thus, the visible Church was divinely guided to accept and teach the truth.[60] More conservative theologians, on whose authority Luther would draw, strongly criticized this line of reasoning, preferring to emphasize the independent value of Scripture as divine revelation.[61]

In his solution, as throughout his career, Turrecremata believed he was defending a body of uniform truths, unfailing and universally valid principles whose acceptance by the faithful was necessary for their salvation. Scripture governed theology, while universal Tradition and local traditions guided the Church's work.[62] Everything necessary for salvation was contained, at least implicitly, in the Old and New Testaments.[63] The Holy Spirit had implanted in Scripture an evident meaning, which could be ignored only by a heretic. Turrecremata therefore regarded the Church as the witness to the valve of Scripture, not as the source of its authority. His understanding of the Augustinian text about Church and Holy Writ was a papalist version of the argument used by Netter and other conciliarists. The Church, in the pope's person, had been divinely guided to accept as canonical only genuinely inspired books, precluding the possibility that truth and the *magisterium* of the Church could be in conflict.[64]

Granted the fundamental agreement of Holy Writ and Holy Church, Turrecremata still had to discuss the second problem—Scripture and Tradition—the relationship of Scripture to other authoritative materials derived from universal Tradition or local traditions. In previous centuries, *hierarchies of authorities* had been created for use in legal and theological argument, and for his own doctrine Turrecremata would draw variously on the past thinkers.

The canonists, whose interest in ecclesiastical discipline had led them to emphasize the value of Tradition, had been in the forefront of developing such hierarchies. One of the most influential lists of authorities was prepared by Huguccio, who listed—after Scripture—the canons of the Apostles and of councils, papal decretals, the Greek and Latin Fathers, and the examples of the saints.[65] Conservative theologians like Thomas Bradwardine were quick to accuse the canonists of making Tradition a rival to Scripture, a criticism violently restated by Wycliff and Hus.[66] William of Ockham, composing antipapal polemics, prepared a different and extremely influential list of authorities, which made Tradition, apostolic or postapostolic in origin, a source of truths that might be used in condemning the pope himself. Ockham listed—after Scripture—doctrines derived from Holy Writ by necessary reasoning, orthodox traditions handed down from apostolic times, truths found in trustworthy ecclesiastical histories, conclusions drawn from these sources by necessary reasoning, and postapostolic revelations—including the Franciscan doctrine of Christ's poverty.[67] In Turrecremata's day, Ockham's hierarchy of authorities was employed by such theologians as the conciliarist Johannes de Breviscoxe and the papalist Gabriel Biel.[68]

Turrecremata's own development of hierarchies of authority responded to the problems he was confronting. Quite early his obvious zeal for orthodoxy caused the Council of Basel to employ him as a theological expert;[69] one commission, to debate the proposed definition of the doctrine of the Immaculate Conception, led Turrecremata to prepare his own hierarchy of authorities for citation in any theological debate. Turrecremata listed—after Scripture—dogmatic definitions of councils, those of popes, and officially approved definitions prepared by learned doctors. In this first list, magisterial authority weighed more heavily than erudition; indeed, he gave no place whatever to Tradition, whether apostolic or postapostolic.[70] Had Turrecremata always employed this hierarchy, he would have belonged to what Heiko Obermann calls "Tradition I," that which emphasized the sufficiency of Scripture.[71] In his later works, however, the dual exigency of defeating Hussitism and conciliarism led him to restate his hierarchy of authorities.[72] Turrecremata began to draw upon both Ockham and Huguccio, borrowings which led him to place greater weight on the value of Tradition, at least in ecclesiological questions.[73] Scripture, and the truths derived from it by necessary reasoning, kept pride of place.[74] After these Turrecremata listed non-Scriptural truths handed down orally by the Apostles to subsequent generations of believers.[75] Such truths did not conflict with Scripture, since there was nothing necessary for salvation that was not taught, to use Turrecremata's curious phrase, "by the gospels or by Christ."[76] The next rank in the hierarchy belonged to the canons of councils, while the fourth place belonged to papal decrees—neither of which could err.[77] After these authorities were ranked the works of the Fathers, portions of which had been sanctioned by the Church as the best refutations of heretical doctrines. Other theological works, although without official approbation, were useful in the interpretation of Scripture, while valuable materials could also be found in the works of learned pagans. (In the *Commentaria,* which is concerned with the sources of ecclesiastical law, Turrecremata also listed trustworthy histories and the examples of the saints—derived respectively from Ockham and Huguccio.)[78]

The high rank Turrecremata gave to conciliar canons had a historical background and demanded further explanation. The pronouncements of the four great councils—Nicaea, Constantinople, Ephesus, and Chalcedon—had been compared by Gregory the Great to the four gospels because of their fundamental importance for the teaching of Christian doctrine.[79] Some conciliarists, upon finding Gregory's words in the *Decretum,* used them to prove that the council was superior to the pope.[80] This interpretation based on Gratian's texts was exactly the sort of error Turrecremata had set out to refute. Turrecremata argued that the four great councils were important because they defined key Christian doctrines, but their theological importance did not infringe on the Roman pontiff's supremacy in matters of positive law, which pertained to his plenitude of power.[81]

Although Turrecremata never thought of changing the accepted emphasis on Scripture, the exigencies of ecclesiological debate compelled him to place increasing weight on Tradition as the Church's guide to right actions and source of truth. It is the change of emphasis, based on the exigencies of papalist polemic, which lies behind George Tavard's claim that Turrecremata contributed to the development of the Tridentine doctrine of the two sources of revelation, a modified version of Ockham's hierarchy of authorities. In Obermann's terms, Turrecremata passed over from Tradition I to Tradition II.[82]

Turrecremata's preoccupation with the nature and extent of papal power obliged him to discuss the third problem agitating his contemporaries: the old belief that a pope could, publicly or privately, fall into heresy.[83] The Councils of Constance and Basel had claimed to have power directly from Christ to decide matters of heresy, schism, and reform. The Eugenians, with Turrecremata in the vanguard, were gradually led to reemphasize the pope's supreme *magisterium*, which displaced the council's authority in matters of faith. In the process, the Dominican cardinal developed his own notable views on infallibility, which have remained a subject of modern controversy and misunderstanding.

Turrecremata's first adumbration of a doctrine of papal infallibility appears in a tract written at Basel, although he placed little emphasis upon that doctrine until he was on legation in Germany.[84] In his debate with Cesarini at Florence, Turrecremata seems to have had second thoughts about combining infallibility and papalist polemic, for he denied ecclesiological implications in the old belief that Mary alone had remained faithful at the time of the Schism, when even Peter, the chosen vicar, had fallen away, since Peter—not Mary—had received the power of the keys:

> Although the blessed Virgin Mary, mother of God, spouse of Christ, queen of the world and lady of the angels, was full of grace and ever unshakable in faith; nevertheless, that does not prove that she was greater than Peter in the power of the keys.[85]

In the *Summa* and *Commentaria,* Turrecremata abandoned this line of argument and returned to the doctrine of infallibility. He expressed himself as willing to believe that providence would not let the Church's chief teacher err in matters of faith,[86] since the alternative was a prospect of the Church drifting into doubt, division, and error.[87]

In Turrecremata's time, there was no common opinion among theologians and canonists on the idea of infallibility. He was therefore free to borrow from the ideas of Olivi and Terreni, while rejecting the excesses of Ockham and the Michaelists. Also, Turrecremata founded his doctrine on an identification of *indefectibility* and *infallibility*—unfailing faith and unerring judgment in matters of faith—again, an identification that was not new. Huguccio and Johannes Teutonicus had interpreted Christ's prayer that Peter's faith might not fail (Luke 22:32) as a guarantee that the Church would adhere to the truth even if the pope fell into heresy. Ockham had argued that even an individual might judge prelates if he alone adhered to the truth. Some conciliarists had assigned the general council the role of unfailing exponent of the Church's unfailing faith.[88]

For his own doctrine, Turrecremata argued that the best location for the Church's unfailing faith was the papacy, the teaching authority which God would not allow to err:

> The pope, head of the Church, teacher and leader of the Christian people, can not err concerning matters of faith which must be held and believed. The apostle [the pope], *by virtue of his public office* [italics mine] of teaching the Christian people, discerns or defines what must be believed and held. The judgment of the apostolic see is indefectible, which is the same thing.[89]

Turrecremata thought the Church's own indefectibility devoid of juridical implications, since (like Mary) it lacked the power of the keys to translate its unfailing faith into unerring decisions.[90] Moreover, the Church's unerring faith belonged only to that body of believers in communion with the Roman see.[91]

To support his position, Turrecremata had to prove that Peter had received infallible *magisterium* along with the governing powers assigned to him by Christ. He argued that infallibility was inherent in the *Tu es Petrus* (Matt. 16:16) and—assuming that indefectibility and infallibility were the same thing—in Luke 22:32.[92] Turrecremata had to dispose of two objections to this argument: Peter's lapse of confidence at the time of the Passion and his erroneous treatment of the gentiles. In the first case, Turrecremata argued that Peter had lost the strength to proclaim his faith, not faith itself, when he denied Christ, and that he did not receive infallible *magisterium* until after the Resurrection (John 21:15–17).[93] Infallibility was thus an attribute of the papal office, not a grace granted the individual pope, and was consequently inherited by all of Peter's successors.[94] In the second case, the conciliarists had used Paul's rebuke of Peter for not eating with the gentiles (Gal. 2:11–14) as a proof that the pope could be corrected for misusing his powers.[95] Turrecremata replied that Peter had committed, at most, a sin but had not fallen into serious error. Paul had administered fraternal correction for that lapse—an incident devoid of juridical significance.[96]

Briefly attracted by Guido Terreni's insistence that God would keep the pope from falling into heresy in the exercise of the *magisterium*, Turrecremata even claimed that God would intervene if the pope tried to teach false doctrine.[97] However, guided by traditional ideas on papal heresy or by his own experience of the Schism, the Dominican cardinal did not leave the matter entirely in God's hands. Like Herveus Natalis, he emphasized the infallibility of the papal office.[98] If the pope attempted to teach false doctrine—Turrecremata's arguement was drawn from Huguccio rather than Terreni—the Pontiff would fall from his see *ipso facto*:

> If the Roman pontiff becomes a heretic, he falls from Peter's chair and see by the very fact of falling from Peter's faith. Consequently, a judgment rendered by such a heretic is not the judgment of the apostolic see.

This recourse to Huguccio's doctrine allowed him to separate the infallible see from the fallible person who might embrace false doctrine.[99] And Turrecremata even gave up his flirtation with Terreni's ideas on papal infallibility, dismissing them as unacceptable:

> Some say that "God would not permit the pope to define heresy, or anything contrary to the faith; but would prevent him by death, by resistance of other believers, by the instruction of others or by internal inspiration, or by other means."

> But we give another explanation . . . namely that, if the Roman pontiff should fall into a condemned heresy, by the very fact that he falls from Peter's faith, he falls from Peter's chair and see.[100]

The First Vatican Council (1869–70) launched an ongoing debate on whether Turrecremata's views agreed with its own definition of papal infallibility, namely, that papal pronouncements on faith and morals, issued *ex cathedra* with the guidance of the Holy Spirit, could not err. Lederer, though noting Turrecremata's distinction between pope and office, assumed that the cardinal had foreshadowed the Vatican Council definition.[101] Pacifico Massi has claimed that infallible office and *ex cathedra* definition are the same thing, while Joseph Fenton, trying to explain away Turrecremata's references to a pope falling from his see, has argued that the errors in question were purely private ones.[102] But Fenton has ignored Turrecremata's argument that heretical pronouncements were not those of the apostolic see, a clear reference to attempted abuse of papal *magisterium*. Moreover, if in Turrecremata's view a Roman pontiff could forfeit his see for issuing an erroneous pronouncement, then the cardinal had no idea of infallible *ex cathedra* pronouncement. Like Fenton, Massi has ignored Turrecremata's fear that the pope might abuse his teaching office.[103] Rather than adumbrating the doctrine of the First Vatican Council, which (like Terreni) emphasized the divine guidance of the pope, Turrecremata presented the incongruity of a pope losing his see by placing himself at variance with his infallible office.[104]

Turrecremata's belief that divine guidance of papal *magisterium* was not automatic is equally evident in his discussion of the power of the keys. The Michaelists, trying to prove *Exiit* an irreformable doctrinal definition, argued that the pope had the "key of knowledge" (Luke 11:52), which they understood as a special, divinely granted *habitus scientiae* (state of knowledge). (This was an unusual use of a scriptural term normally applied by theologians and canonists to the pope's magisterial authority or to the confessor's power to inquire into a penitent's state of soul before granting absolution.) In reply to the Michaelists, John XXII hotly denied that the pope had special *habitus scientiae*.[105] Turrecremata, writing with an eye to past controversies, maintained that the power of the keys consisted of keys of knowledge and of power, that is, the powers of inquiry and absolution. But he denied that the key of knowledge conferred a special gift of knowledge.[106] Thus, although it seems that Turrecremata did not apply this argument directly to papal *magisterium,* evidently there was no room in his ecclesiology for a belief that the Roman pontiff received a special *habitus scientiae* for teaching the faithful.

Eventually Turrecremata concluded that divine guidance of a general council was, similarly, not automatic unless pope and council reached unanimous agreement. Increasingly hostile to the conciliarist emphasis on the corporate Church, Turrecremata denied that a general council acting alone could translate the Church's unfailing faith into infallible doctrinal definitions. Even in his early polemical treatises, he expressed a preference for decisions made by pope and council acting together.[107] In his mature works, Turrecremata still argued that a council separate from the pope could fall into error, citing the examples of the Council of Rimini and the Second Council of Ephesus.[108] Nevertheless, he did not deny the value of a general council, which—with the advice of learned doctors and the prestige of consultation with leading prelates of the Church—could lend much to the decisions of the Roman pontiff. No good Christian could argue with the decisions of a pope in council.[109] Moreover, the council became indirectly involved in Christ's promise to Peter of unfailing faith,[110] helping to preserve the Church from doubts and dissensions.[111] Turrecremata shared with Nicholas of Cusa this preference for unanimous agreement of pope and council, which would provide an unfailing assurance that God had guided the Church to the acceptance of the truth.[112]

All in all, Turrecremata's doctrine differed significantly from that defined by the First Vatican Council. It was, rather, the cardinal's coherent response to the dual problem of identifying an unquestionably reliable teacher of sound doctrine and preventing an erring pope from harming the Church—replacing his unsuccessful polemical attempt to include the ideas of Guido Terreni in his system.[113]

The Doctrine of Hierarchy

Johannes de Turrecremata was deeply concerned with the preservation of ecclesiastical unity, a preoccupation based on his own experience of the Church's troubles, as well as on traditional ecclesiological concepts. The Dominican cardinal saw his chief foes, conciliarists and Hussites, as threats to this ideal of oneness. So he sought some unifying principle that would harmonize his discussion of the distinct but interrelated powers of orders and jurisdiction. (He referred to possible ambiguities in the distribution of these powers with the usual canonistic example: an archdeacon superior to an archpriest in jurisdiction but inferior to him in orders.)[114]

As one such unifying principle Turrecremata employed the canonistic concept of *majoritas,* an idea of superiority closely linked to obedience. (Boniface VIII's bull *Unam sanctam,* declaring obedience to the pope as necessary for salvation, would appear in the *Extravagantes communes* under the title *De maioritate et oboedientia.*)[115] Thus, Turrecremata assigned the papacy a share in both the priestly superiority in orders and the episcopal superiority in the conferral of orders. Also, the Roman see was senior to all other bishoprics in time of founding because of Peter's selection by Christ as a bishop. Moreover, the papacy held unrivalled *majoritas* in the realm of jurisdiction, the power of governing the Church and maintaining its unity.[116]

But Turrecremata leaned far more heavily on another proof that unity involved subordination to the Roman see: the doctrine of hierarchy. The idea of orderly subordination to higher powers was common in medieval thought, with roots in Christian tradition and in the actual ordering of Christendom. This principle was most evident in the Neoplatonic writings that formed the Pseudo-Dionysian corpus.[117] Thus, Turrecremata readily embraced the doctrine of hierarchy, arguing that the Hussites threatened the Church with chaos when they denied its validity.[118] The Church was a microcosm of the universal order, which imitated the hierarchic disposition of angels beneath the divinity. Jesus, a prudent legislator, had created a hierarchy of orders and had given Peter the authority to create a hierarchy of jurisdiction, the most efficient and decorous pattern for ecclesiastical government.[119] The pope presided over the Church Militant as Christ presided over the Church Triumphant, or as God presided over the angels. There was no power of jurisdiction that did not descend from above, that is, from the pope to the lower ranks of the ecclesiastical hierarchy.[120] As a good Thomist, however, Turrecremata did not think the ecclesiastical hierarchy was a perfect reflection of its celestial exemplar. Individual details had to be flexible, so that the pope might make arrangements that promoted the Church's saving work.[121]

Antony Black has described hierarchy as the fundamental principle of Turrecremata's ecclesiology.[122] But in an attempt to fit Turrecremata into Walter Ullmann's paradigm of ascending and descending theories—categorized, respectively, as Aristotelean and Platonic[123]—Black has described the cardinal as a Neoplatonist led by his metaphysics to adopt a monarchist political theory. Turrecremata's references to Aristotle and Aquinas thus become mere proof-texts for a descending theory of government.[124] This assessment overemphasizes Turrecremata's use of Pseudo-Dionysius, one of many authors cited by medieval polemicists for different ends. Moreover, Turrecremata's analogies between the angelic hierarchy and the ordering of human society are little more than commonplaces.[125] Turrecremata was a Thomist more interested in the Church's mission than in political theory. And he discussed the limits of papal power alongside his affirmation of papal primacy in order to safeguard the right functioning of the ecclesiastical institution.[126]

Turrecremata shared in the common medieval polemical technique of piling up citations to all relevant authorities. He made more use of Scripture than of philosophy and at least as much use of law and theology.[127] Nor were the works of the pseudo-Areopagite susceptible to a single ecclesiological interpretation, that of the papalist comparison of the Roman pontiff's status to that of the godhead. Pseudo-Dionysius, despite the special status he accorded Peter, considered the episcopate, not the papacy, the highest level of the ecclesiastical hierarchy. Episcopalists had argued that this proved the bishops were immune from papal meddling in the right order of their sees, and Gerson had placed the ecclesiastical hierarchy within the common body of the Church, to which Christ had given the supreme governing power.[128] While Turrecremata used the doctrine of hierarchy to support papal power, Nicholas of Cusa employed it in both his conciliarist and papalist writings with no apparent worry that mention of Pseudo-Dionysius bound him to accept one or another ecclesiological doctrine.[129]

Turrecremata and his contemporaries were not blind ideologues. Conciliarism might be termed nominalist or realist,[130] ascending or descending,[131] but its real focus was the reunification and reform of the Church, not system building. Papalism, too, despite its excesses, was concerned with the unity and good order of the ecclesiastical institution, promoting its work for the welfare of souls.[132] Whatever the varying ambitions, fortunes, and ideas of men like Turrecremata, Cusa, Piccolomini, Panormitanus, and John of Segovia, they had a lively concern for the welfare of the Church that precluded their maintaining rigid doctrinal postures. Whenever the welfare of the Church seemed to dictate a change of ecclesiological stance, even the rethinking of cherished ideas, Turrecremata and his contemporaries were quick to do that thinking and to make that change.[133]

4

THE

PAPACY

A Papalist View of the Roman Church

The papalism of Johannes de Turrecremata must always
be seen against the background of his times. As we have
noted, he wrote to refute two assaults on papal
primacy—Hussitism and conciliarism. To his mind, Hussites shared with Lollards the antipapal errors of the Waldensians: thus, Hus had claimed that Christ, not the pope,
was head of the Church, and Hussite envoys to the Council
of Basel had twitted the fathers for defending papal primacy in theory while denying it in practice.[1] Nor was this
last criticism without foundation. Conciliarists, like Gerson,
Cusa, and Panormitanus, thought that the pope had wide,
but not unlimited, powers; but the Council of Basel, afraid
that Eugenius IV would defeat its reforming efforts, tried
to disestablish the Roman curia, an action rendered suspect
by the foundation of a conciliar curia.[2] Under such pres-
sures within and without the Catholic fold, papalists were
driven to make or remake claims about the exalted nature
of papal power, which in some cases sounded quite extreme. Nevertheless, remembrance of the Schism made the
more responsible papalists, the Dominican cardinal foremost among them, retain traditional safeguards against the
abuse of papal power.[3]

But Turrecremata's papalism was also related to the inherited writings of generations of papal apologists, which
he had to sift well. One of the worst conceptual tangles in

the papalist tradition concerned the meaning of the term
Romana ecclesia, which could denote the pope, pope and
cardinals, the diocese of Rome, or—its most common meaning—the universal Church. Furthermore, canonists and
publicists had ascribed to the Roman Church the supreme
power of ecclesiastical government and unfailing faith.
Here indeed was fertile ground for ecclesiological controversies. One dispute raged between Hus and his former
colleague Stanislav of Znojmo, who described the Roman
Church, composed of pope and cardinals, as the supreme
ecclesiastical authority. Hus's own argument that the Roman Church was merely a local part of the universal
Church, though it was not dissimilar to arguments used by
fellow Hussites, was viewed with suspicion by Catholic
apologists.[4] The parallel conciliarist argument rested on
the Decretists' identification of Roman Church and universal Church, which Huguccio and others deemed the
only *ecclesia* free of stain and wrinkle. Zabarella and other
conciliarists argued that a council represented this pure
Roman Church when it met to act for the good of the whole
ecclesia.[5] This general form of argument allowed the specific
contention that Jerome's description of the world as greater
than the city—"Orbis maior est urbe"—proved that a council, representing the Church (world), was greater than the
pope (city).[6]

Countering these conflicting definitions, Turrecremata
proposed instead a consistent papalist interpretation of
Romana ecclesia. In glowing terms he described the Roman
Church as the head of the congregation of the faithful, the
guardian of ecclesiastical unity, the unerring teacher whose
faith and authority would not fail to the end of time. In
sum, all other ecclesiastical dignities were founded on the
Roman Church, any denial of whose vital importance was
heretical.[7] Of course, Turrecremata carefully chose to identify this Roman Church with the papacy: any identification
of Roman Church and universal Church rested on the supremacy in jurisdiction that Christ had given to Peter and
his successors, who founded all local churches and insti-
tuted all local prelates:

> All other churches diffused throughout the world were in-
> stituted and founded by the Roman Church; therefore, all

the authority of ecclesiastical jurisdiction of prelates was derived from the pope or Roman pontiff.[8]

Like infallibility this dignity pertained to the pope's office,
not to his person. It was the office that raised the pope
above all other men, making him, in the sphere of ecclesiastical government, virtually the whole Church.[9] On this
basis Turrecremata brushed aside the conciliarist version
of Jerome's "Orbis maior est urbe" as a mere reference to
local Roman customs compared with those of the whole
Church.[10]

According to Turrecremata, pope and Roman Church
had supreme power of ecclesiastical government by Christ's
own mandate. Although he largely ignored Peter's mar-
tyrdom in Rome and the presence of his relics there, factors
which had weighed heavily in the establishment of papal
supremacy in the West,[11] Turrecremata did cite the *Quo
Vadis?* story to prove that Christ had chosen Rome as the
seat of the papacy.[12] However, the *sedes,* or office of the
pope, could be moved temporarily if such a transfer would
serve the welfare of the Church. As an example Turrecremata cited the common practice of removing the papal
court to the countryside in a plague year.[13]

In elaborating his papalist definition, Turrecremata also
faced the controversial idea of *Romana ecclesia* as comprising
pope and cardinals. And the heritage concerning the cardinalate was especially complex, involving as it did the in-
terplay of a changing institution and evolving theories right
up to Turrecremata's times.

Originally the cardinals were those bishops of the Roman
province, and clergy of Roman churches, who officiated at
services in the major basilicas. As papal power increased,
the cardinals became the pope's chief assistants in the government of the Church. The reign of Leo IX marked an
important stage in this development, when the prestige of
the Sacred College was increased by the inclusion of such
eminent churchmen as Peter Damian and Humbert of Silva
Candida. In 1059 Nicholas II gave the cardinals sole right
to elect the pope, and in the thirteenth century, the con-
sistory—pope and cardinals together—heard important
lawsuits and decided matters touching laymen and clerics
alike. During the Avignon period these "princes of the

Church" gained a regular share of the curia's revenue and had their own particular tribunals. Princes, prelates, and religious communities, as well as humbler suitors, found the friendship of cardinals an effective means of advancing their own interests. Moreover, since kinsmen of popes, servants of kings, and well-born clerics were made cardinals, the Sacred College became one of the proudest, as well as one of the most influential, institutions in Europe.[14]

These historic developments had their parallels in the realm of theory. Peter Damian termed the cardinals the "Church's senators"; Humbert of Silva Candida attributed a divine origin to the Sacred College. Some early canonists described the Roman Church as pope and cardinals sharing governance of the Church Militant, since cardinals were parts of the pope's body, his most intimate collaborators. If the pope fell into heresy, the cardinals could judge him.[15] The Decretists were quite interested in the role of cardinals in the ecclesiastical government, particularly when the papal chair was vacant and the Sacred College might be considered the head of the Church. Huguccio's dominant opinion denied such wide powers to so new an institution as the Sacred College, but the Decretalists, particularly Hostiensis, saw pope and cardinals as a corporation whose powers did not lapse upon the death of its leading member, the pope. So, Hostiensis claimed for the cardinals a share in the papal plenitude of power during the Roman pontiff's lifetime (including a voice in deciding important questions), as well as in the exercise of that power after his death.[16] Johannes Monachus, a canonist cardinal often at odds with Boniface VIII, supported this line of argument,[17] which did not, however, gain universal support among canonists.

When the cardinals convoked the First Council of Pisa, this drift toward cardinalatial oligarchy was temporarily grafted onto conciliarism. Zabarella argued that the cardinals, representing the Church, might depose a heretic pope or summon a council to do so.[18] At Constance, d'Ailly wrote tracts intended to prove that the cardinals should direct the council's proceedings. Like Humbert, d'Ailly thought that Christ had founded the Sacred College in the persons of the Apostles, his companions, and that cardinals succeeded to that position just as the pope succeeded to Peter's role as Vicar of Christ.[19] (D'Ailly found support for his theory in the works of publicists like Giles of Rome, Augustinus Triumphus, and Petrus de Palude, who were more concerned with jurisdiction—a power in which all cardinals might claim a share—than with orders, in which some of them were inferior to bishops.)[20] But the alliance between conciliarism and cardinalatial pretensions was tenuous and short lived. At Constance the fathers carefully limited the role of cardinals in the decision-making process, even in the election of Martin V, while at Basel they tried to restrict the numbers, powers, and revenues of the cardinals.[21]

While this breach was growing, Eugenius IV ruled that cardinals outranked all bishops, even when the cardinal was not a bishop and not resident in Rome.[22] For their part, the cardinals transferred their pretensions back into curial politics, usually manifesting them in the form of electoral capitulations, in which each cardinal in a conclave promised, if elected, to increase the powers and revenues of the Sacred College. During the Schism there was some excuse for such capitulations, since they bound each new pope to work for ecclesiastical unity; after the Schism, however, bitter struggles ensued between popes and cardinals over broken promises made in conclave. (At one point Dominicus de Dominicis advised Calixtus III to make concessions to the cardinals but then withdrew the suggestion during the reign of Pius II.[23] Paul II forced the cardinals to renounce the capitulations made before his election and employed writers like Theodoro Lelli and Andreas Barbatia to defend his actions; these polemicists went so far as to question the belief that Christ had founded the Sacred College.)[24]

Turrecremata's only recorded role in all of these papal-cardinal proceedings was his ready cooperation with Pius II in the pontiff's dealings with the College of Cardinals. Yet, our cardinal, borrowing from d'Ailly's works, wrote about the Sacred College in very lofty terms. Accordingly, Hubert Jedin has suggested that Turrecremata's works on ecclesiology, with their exaltation of the cardinalate, contributed (at least indirectly) to the oligarchic movement in the Sacred College[25]—an opinion that requires some reexamination.

According to Turrecremata, the Sacred College was founded by Christ in the persons of the Apostles. They served Peter in the same way before undertaking their separate missions; then a separate College of Cardinals, with its own apostolic succession, was created to assist Peter's successors, the popes. Therefore the cardinalatial dignity anteceded the episcopal and took precedence over it. Cardinals advised popes, aided them, and elected their successors; through their pastoral labors bishops assisted popes less directly. As the pope's direct assistants in Church government, the cardinals could be described as parts of his body or, figuratively, as the Church's representatives and its Senate. Because of the cardinals' collaboration in the papal work of ecclesiastical government, their powers could be termed universal.[26]

Although such general statements lend some substance to Jedin's assessment of Turrecremata's influence, they should be counterbalanced by the cardinal's specific ideas on the role of the Sacred College. For Turrecremata the most signal function of the cardinals was the election of the pope. Certain conciliarists, notably Zabarella and Panormitanus, thought the Sacred College represented the whole Church in performing this task.[27] Turrecremata, on the other hand, thought that since the power of election had been conferred on the cardinals by God alone, no one, not even a reigning pope, could take it away. Neither could a pope circumvent normal procedures by nominating his own successor, an act which would undermine the *status ecclesiae*, nor even a saint become Christ's Vicar by different means.[28] Whomever the cardinals chose, following proper procedures and unswayed by corruption, became pope. And the pope-elect would succeed immediately to the jurisdictional powers of his office even if he were a mere layman lacking priestly ordination and episcopal consecration. (Here Turrecremata followed the canonists and such publicists as Augustinus Triumphus, ignoring the ancient idea that all episcopal powers were inherent in consecration—a concept of prelacy revived by Jean Gerson, as noted above.)[29] Moreover, since the pope assumed an office—and did not, as in the ancient concept of episcopate, marry his see—he could resign if he thought that would promote the Church's welfare. (Here Turrecremata echoed the arguments that had surrounded the abdication of Celestine V, when legists and the Franciscan theologian Peter Olivi had defended the concept of office from the spiritual Franciscans' more traditional arguments against abdication.)[30]

If the cardinals were to become entangled in a disputed election, they should not resolve the dispute themselves, thought Turrecremata, since judging their own case would violate all norms of justice. Decision between claimants belonged to a general council. Looking to the precedent set at Constance, Turrecremata said that a council's combination of power and prestige could best establish an indubitable pope on Peter's chair.[31] When discussing problems arising from a conclave, he failed to mention electoral capitulations but made it clear that it was not the choice of the cardinals that conferred the power inherent in the papal office: upon election the pope-elect received his official authority from Christ. Thus, it was inconsonant with Turrecremata's ecclesiology that the new pope be bound to carry out the cardinals' will.[32]

So much for the electoral role of the cardinals. But what did Turrecremata view as their role in ecclesiastical government during a vacancy of the Roman see? Hostiensis, as we have seen, had argued that the plenitude of power devolved onto the cardinals, a claim butressed by the idea that the *Romana ecclesia* consisted of pope and cardinals.[33] And some conciliarists even thought that the plenitude of power reverted to the universal Church and its representative, the general council.[34] But Turrecremata consistently denied that anyone but a new pope could succeed to the plenitude of power inherent in the papal office identified as the true Roman Church. The cardinals were only figuratively parts of the pope's body, and thus they were unable to exercise papal power during a vacancy. The plenitude of power simply lay dormant in the immortal office for want of a proper administrator. (Likewise a cathedral chapter could not exercise the episcopal powers of a dead bishop.)[35] Turrecremata specifically criticized an aspect of Hostiensis's oligarchic theory by denying that cardinals could coopt new members into their own ranks during vacancy.[36] Yet the Church was not helpless or illprovided during such a period. The sacramental functions of the clergy, dependent directly on Christ, never lapsed, and the ordinary exercise of jurisdiction *in partem sollicitudinis* still belonged to bishops and other prelates. Their powers were, after all, derived from the immortal papal

office, not from the mortal person of the pope.[37] A brief
interregnum was unlikely to see the eruption of a major
crisis; Turrecremata provided for an emergency, however,
in claiming that the prelates of the Church had sufficient
authority to meet in general council in order to provide
any necessary remedies. The cardinals could convoke such
an assembly, not on their own authority, but *vicem capitis*.[38]

Finally, oligarchic ideas espoused by Hostiensis and Johannes Monachus included the suggestion that cardinals
should consent to important papal decisions.[39] Turrecremata (his attitude toward this pretension is the best guide
to his view of the oligarchic movement) thought that the
cardinals were the pope's assistants and chief counsellors,
forming with him the highest tribunal of the Church. This
share in the pope's governing responsibilities served as further proof that the cardinalate was the second rung of the
ecclesiastical hierarchy.[40] But all these marks of status were
purely derivative, because the cardinals "are assumed by
the supreme pontiff, the Vicar of Christ, to his assistance
and co-operation in the rule of the Christian common-
wealth." Any share the cardinals had in the exercise of the
papal plenitude of power was a matter of delegation only.[41]
Thus, the pope did not need the cardinals' consent to any
decision: the pope could do without the cardinals whatever
he can do with the cardinals. The advice of the Sacred
College might add the prestige of learned counsel to papal
pronouncements but nothing more.[42]

To resume, although Turrecremata exalted the Sacred
College, he rejected its more extreme oligarchic pretensions, those associated with such great names as Hostiensis,
d'Ailly, and, in his own day, Nicholas of Cusa. He believed
that the College of Cardinals was indeed founded by Christ,
with a great dignity and an important role in ecclesiastical
government. Nevertheless, Turrecremata's rejection of
what he felt were unnecessary limits on papal power left
him outside the camp of those who favored cardinalatial
oligarchy.[43]

The Office of Vicar of Christ

In his consideration of yet another historically evolved
concept of the papacy—the pope as the Vicar of

Christ—Turrecremata characteristically avoided extremes and acknowledged limits, while exalting the papal office.

Just as the Roman see had experienced varying fortunes, so too the very concept of papal power had changed gradually during the ages before the Dominican cardinal wrote his treatises. The earliest theoretical emphasis lay on the continuing presence of Peter in Rome, through his relics or through the pope as his successor and representative *(vicarius Petri)*. In the later Middle Ages, papalists went far beyond this doctrine, claiming that the Roman pontiff was Christ's representative on earth *(vicarius Christi)* and possessed the plenitude of power. The term *"vicarius Christi,"* adopted by Innocent III from the writings of Bernard of Clairvaux into the official vocabulary of the papal chancery, was adopted by canonists like Alanus and Hostiensis, by publicists like Augustinus Triumphus, and by theologians like Petrus de Palude and Herveus Natalis. The most extreme of these theorists ascribed to the Roman pontiff a quasi-divine status with minimal restrictions on the exercise of his powers.[44] It was exactly this confidence in any reigning pope which upset Hus. Not being a lawyer given to distinguishing between office and person, the Czech reformer, and many like him, could not believe that tenure of office conferred on the Roman pontiff a quasi-divine status independent of his individual sanctity. Hus therefore demanded that the pope's conduct be so pure as to demonstrate that he was Christ's representative.[45]

In his writings Turrecremata ascribed a wide variety of titles to the pope as an illustration of papal preeminence. A few, such as "father," referred to the primacy of honour held by the pope,[46] but most involved the plenitude of power, through which the hierarchy was founded and directed. The pope was the head through which the body (the Church) received all sense stimuli, that is, all jurisdiction, the power in which the pope was virtually the whole ecclesiastical body.[47] Like many Thomists Turrecremata considered monarchy the best form of human government and the best promoter of both unity and peace. Following this version of Aristotelean political theory, he argued that God had wisely founded the Church as a papal monarchy.[48] In fact, after Christ the pope was the second founder of the Church. As Christ was the rock on which the Church rested, so Peter was the cornerstone of the edifice.[49]

As heir to the papalist tradition, Turrecremata placed the greatest emphasis on the papal title "Vicar of Christ." Thus, he wrote that "the pope holds the place of Christ in the Church."[50] In more cautious terms, he described Peter and his successors as holding Christ's place as visible head of the Church—uniting, ruling, and teaching the faithful by virtue of his office.[51] Although the interior influx of grace depended directly on Christ, the exterior influx of jurisdiction came through the office of his Vicar.[52] Turrecremata denied that this doctrine left the Church with two heads and so violated its unity or (what was blasphemous in Hussite eyes) that it closely identified Christ and the pope. The Roman pontiff held a juridical office as Christ's representative on earth, and only within the scope of this commission were his judgments to be considered those of Christ himself.[53]

The powers assigned the pope were such that they could only come from God, not men. Indeed these powers were so great that papal acts could be described as those of the Church itself.[54] Consequently, the pope's ability to act for the welfare of the Church could not be impeded by the wishes of the faithful. The Vicar of Christ was supposed to serve their best interests, not their whims.[55] To preserve this freedom of action, Turrecremata denied all other theories of the origins of papal power, whether they were propounded by heretics like Marsilius, by conciliarists, or even by past papalist writers. He even rejected the hoary term *"vicarius Petri,"* because it inserted an intermediary between Christ and the reigning Roman pontiff.[56] Papal power was universal, unconfined by local ecclesiastical boundaries; if it were only local, the Church would be headless and disordered. With the Hussites in mind, Turrecremata claimed that rejection of this unifying principle was tantamount to heresy and treason.[57] Moreover, papal power was immediate to each member of the Church. Despite the use of subordinates to tend his scattered flock, the pope could minister to the needs of any Christian anywhere. Answering the old episcopalist argument that local prelates were more immediate to the faithful, Turrecremata argued that the pope, font of all jurisdiction, was more immediate than any lesser prelate, whose authority was local and derivative; others, that is, the friars, could be assigned to help bishops care for the neglected spiritual needs of the faithful without the friars' privileges violating any fundamental ecclesiological principle. Defiance of papal decisions designed to save souls was a schismatic act.[58]

Practical ramifications of this papal power were multiplex in theory and practice; they included disposition of cures of souls, collation of benefices, exemptions, and the like. The pope could dispose of all ecclesiastical offices, even by granting reservations in the lifetimes of their tenants. (Here Turrecremata placed the governmental supremacy of the Roman see ahead of demands made at Constance and Basel for reform of the much abused papal patronage system.)[59] Moreover, all indulgences flowed to the faithful from the Roman pontiff through his agents, the clergy.[60]

The sacraments and dogmatic canons derived their validity directly from Christ, of course, but the positive law of the Church, canon law, was established by the pope, directly or through lesser prelates. As founder of the law, the Roman pontiff was untrammelled by its provisions *(legibus solutus)*, like the emperor in Roman law. The pope, therefore, could change even the most ancient regulations handed down by the Fathers, alter conciliar canons, and revoke the decretals of his predecessors whenever such changes served the welfare of the Church. Nevertheless, the pope was not exempt from divine law or natural law:[61] though not bound in positive law by his predecessors' enactments *(par in parem non habet imperium)*, a heretic pope, as Johannes Teutonicus had noted, fell under any condemnation of false doctrine issued by a previous pontiff.[62] Even in matters of positive law, the pope should set an example of obedience for his subjects.[63] However great were papal powers in matters of law, Turrecremata's discussion of them was designed to promote the welfare of souls, not just papal absolutism.

Moreover, as founder of canon law, the Roman pontiff was also its chief interpreter and the source of dispensations from its provisions. This latter power extended to dispensation from (though not abolition of) the canons of the Apostles and other fundamental ecclesiastical regulations.[64] Similarly, the pope was the chief judge of the faithful. By virtue of his plenitude of power, he was the *ecclesia* of Matt.

18:17, "If he [your brother] refuses to hear them, tell the Church." Conciliarists understood this text as referring to the powers of a council, since a council represented the Church. Turrecremata replied that most disputes could not easily be referred to such an assembly, let alone to all the faithful; thus, the pope was the chief judge of ecclesiastical causes, even those involving his fellow bishops. Furthermore, the chief judge was also the chief reformer of abuses.[65] Though papal judgments primarily concerned spiritual matters, they could extend to secular affairs relevant to the salvation of souls.[66] The attempt of Basel to impede appeals from council to pope was an unjust assault on this papal judicial supremacy.[67]

The offices of pastor, legislator, and judge required coercive power to insure obedience. Thus, Turrecremata argued that the pope had at his disposal the *two swords* (Luke 22:38), temporal as well as spiritual force, to be wielded for the welfare of the Church. This Biblical metaphor had been used by Gratian and Bernard of Clairvaux to demonstrate the availability of both spiritual and temporal coercion to help end a schism. Huguccio wrote that the pope possessed the spiritual sword but that the temporal sword was in the emperor's hand. Alanus replied that the pope held both swords and bestowed temporal power on princes, an argument taken up by such extreme papalists as Giles of Rome. Turrecremata reverted to the earlier theory of Gratian and Bernard, arguing that the pope possessed the spiritual sword and could direct the employment of its temporal counterpart.[68] While rejecting the hierocratic extreme of Alanus and Giles, Turrecremata also eschewed its opposite. Critics of the papacy, like Marsilius, Wycliff, and Hus, had argued that the Church had no right to temporal power. Turrecremata replied that the pope could employ force against heretics, schismatics, and other obdurate malefactors and even censure princes who failed to coerce them.[69] Coupled with these temporal concerns was the pope's role as chief administrator of the Church's goods. Although ownership of material goods, according to Turrecremata and most canonists, belonged to the faithful for the support of good works, the pope could dispose of these goods as he saw fit, without the consent of others.[70]

Turrecremata's enumeration of such papal powers and

titles was hardly new. Any papalist of the preceding century—Petrus de Palude, Giles of Rome, Augustinus Triumphus—had used expressions either as strong or stronger to describe papal primacy. And Turrecremata's younger contemporaries, Arévalo or Theodoro Lelli, for example, were less cautious papalists than he. Only the conciliar epoch—a backdrop of theories designed to limit the exercise of papal power—made Turrecremata's defense of the papacy, against severe checks on its work for the welfare of the Church, appear to be absolutist theorizing.[71]

The Limits of Papal Power

As we have seen, for Turrecremata the papal office was the true Roman Church, and tenure of that office made the pope the highest ecclesiastical authority, one with a right to command princes to certain correct actions. But tenure of that office also imposed limits on the pope's actions. If the pontiff passed these bounds—violating natural or divine law, teaching heresy, or otherwise threatening the welfare of the Church—he was a tyrant who could lose his see and be punished.[72] Turrecremata was hard put to balance his defense of papal power with this very real concern for the welfare of the Church. He contended that the pope was subject only to Christ, whose vicar he was, and providence would preserve the Church, even by striking the pope dead. Yet Turrecremata could not rest content with this assertion of trust in Providence. From reverence for traditional ideas about the possibility of papal heresy, or moved by memories of the Schism, Turrecremata created safeguards on the exercise of papal power, designed to protect the Church's welfare without destroying the pope's freedom of action.[73]

Two key questions had long been involved in limiting the abuse of papal power: what crimes could be punished and how that punishment should be administered. Throughout the Middle Ages there was no single accepted solution to either problem but, rather, two major traditions about each, which are best represented by the conflicting opinions of the canonists Huguccio and Alanus. Whereas Huguccio believed that the pope was subject to punishment for heresy and other crimes that, because they scandalized the faithful, were tantamount to heresy, Alanus, intent on preventing irresponsible attacks on the pope's orthodoxy, argued that only obstinate adherence to false doctrine could be punished. Huguccio's doctrine described the pope as automatically falling from his see when he erred grievously: the erstwhile Vicar of Christ became less than any Christian and subject to punishment since his errors had cost him the papal judicial immunity. Alanus demanded a formal judgment of the erring pope by a general council: at the time he wrote, there was less likelihood for such a judgment to be unjustly rendered than for enemies of the Roman see to claim that the pope had deposed himself through misconduct or error; nor could those foes summon a council; for, under canon law, that was the prerogative of the pope. Most canonists, like Guido de Baysio, were inclined to accept Alanus's doctrine. Huguccio's doctrine, however, found advocates in diverse figures like the Franciscans Peter Olivi and Michael of Cesena, who feared abuse of papal power, and papal apologists like Augustinus Triumphus and Petrus de Palude.[74]

By Turrecremata's time, the Schism made these questions of immediate importance to responsible ecclesiastics. They sought means to rid the Church of conflicting pretenders to the papacy—claimants who, though orthodox, endangered the welfare of the institution. Thus, most conciliarists adopted Huguccio's doctrine on crimes which made the pope vulnerable to judgment. Jurists like Zabarella and Conrad of Gelnhausen were willing to judge the pope's fitness to reign by potentially subjective standards, a theme taken up by Panormitanus and Cusa, who argued that a pope could be deposed for scandalizing the faithful or for impeding his own work for the welfare of the Church. Cusa even suggested that a pope could be deposed for incompetence. But it is worth noting that Cusa became the Hercules of the Eugenians and Panormitanus opposed, on behalf of the House of Aragon, any rash attempt to depose Eugenius IV. In the crucial debate on deposition, canonists proved less willing than theologians to believe Eugenius guilty of crimes against the Church.[75]

For his part, Turrecremata reacted strongly against any too close identification of moral failings with heresy, arguing (with Hussites as well as conciliarists in mind) that subjective standards for judging prelatial acts could reduce the Church to chaos. In such a case each man would be faced with a choice of which commands he would obey. Nevertheless, Turrecremata did not embrace the fullness of Alanus's doctrine. He permitted denunciation of the pope for any crime which, by its very nature, deprived him of his immunity.[76] According to Turrecremata the chief of these crimes was heresy, the stubborn contradiction of Scripture or defined dogma; an erroneous pronouncement violated the pope's duty of teaching the truth to the faithful.[77] Further, the pope was supposed to maintain the *status ecclesiae*, the good order of the ecclesiastical institution, so that it could function for the salvation of souls.[78] Included under this rubric was the observation of all divine ordinances: divine law, natural law, the order of the sacraments, and the fundamental principles of Christian morality. A pope could never deliberately contradict any of these without harming the Church and making himself liable to judgment.[79] Scholars have often emphasized the way in which the concept of office freed the pope from control by his inferiors, but Turrecremata thought that the papal office itself also had limiting effects. The pope could not act contrary to the saving purpose for which his office existed without risking loss of his judicial immunity.[80]

Turrecremata's doctrine on the punishment of an erring pope varied with his personal experiences. At Basel he began by admitting that, as was stated in *Haec sancta*, a council could overrule a pope in matters of heresy, schism, and reform of the Church in head and members. By the time of his break with the Council of Basel, however, Turrecremata was near to rejecting all limits on papal power. In his *Flores sententiarum*, ignoring relevant materials in Aquinas's works, Turrecremata's last word on an erring pope was concerned with fraternal correction, not deposition. During his debate with Cesarini at the Council of Florence, Turrecremata reaffirmed the possibility of deposition, and thereafter he carefully described and circumscribed the machinery for calling to account an erring pope.[81]

This machinery is best studied in the context of doctrinal deviation, where conciliarists and papalists followed dif-

ferent legal opinions. In a period of crisis like that of the
Schism, the Church resorted to the convocation of general
councils to deal with its problems. In such an atmosphere,
it became possible for a pope to be accused and tried before
a council in accord with the doctrine of Alanus, echoes of
which can be found in the works of Turrecremata's contemporaries, among them Panormitanus, Nicholas of Cusa,
and John of Segovia. The Councils of Constance and Basel
actually conducted the sort of trials these described.[82] Turrecremata deliberately avoided this approach, instead
adopting the doctrine of Huguccio, who thought that the
pope could automatically lose his see through doctrinal
deviation. That doctrine gave the Church some measure
of safety against abuse of papal power but left no space for
conciliarist pretensions to formally judging the pope.[83]

Accordingly, Turrecremata established a set of procedures by which the presumption of self-deposition could
be reached. Strict limits were placed on the first step, accusation, the point on which Huguccio's doctrine left the
pope most vulnerable, since many crimes could be equated
with heresy. As we have noted, Turrecremata narrowed
the possible charges to those most closely connected with
faith or the welfare of the Church. Not even the notorious
crime of simony was a ground for accusation, since it was
a moral rather than a theological problem. Even a heresy
case was supposed to concern errors already condemned.[84]
Nor could just anyone accuse the pope of heresy. Charges
had to be brought by trustworthy and learned men, such
as the cardinals, to whom the truth of the accusation was
painfully obvious. Mere suspicion did not justify subjecting
the Church to a crisis of leadership.[85] Moreover, the pope
should be allowed every opportunity to clear himself of the
charges by making a profession of faith and, if necessary,
doing penance; to obviate scandal, he could even resign his
see. But the Roman pontiff could not merely dismiss the
charges. It was best for the accused to consult responsible
individuals or, preferably, to call a general council.[86]

If the pope failed to clear himself voluntarily, the cardinals could demand convocation of a council to inquire
into the case. Turrecremata could hardly believe that an
accused would fail to call a council, since a refusal would
lend credibility to the charges. If, however, the pope also

refused to call a council, the power of convocation devolved on the cardinals, who could, as true guardians of the Church, provide for its welfare in such a crisis.[87] The Sacred College could confer upon a council's proceedings its own immenese prestige.[88] (Should even the cardinals fail to act, the power of convocation devolved on the emperor, other Christian princes, or even lesser prelates, for the Church's safeguards against papal heresy could not be allowed to fail because someone shirked his duty.)[89] Despite the role assigned the cardinals, Turrecremata wanted to justify more fully a council's ability to examine the case of a pope it could not formally depose. He hoped to provide a minister for the law that safeguarded the Church's welfare, without creating (like the conciliarists) a rival to the papacy.[90] He therefore denied the claim of both Constance and Basel to have received some sort of general commission from Christ to oversee ecclesiastical government. Nor was a council, despite its emergency powers, to become the highest ecclesiastical tribunal: that would make the council the pope's rival when in session, turning the Church into a two-headed monster.[91] Rather, Christ's law lent authority to the council to deal with specific crises. Under this law, the very fact of accusation made a pope, even if innocent, subject to proceedings to determine his true status.[92]

Such council proceedings, Turrecremata insisted, were to be conducted in the most discreet manner possible. If the fathers found any truth in the charge, they should patiently explain to the pope his errors, while employing Scripture and the decisions of the Church.[93] Just as Paul rebuked Peter (Gal. 2:11), even so a council, moved by the truth and pastoral concern, could offer a pope fraternal correction.[94] If the pontiff obstinately refused to accept correction, he was an obstinate heretic who had lost the true faith necessary to hold his office. Without membership in the Church through faith, it was impossible to hold the power of the keys, and thus a heretic pope ceased to be head of the Church. Fallen from the rock of Peter's faith, he lost his judicial immunity along with his tenure of office, making him subject to the jurisdiction of lesser prelates assembled in council. This was true even in a case of secret heresy, since God would make hidden errors public.[95]

In certain passages, Turrecremata actually said that the

council "deposed" a heretic pope; if meant literally, this would have been a major concession to conciliarism.[96] But Turrecremata usually made it clear that he intended a declarative procedure, in which the council would announce that the pope had lost his office, rather than a formal condemnation. Like John of Paris and Herveus Natalis, Turrecremata thought that a council announced to the faithful the fact that a pope had forfeited his see. The council's power of inquiry thus allowed it to "depose" a pope. This concept of deposition limited possible abuses of papal power but made no real concession to conciliarism.[97] Moreover, Turrecremata tried to deflate conciliarist claims that councils had judged erring popes in the past, by proving that even the safeguards he had outlined had never come into play. The classic cases of papal heresy were those of Anastasius II and Marcellinus, both mentioned in the *Decretum*, and of Pope Honorius I, cited in a *palea*.[98] Turrecremata argued that Marcellinus had repented his errors; Anastasius was punished by God, not man; and Honorius was not a Monothelite. As in his doctrine of infallibility, Turrecremata wanted to believe the papacy was unstained by error, though he would not abandon traditional safeguards against it.[99]

Turrecremata treated crimes against the *status ecclesiae* in the same way that he treated papal heresy. If the pope tried overtly to upset the ecclesiastical constitution, for example, by deposing all other bishops, he could be regarded as a self-deposed heretic.[100] But Turrecremata's approach to other crimes was more cautious in that it encouraged resistance to tyrannical acts without infringing on the pope's judicial immunity. Papal commands dangerous to the welfare of souls, those which violated divine law or natural law, could be ignored because the pope had exceeded his powers.[101] If the pontiff persistently issued such commands, the cardinals could call him to account, offering fraternal correction and insisting that he swear an oath purging himself of the charges. If these actions failed to secure amendment of the pope's conduct, the cardinals could renounce obedience. Their resistance would be virtuous, since it served the welfare of the Church, and could be reenforced through convocation of a council to win support of other prelates and the secular arm.[102] If even this did not end the crisis, the Church had one further hope, short of a providential event. The pope could persevere in his wrong actions but not defend them: should he do that, he would fall into the heresy of describing evil as good, for which he could lose his see! This, Turrecremata said, was the true meaning of Johannes Teutonicus's declaration that a scandalous pope was a heretic in the eyes of God.[103]

Finally, Turrecremata tackled the problem of papal schism—a grave threat, not only to the good government of the ecclesiastical institution, but to its very unity, one of the marks of its divine origin. Since Christ had established the papacy to settle divisive disputes, there could not be two popes.[104] Turrecremata distinguished between different types of schisms: an attempt by an intruder to oust a licitly elected pope and a dispute between two pretenders whose claims to the papal office were difficult to judge. In either case a council was the best forum for settling the dispute. If it found the case to be one of intrusion, the council could expel the false claimant.[105] If, however, the intruder could not be compelled to give up his pretensions, perhaps because he had not been apprehended by a prince or prelate, Turrecremata denied that the true pope could be removed from office as a sacrifice to the cause of unity, denouncing such a suggestion as a source of further scandal and division[106] (the pope's conscience might move him to abdicate, however, if it would serve the welfare of the Church).[107] In the case of two claimants, certain gambits might be tried to bring an end to the crisis. Turrecremata reviewed all the suggestions made before the convocation of the Council of Pisa: simultaneous resignation of both pretenders, election of one pretender by both obediences after the other pretender's death, a conference between the pretenders, even armed conflict.[108] As a former participant in the reunifying work of the Council of Constance, Turrecremata readily concluded that the best recourse was the convocation of a general council. If neither claimant could make a convincing case for himself or was thought worthy of being pope, the council could set both aside to make way for a new election. That he granted a council such a great power over pretenders to the Roman see shows the extent to which Turrecremata shared common ground with his conciliarist contemporaries.[109]

Certain scholars have unfavorably judged Turrecremata's doctrine of the limits of papal power, either because he did not teach pure papal absolutism or because he granted the pope excessive immunity from formal condemnation.[110] Both criticisms demand from Turrecremata an uncompromising purism foreign to his works. The Dominican cardinal had to pick his way between reaction against the Council of Basel, which often justified its excesses by an appeal to equity,[111] and his concern for the welfare of the Church. Furthermore, the defense of papal judicial immunity and the imposition of limits on the abuse of papal power were both part of the tradition in which he was working.[112] Because he bore all these concerns in mind and did not try to stand firmly in any one narrow, ideological camp, Turrecremata was able to formulate a coherent and balanced, if complex, theory of papal power.

5

THE
GENERAL
COUNCIL

Debating the Constance Decrees

Perhaps no aspect of Johannes de Turrecremata's ecclesiology has impinged upon more ancient and modern controversy than have his views about the general council. As usual, however, we shall find that his ideas were first formed amid the conflicts of his own era, then gradually shaped by him into a coherent doctrine. This development began with his changing positions on the Constance decrees, primarily *Haec sancta* and also *Frequens*—decrees which have been the subject of debate from his time till our own.

In Turrecremata's troubled age, the Basel conciliarists used many arguments to prove council superior to pope. But it was on the precedent set at the Council of Constance—which ended the Schism, condemned Wycliff, executed Hus, and tried to reform the Church —that their case rested solidly. In the decree *Haec sancta*, Constance had claimed a common reponsibility for the welfare of the Church and made a council superior to a pope in matters of heresy, schism, and reform. Although the decree was originally drafted to meet the emergency created by the flight John XXIII, it was widely understood to be the definitive statement of conciliar supremacy in ecclesiastical government. Its claim was implemented in the decree *Frequens*, which provided for a regular series of councils to watch over the Church. Throughout its troubled history, the Council of Basel acted with these decrees in mind; and Cesarini and his colleagues, when they cited them in open debate to defy Eugenius IV, reaffirmed the Constance decrees as binding upon the whole Church. Even at Florence, Cesarini's statement of the conciliarist case made extensive use of *Haec sancta*.[1] It was the failure of Basel to reform the Church—producing a schism instead—that seriously diminished the prestige the decrees enjoyed more than did Turrecremata's answer to Cesarini, which we shall examine in due course.

But the demand for a reforming council never entirely died out. Louis XII of France used that demand as a weapon against Julius II in the so-called *conciliabulum* of Pisa. Even the papacy, which held conciliar agitation in suspicion, twice resorted to the convocation of general councils, the Fifth Lateran Council and the great Council of Trent. After Trent, however, the desire for a general council became identified with Gallicanism, which caused the First Vatican Council's condemnation of appeals from pope to council.[2] After that condemnation, Catholic historians, who always had some qualms about the proceedings of the Council of Constance, tended to dismiss *Haec sancta* and *Frequens* as short-lived mistakes produced by the passions and uncertainties of the Schism.[3]

When the Second Vatican Council reawakened interest in the conciliar crisis, *Haec sancta* became once more the subject of much controversy. Paul de Vooght has claimed that the decree had been defined as dogma by a general council and accepted as such by the popes of the times;[4] his contention has aroused much passion and stimulated no less research. Hans Küng has argued that, as a conciliar decree, *Haec sancta* was valid on its own merits and without papal approval. Joseph Gill replied by calling it the invalid decree of one obedience of the Schism. Between these extremes, noted scholars like Hubert Jedin, August Franzen, and Brian Tierney have sought to place the decree in its temporal context, as a preliminary of determining its place in ecclesiology and political theory. But there is still no consensus.[5]

A side effect of this controversy has been that of drawing Turrecremata into the argument. Vooght has charged that Turrecremata (from whom Gill drew his argument) initi-

ated a deviation from sound doctrine—a claim copied zealously by generations of Catholic historians—when he
attacked *Haec sancta* in his debate with Cesarini, even
though he had accepted it at the beginning of his career.[6]
Turrecremata's change of opinion was part of a gradual,
pragmatic development. He at first readily accepted the
decree, which had, after all, a key place in the reestablish-
ment of ecclesiastical unity. In his early days at Basel, Turrecremata admitted the council's ability to overrule the
pope in matters of heresy, schism, and reform (perhaps,
as we have noted, he understood "reform" as refering to
the *status ecclesiae*). But Turrecremata reproved those who
thought reform included meddling with papal prerogative.[7] As he fought a losing fight at Basel, he began to
question the validity of *Haec sancta*.[8] After leaving Basel,
he decided that conciliarism had to be rooted out of the
Church, and especially by refuting *Haec sancta*'s explicit
claim that Christ gave the council power apart from papal
power. Thus, in his debate with Cesarini Turrecremata
made the first explicit, effective attack on the degree, an
assault which set a precedent for later Catholic interpretations of it.[9]

Because *Haec sancta* commanded the respect of many
churchmen, as it once had his own, Turrecremata avoided
terming it heretical. Instead, with papal encouragement,
he developed the line of argument first adumbrated at
Basel: a description of *Haec sancta* as the act of one obedience of the Schism.[10] Thereafter, Turrecremata always
described the decree as issued by the followers of John
XXIII in the absence of the other obediences and, consequently, not the act of a true general council.[11] This denial
required a reinterpretation of the Council of Constance.
Despite that he once suggested that convocation by Gregory
XII legitimized the assembly,[12] Turrecremata's doctrine
emphasized the importance of the gathering of all three
obediences. The council became valid only after the former
followers of Benedict XIII arrived and remained valid long
enough to depose the Avignon claimant, enact *Frequens*,
and arrange for the election of a new pope.[13] According
to Turrecremata, the Council of Constance did not depose
a true pope; it disposed of two unworthy claimants to the
Roman see, John XXIII and Benedict XIII. Although John

was removed from office before the three obediences were assembled, he, like his opponent, was suspect of heresy and thus readily removable.[14] Turrecremata defended on similar grounds the condemnation of Wycliff and Hus of the same period. Moreover, Martin V had confirmed these sentences in the bull *Inter cunctas,* which also reaffirmed the status of belief in papal supremacy as an article of faith.[15] Perhaps Turrecremata's strongest secondary argument against the conciliarist use of *Haec sancta* was his contention that the Council of Constance had rejected it by placing the reform of the curia in the pope's hands.[16] Turrecremata's attack on *Haec sancta* left only one key question unanswered, that of the legal right of one obedience to try John XXIII, Wycliff, and Hus in the absence of the other two.

In addition to refuting *Haec sancta,* Turrecremata found it necessary to attack *Frequens.* Not only did that decree provide for a regular series of councils to supervise the governance of the Church, but it stipulated that these assemblies could not be transferred or dissolved without the consent of their participants. *Frequens* thus remained a latent threat to papal power throughout the fifteen century: the French based their demand for a third, neutral council on the contention that Eugenius IV had violated *Frequens* when he transferred the Council of Basel to Ferrara without the consent of its members; whenever the King of Bohemia or the German princes conflicted with the curia, they appealed to a future council. These appeals overshadowed suggestions by responsible churchmen like Cusa and Henricus de Campo to call a reforming council. And papalists like Gabriel Biel, Theodoro Lelli, and Rodrigo Sánchez de Arévalo answered the more political appeals by questioning the value of a general council. Finally Pius II, while at Manuta, issued the decree *Execrabilis* that actually forbade appeals from pope to council.[17]

It is small wonder in this context that Turrecremata attacked *Frequens,* particularly when he refuted Charles VII's arguments in favor of a council on a third, neutral site. Turrecremata argued that *Frequens* lacked legal status. Neither had the papacy accepted it, nor had the fathers at Constance given it their unanimous consent. Even if they had, the pope would not be bound by *Frequens,* since it concerned only positive law, which did not bind Christ's vicar. Once the conciliar crisis had died down, Turrecremata rescinded the first of his arguments. *Frequens* had, after all, been issued by the three obediences, and Martin V had convoked the councils it mandated. So Turrecremata simply maintained that the pope was not bound by the decree, since it was not concerned with dogma.[18]

Even as a member of the Council of Basel, Turrecremata rejected certain of its decrees as perversions of ecclesiastical law. He later argued that the more radical decrees had never received papal approval. (Eugenius IV reinforced this position when he told Turrecremata that his bull *Dudum* [1433], which sanctioned the proceedings at Basel, was worthless because his approbation had been obtained by coercion. Eugenius maintained, moreover, that he had always reserved his rights from any infringement by conciliar legislation.)[19] But his harshest words were those directed against the decrees the Council of Basel issued after breaking with the pope: these were the illegal acts of a headless assembly abandoned by its more responsibile members, and at least one of them, which approved the doctrine of the Immaculate Conception, was a deviation from sound doctrine.[20]

The Desirability of a Council

Turrecremata nevertheless did not deny the desirability of a general council, even though the papal apologists, like Arévalo, tended to question the value of any such assembly on the grounds that reform was the pope's business in which a council would be useless.[21] Yet, one modern scholar, John Hine Mundy, has interpreted Turrecremata's attack on conciliarism as an attempt to discourage convocation of future councils.[22] Nor is this an idle question, for, as already noted, the late fifteenth and early sixteenth centuries heard much talk of reform and saw abortive attempts to implement such schemes; there was also a less fervid continuation of the ecclesiological debates of the Conciliar Crisis.[23] Turrecremata's ecclesiology, as we shall see, had an important place in these debates, especially in the writings of Cajetan.[24] Mundy's question about Turrecremata's attitude toward a general council is thus of no small importance.

The bitterness of Turrecremata's anticonciliar polemics is evident in such diatribes as his contention that the electors of Felix V had followed the antipapal errors of the Waldensians.[25] The Dominican cardinal never entirely despaired of the value of a general council, however. While denying that an assembly should settle all problems, he admitted that it was an excellent place for resolving the most serious ones.[26] Although a general council could not create a new, nonpapal power to deal with emergencies,[27] its uses were manifold. Among the reasons for calling a council Turrecremata listed condemnation of false doctrine, inquiry into the pope's orthodoxy, termination of a schism, reform, enforcement of another council's decisions, and deep deliberations concerning the welfare of the Church.[28] The value of a council in such circumstances rested on its prestige and on the aggregate wisdom of assembled prelates and doctors. Even papal decrees were more readily received by the Church when formulated in a council.[29] Thus, unlike some younger papalists, Turrecremata thought a council useful to the Church—if it acted like Constance or Florence, not like Basel. Mundy, therefore, has overstated the Dominican cardinal's anticonciliar position. Turrecremata was warning against abuses, as in his contention that a council called in a vacancy should limit itself to the urgent business at hand and not meddle in other matters. What he did do, as we shall see, was describe the ideal general council in terms compatible with papal supremacy in ecclesiastical government.[30]

The Nature of the Council

Since he thought a council was useful to the Church, Turrecremata had to define both the true nature of a council and its proper procedures. He portrayed an assembly that would aid the pope in governing the Church rather than one interested in claiming the highest possible position. This is obvious from Turrecremata's definition of a universal council:

> A universal council is an assembly of the greater prelates of the Church, specifically called by the authority of the Roman

pontiff, to do something for a common purpose concerning
the Christian religion, under the pope's presidency or with
another [a legate] in his place.[31]

The Dominican cardinal believed that only this definition
was wide enough to include all legitimate councils, from
those held by Peter in Jerusalem to the Council of Florence.
Moreover, it left no room for conciliarist definitions that
made the council the Church's representative and consequently the pope's potential rival. The chief elements he
emphasized were the welfare of the Church, the authorization given by the pope, and the presence of the greater
prelates.[32]

Representation of the Church was not simply an abstract
idea mentioned in *Haec sancta* or conciliarist polemics;
princes could make practical use of the concept to put pressure on the papacy. In support of the demand for a third,
neutral site for a council, the French ambassadors told Eugenius IV that neither Florence nor Basel was the un-
questionable supreme authority in the Church, since neither
represented the whole Church; a third council that ab-
sorbed the rival assemblies would have that virtue. In his
reply to the French ambassadors, Turrecremata had to explain how a council could be universal in authority though
not in membership. He argued that the presence of the
true pope, supported by the cardinals and leading prelates
of both Latin and Greek Churches, proved the universal
validity of the Council of Florence. All other prelates were
welcome, but their adherence would give the council no
additional powers.[33] In his later works, Turrecremata ex-
panded this argument into a distinction between two types
of general councils—a plenary council of all prelates and
a universal council: the former had greater prestige because it had greater numbers; the latter, though not at-
tended by all prelates, was granted full governmental
authority by the pope.[34] But there was no real difference
between the two types of assembly in jurisdiction. Both
received broad powers from the Roman see, an authorization which distinguished any form of general council
from a local ecclesiastical assembly.[35]

According to Turrecremata, the council had no source
of power other than the pope. Contradicting *Haec sancta*
and writers like John of Segovia, he denied that it had

power directly from God. Peter, not Christ, had called the first council.[36] Panormitanus and others had claimed that the councils described in the Acts were authorized by all of the Apostles; as successors of the Twelve, the episcopate could bestow on a council the power the Apostles had received from Christ.[37] Turrecremata replied that the Apostles were Peter's subordinates, not his equals, in the power of jurisdiction. Likewise their successors, the bishops, were inferior to the pope. Neither the Apostles nor their successors were able to confer on a council a power superior to that of the pope, since they themselves possessed no such power.[38]

Many other conciliarists, including John of Segovia and Panormitanus, believed that the Church possessed the plenitude of power. This power could be exercised through the Church's representative, the council, and was superior to that held by the pope. Conciliarists usually failed to explain in what manner the council did represent the Church.[39] Only Nicholas of Cusa, who thought that the council represented the Church imperfectly, suggested that delegates be selected from every province of Christendom.[40]

Turrecremata, as we have seen, challenged the corporate concept of the Church that was so fundamental to these doctrines. While he was a papal diplomat, he openly denied that the Council of Basel represented the Church when it tried to depose Eugenius IV.[41] In the *Summa de ecclesia*, Turrecremata carried this attack through to its logical conclusion, arguing that no close connection existed between the universal Church and the council separated from the pope. True representation would require the presence of all the faithful to exercise their share of the power of jurisdiction; and, under such a "nominalist" concept, any representation of the whole, virtually or by delegation, was impossible.[42] Even granted that the Church could be represented by a council, the fathers would still represent the flock of Christ subordinate to its visible shepherd, the pope.[43] Representation of the Church by a general council could be meaningful, according to Turrecremata, only when the fathers acted in consort with the pope, the font of all jurisdiction. While they did not constitute the whole Church or its representatives in any legal sense, the fathers would nevertheless share in the exercise of the supreme power of ecclesiastical government and thus represent the Church.[44]

Under this limited idea of representation, Turrecremata could restrict the number of those who were true members of a council. Since the essential element in a council's authority was its convocation by the pope, there was no need to assemble lesser clergy, let alone laymen, to sanction the proceedings. The only necessary participants in a council were bishops and other prelates, the chief holders of jurisdiction *in partem sollicitudinis.*[45] Here Turrecremata touched a sore spot of the conciliar movement, the latent tension between its corporate and episcopalist strands. Between them was no real agreement whether the Church was represented by prelates alone or whether the rest of the clergy and the laity were also vitally important. Representatives of the lesser clergy often dominated the Council of Basel and twice overruled the prelates on the key issues of the site of a council with the Greeks and the deposition of Eugenius IV. In the latter case, Panormitanus, as ambassador of the house of Aragon, claimed that only prelates had the right to vote; Cardinal d'Aleman replied that that right belonged to all ecclesiastical orders. When the final vote was taken, d'Aleman packed with the relics of saints the seats of those prelates who absented themselves before the majority of lesser clerics voted to depose Eugenius from his see.[46]

For his part Turrecremata claimed that in the strictest sense only bishops had the right to participate in a council: they were the leaders of the Church and charged with promoting its welfare through their share in the power of jurisdiction.[47] Other prelates, such as abbots, might receive a special invitation from the pope; however, their presence could be dispensed with if they imitated the follies of the Council of Basel.[48] Lesser clerics could only attend a council as theologians, canonists, minor functionaries, proctors, or participants in suits.[49] Turrecremata discouraged the attendance of laymen without cases to plead, but princes both represented their interests and had their own duty of protecting the Church by force of arms. The idea of the universal consent of the laity to ecclesiastical enactments, controversial even in conciliarist circles, had no place in

Turrecremata's ecclesiology.[50]

As we have seen, *Haec sancta* described conciliar power as superior to papal in any crucial juncture, and this was also the burden of diverse streams of conciliarist thought.[51] In the course of his career, Turrecremata inclined increasingly to the opposite tack: the council depended on the pope, font of jurisdiction, in all ordinary functions.[52] Accordingly, he restated the canonistic doctrine that only the pope could call a council except when the pontiff fell into error or the Roman see was vacant. Any assembly called in defiance of the law and without such unusual circumstances to justify it was clearly schismatic.[53] Papal convocation gave a council a mandate to deal with certain specific problems, and the fathers could not pass the bounds of that mandate without being guilty of attempted usurpation of papal prerogative.[54] If the council tried (like Basel) to tie the hands of the papal legates or, worse still, to act without them, then it was headless and unable to act legally for the welfare of the Church.[55] The pope's presidential powers allowed him to move or dissolve a council and to punish any participants who promoted illegal courses of action.[56] In the exercise of this presidential power, the pope was not hampered by *Frequens* unless his acts were harmful to the Church's welfare within the strict bounds of Turrecremata's doctrine of the limits of papal power. Thus, the pope could not, if justly suspect of heresy, terminate a council's inquiry into his orthodoxy. Once again the Dominican cardinal showed that the welfare of the Church meant more to him than any puristic idea about untrammeled papal power.[57]

All writers of the conciliar period preferred that an assembly agree unanimously upon the canons it promulgated;[58] however, they could not agree on the procedures to be followed when agreement was impossible. Many conciliarists, including John of Segovia, believed in majority rule, a principle previously elaborated in order to deal with disputes in cathedral chapters and monasteries. But that belief existed side by side with the one that the *sanior pars*, the wiser element, should prevail however small its numbers.[59] Turrecremata rejected the idea of majority rule, arguing that papal plenitude of power included the authority to promulgate conciliar canons; the rest of the assembly merely advised the pope what actions would best serve the welfare of the Church.[60] If there were open disagreement on a matter of positive law, the pope's will was to prevail. This did not, of course, include actions injurious to the *status ecclesiae*, for which the pope could lose his see.[61] Since the pope's office gave him no special gift of knowledge, other participants in a council might be wiser than he in matters of faith and their prestige and learning prevail over his opinion if he stood alone against them.[62] Like Alanus, Turrecremata thought that the fathers had to be both in complete agreement among themselves and supported by Scripture and Tradition. As for Huguccio's idea that the pope's opinions should prevail unless in conflict with defined doctrine, Turrecremata restricted this to a case where neither pope nor council was obviously right. Any pope who persistently ignored sound advice on theological matters was in danger of falling from his see and being punished as a heretic.[63]

It is important that we not read too much into his doctrine. Turrecremata did not, as we have seen, teach the First Vatican Council's doctrine of infallibility; however, he did not intend to set up the council as the pope's superior in matters of faith.[64] Rather, he was asserting the supreme authority of the Catholic truth. Alongside his statements about a council's ability to overrule the pope in matters of faith he placed cases in which popes overruled erring councils. Turrecremata often mentioned the Second Council of Ephesus and the Council of Rimini. If the pope had reason and revelation on his side, he could overrule a council and resist implementation of its decisions.[65] Though the assembly might surpass the pope in knowledge and prestige, it never could possess a power of jurisdiction greater than his *plenitudo potestatis*.[66]

Turrecremata expected that a council end with a display of this papal preeminence in jurisdiction, a confirmation of its canons by the Vicar of Christ. This was particularly important for a council, like that at Basel, that the pope was unable to attend or one, like Constance, held in an emergency. The canons did not bind all believers until they had been confirmed, and this was an illustration of the council's dependence on the pope; after all, confirmation would be needless if the assembly received its authority directly from Christ or the Church.[67] The applicability of this rule to a council held during a vacancy tied up a loose end in Turrecremata's discussion of the Council of Constance. Confirmation of the council's canons by Martin V ratified the condemnation of Wycliff and the death sentence imposed on Hus.[68]

Since the pope was the supreme authority in matters of positive law, he could alter the disciplinary decrees of councils and grant dispensations from their provisions. This did not imply an ability to tamper with dogmatic definitions made by general councils.[69] At Basel Turrecremata had defended the right of litigants to appeal from council to pope, particulartly in the case of an unconfirmed canon someone thought was unjustly formulated. The pope could hear such an appeal even if he had sat in the assembly as a mere bishop, just as a bishop could sit with his chapter as a mere canon. But no one could appeal from pope to council, since the council received its power of jurisdiction from the pope.[70]

Turrecremata's ideas about the proper conduct of a general council were designed to prevent future councils from imitating the follies of the Basel assembly. In most cases the pope could call or dismiss an assembly at will, direct its actions, and ratify its canons. Unless he erred in faith or committed some enormous crime, the Roman pontiff had no need to fear that such a council would turn on him.[71] This concept of the general council was a large part of Turrecremata's contribution to Roman Catholic ecclesiology. Through Robert Bellarmine it became the standard Roman doctrine and endured as such down to the time of the Second Vatican Council.[72]

6
CHRISTENDOM

The Temporal Sphere

A final aspect of Johannes de Turrecremata's ecclesiology concerns his doctrine on the relation between the spiritual and the temporal powers—a compromise position which reflects his view of the place of the temporal power in Christendom. As we would expect, Turrecremata's theory responded to conditions in his own age, but in this case it was a typically Dominican answer to a controversy that had developed during a millenium.

By Turrecremata's day, Western Europe—a region guided by popes and princes—had been nominally Christian for a thousand years. In the beginning Western theologians, unlike their Eastern counterparts, had adopted a cautious attitude toward Christian princes. Neither Ambrose nor Augustine identified the Church with the Christianized empire, and Gelasius warned the emperor against meddling in the affairs of the more exalted ecclesiastical power. But emperors and popes soon entered the ideological fray. Imitating their Byzantine counterparts, the Holy Roman emperors patronized writers who closely identified empire and Church and envisioned the emperor (as Christ's anointed) guiding and guarding a united Christendom.[1] And many ecclesiastical reformers, including Leo IX and Peter Damian, similarly accepted lay intervention that served the welfare of the Church. But others, led by Humbert of Silva Candida, argued that pernicious lay influence

107

bred evils, such as simony. Acting on this supposition, Gregory VII challenged Emperor Henry IV by opposing imperial pretensions with a claim to papal supremacy over princes.[2] After the Investiture Controversy, popes claimed an ever greater political role in Christendom as guides of princely acts, even those whose bloody nature barred their direct exercise by clerics. Innocent III and Innocent IV broadened and systematized these claims, basing them on solicitude for the welfare of the sinful laity. And Innocent IV described this papal temporal power as an indirect consequence of spiritual primacy.[3]

In subsequent centuries, papal temporal power won support from canonists and theologians. Decretists, particularly Huguccio and Alanus, argued about the extent and legitimacy of temporal power: one thought that princes received their powers directly from God; the other made the pope an intermediary between the divinity and the secular power.[4] Decretalists, glossing the decrees of Innocent III, described the pope as the chief judge of Christendom, able to use his plenitude of power to correct evils.[5] Among theologians, Bernard of Clairvaux and Hugh of St. Victor developed papalist arguments subsequently taken up by the friars. Some mendicants, like Aquinas, kept papal temporal power in perspective; others, especially the Augustinians, carried papalism to a hierocratic extreme.[6] These various strands of papalist polemic were woven together by Boniface VIII in his decree *Unam sanctam*, which made spiritual and (indirectly) temporal dependence of all Christians on the pope an article of faith.[7] On the other side, however, the princes never lacked apologists. Frederick Barbarossa tried to reassert imperial power over Rome; his grandson Frederick II, locked in a death struggle with Innocent IV, claimed that wealth and power had perverted the Church's spiritual mission. Philip IV of France, who totally defeated Boniface VIII, enjoyed the support of apologists like the Thomist John of Paris. And in the fourteenth century, the empire was supported by such formidable polemicists as Dante, Marsilius, and Ockham.[8] All told, centuries of argument had produced two camps; papalist claims that the spiritual power served the higher end of man opposed ancient claims that the secular power was God's agent (or the Church's strong arm).

Into this polemic, Aristotelean ideas and Thomism introduced a new element that would be strongly developed by our protagonist. Aristotle's notion that civil society promoted temporal felicity gave the nascent state a separate rationale for its existence—a rationale conducive to our present Church and State dichotomy. To be sure, there was no single, unwavering use of Aristotle even among Thomists. But most Dominicans, from Aquinas through Petrus de Palude to Turrecremata, thought that the spiritual and temporal ends of human life were best served by *a coordinated effort of the two powers*. However, Tolemy of Lucca and Antoninus of Florence taught more hierocratic doctrines; John of Paris was more favorably inclined toward the independence of princes. Arguments adverse to papal power, by Dante and Marsilius, made other uses of Aristotle; and those of Marsilius were so extreme that they were condemned by the papacy.[9]

Modern assessments of these thought currents have varied widely, from emphasis on the monarchic papacy[10] to emphasis on the coordinate role of the two powers.[11] Perhaps the most judicious assessments underline the pope's role as guide of Christendom toward its higher end, at the same time that they point out that few medieval authors went to either hierocratic or cesaropapist extremes.[12] Turrecremata's own time, when princely power was resurgent, was inopportune for a reassertion of hierocratic theories. Like his predecessors, the Dominican cardinal could presuppose that there was a *respublica Christiana* in which the pope played a leading role, but he had to compromise with the realities of the age. For Johannes de Turrecremata, the Thomist vision of coordinate powers promoting coordinate ends was an ideal framework for such compromises—though perhaps, in the light of the religious politics of later princes, he and other papal apologists too readily made these accommodations.[13]

Like Huguccio and Aquinas, Turrecremata thought that the temporal power derived its legitimacy from God separately, without ecclesiastical intermediary. In Thomistic terms he argued that each power existed to promote an aspect of human welfare: the temporal for the lesser end, the spiritual for the greater. Man was a social animal, who drew from reason those principles of natural law necessary to found families and governments. Governments provided the blessings of peace, the essence of temporal felicity according to Augustine, Aquinas, and Dante.[14] Moreover, a Christian society was the best peacemaking agency, since good government required the true justice inspired by Christ. Similarly, man could not attain temporal perfection, the life of virtue, without also seeking the spiritual perfection promoted by Scripture and the Church. The temporal power thus best achieved its end in collaboration with the spiritual.[15] Turrecremata also believed that the Church needed the services of the State to supplement with coercion its own persuasive efforts. Only thus could Christian ideals be put into practice; moreover, the clergy would not need to perform unworthy labors or stain their hands with blood.[16] Ideally the two powers were coordinate, each promoting the other's end while serving its own. Turrecremata compared the two powers to the pillars of Solomon's temple, composed of different materials but supporting the same edifice.[17]

While working out this doctrine, Turrecremata tackled several disputed topics—first, the basis of secular power. Papalists had never agreed on the role of the Roman see in the creation of secular regimes. The more extreme, including Alanus Anglicus and Giles of Rome, argued that the pope played a major *constitutive* role in this process. Others, like Huguccio and Aquinas, thought the pope guided princes in their exercise of God-given powers. In Turrecremata's day, both he and Nicholas of Cusa taught the latter doctrine, while Antoninus of Florence and Rodrigo Sánchez de Arévalo taught the former.[18] According to Turrecremata the secular power had been valid from its inception. He defended in particular the Roman empire against Arévalo's contention that it was a mere usurper of royal powers. Peter, said Turrecremata, had been born the empire's subject; thus the papacy had played no role in the creation of the empire.[19] The empire's legitimacy was founded on natural law, its conquests being legitimized by the consent of subject peoples to its just rule.[20] Moreover, Christ himself had recognized the legitimacy of the Roman empire when he submitted to Pilate's sentence.[21] The appeal to natural reason aligned Turrecremata with Aquinas, Innocent IV, and Zabarella in defense of the legitimacy of pagan regimes. He attacked the contrary argument of Hostiensis, Duns Scotus, and Falkenberg that belief was a precondition for valid tenure of political power (pagan kings could even rule Christians, so long as they did not tamper with the true faith). The pope could not simply abolish pagan principates, though he could turn back their attacks on Christendom and stop persecutions. This line of argument was adopted from Turrecremata's works by Francisco de Vitoria for his defense of the Indians.[22]

The structure of civil society was also the subject of many disputes. On one side the empire had a broad claim to supremacy over all princes—a claim based on Roman law and past history. (Dante was the most noted apologist for the idea of a universal empire as the guardian of peace.) But a strong body of support for the autonomy of local rulers developed among the canonists, encouraged by Innocent III's decretal *Per venerabilem*, which mentioned the French king's refusal to acknowledge a temporal superior.[23] Turrecremata tried to balance these conflicting claims, arguing that local governments and laws provided for local needs without needing a higher power's intervention. Christendom did not need a temporal monarch with sweeping powers like those held by the pope in spiritual affairs. For, as *Per venerabilem* demonstrated, the kings of France and Spain (Castile) were autonomous princes, though the emperor did have a supranational role as guardian of the Church and promoter of peace.[24] Late in life, when attacking Arévalo's antiimperial polemics, Turrecremata placed added emphasis on the emperor's peacemaking duties and even suggested (as Johannes Teutonicus had said in his gloss on *Per venerabilem*) that kings had an autonomous status *de facto*, not *de iure*.[25] Yet Turrecremata still insisted that the French and Spanish kings had autonomy, since they had averted heathen invasions without imperial aid. In Turrecremata's thought the emperor appears more as a mediator than as a universal monarch.[26] Within his own realm, each prince had the sovereign rights of legislation, justice, and maintenance of order through coercion. The prince was master of his subjects so long as he did not become a tyrant, whose commands could rightly be resisted. Perhaps from lack of interest in the question, or out of deference to princes whose goodwill the papacy needed,

Turrecremata said little about remedies for the abuse of secular power.[27]

Papal Power in Temporal Affairs

Since Turrecremata considered the two powers part of one Christian society, he felt free to make a point about one (usually the value of monarchy) with analogies drawn from the other. Nonetheless, he devoted much more attention to the difficult problem of the interrelationship of the two powers. As we have seen, any writing on that subject involved picking one's way through a tangle of conflicting opinions that had arisen from past controversies and were supported by a mass of authoritative source materials: Scripture, the Fathers, theology, philosophy, and law.[28] Moreover, few past authors had presented schemas of possible opinions on this subject. The most famous schema was produced by John of Paris in his defense of Philip the Fair—an attempt by that Dominican theologian to present his doctrine as a *via media* between Herodian papalism and Waldensian denial of any ecclesiastical direction of temporal affairs. John of Paris described the two powers as coordinate, interacting only indirectly in their pursuit of distinct ends. Petrus de Palude adapted this schema to prove that the pope could direct the actions of princes without usurping their powers.[29] Turrecremata, though familiar with John of Paris's works, adopted Palude's version of this schema as a means of giving order to all the diverse materials on the relationship of the two powers. He seemed pleased to think of himself as a moderate caught between two extremes.[30]

In Turrecremata's times, these extreme opinions were not mere stalking horses. The Herodian doctrine was present in the works of such distinguished fellow papalists as Antoninus and Arévalo. The Waldensian doctrine was represented by the Hussites, many of whom were influenced by Manicheism and thought papal temporal power a mark of Antichrist.[31] And the Domincan cardinal countered each in turn.

Turrecremata answered the Herodians on both theological and practical grounds. The two powers had once been united in the Jewish priesthood; but Jesus, a prudent leg-

islator, had severed that bond.[32] Although Christ had possessed all power on earth, he did not grant the temporal
aspect of his supreme authority to Peter, sparing the popes
excessive concern with temporal goals and allowing them
concentration on their spiritual labors. Turrecremata used
the Donation of Constantine to illustrate the pope's lack õf
temporal supremacy, pointing out that it would not have
been a donation if the emperor merely returned to the
pope something that was his by right.[33] Thus, the papacy
bestowed on men neither property rights, as Giles of Rome
had argued, nor legitimate governments. Men earned their
possessions by the sweat of their brows; kings, though annointed by clerics, founded their governments on natural
law.[34]

Turrecremata's answer to the Waldensian doctrine began
at Basel, when he collaborated with Juan Polemar to defend
ecclesiastical temporal power in open debate with the Hussites. Thereafter Turrecremata was ever ready to argue
that power and possessions were necessary for the welfare
of the Church. The papacy, according to Bartolus's definition, was a perfect principate, able to enforce its decisions
with material coercion (even though it could not actually
shed blood). Although Christ had not given him the fullness
of earthly power, Peter had possessed this principate.[35] The
Church used its property and revenues to support the poor,
the clergy, and the liturgy, as well as crusades against enemies like the Turks. The goods of the clergy were subsumed into the ecclesiastical sphere and so passed out of
temporal jurisdiction.[36]

Since Turrecremata felt that the temporal, as well as the
spiritual, end of man was best fulfilled in a Christian society,
he deemed the two powers coordinate (as we have noted):
but coordination required some single directive force able
to regulate both powers; and, naturally, Turrecremata assigned this role to the pope, head of the spiritual power.[37]
His proof of this contention rested on all the old arguments
of past papal apologists. Following Boniface VIII's interpretation of Gelasius's doctrine, he argued that the superiority of the spiritual over the temporal involved power
as well as dignity.[38] Following Innocent III and James of
Viterbo, he claimed that the spiritual power was as superior
to the temporal as the soul was to the body, an argument

meant to demonstrate the pope's power over princes.[39] While secular governments were not created by the pope, they could not perform their own work well without his aid. Turrecremata compared the pope's role in these matters to that of an architect, who directs the work of the artisans constructing a building but does not interfere in the practice of their crafts.[40]

Such authority was a secondary aspect of the papal plenitude of power, which was primarily concerned with spiritual matters.[41] The scope of this secondary power was wide but not unlimited, extending to all Christians because of their sins, which included crimes. On this basis, the pope could act anywhere to preserve the unity and peace of Christendom—to repel invading infidels, to promote justice, and to safeguard the clergy. Papal intervention in temporal affairs, when inspired by spiritual motives, was an act of charity and not simply meddling.[42]

But although the pope possessed a perfect principate, he could not wield powers proper to the temporal sphere, particularly those involving bloodshed. Instead, he could move princes to act for the welfare of Christendom by warring against its enemies or imposing capital sentences on malefactors. The temporal sword for the defense of the Church was, therefore, at the pope's disposal, but not in his hand.[43] Any king who could not, or would not, follow these orders was useless to the Church and, accordingly, could be deposed by the pope.[44] The pope was also concerned with preventing dissipation of princely power in useless wars, imposing truces on warring powers, and, as guardian of oaths, overseeing the maintenance of treaties. (This was the doctrine used by Innocent III to justify his intervention in the wars of France and England.)[45] The pope, however, could not meddle in purely secular business, such as cases involving technicalities of feudal law; he might correct any totally unjust decision but could not hear the case in the first instance.[46] Like Innocent III, Turrecremata believed that canon law displaced other legal systems where their jurisdictions overlapped; the pope could strike down laws harmful to the Church, but he could not quash an innocuous law by an arbitrary exercise of his plenitude of power.[47]

Over and above all these powers Turrecremata placed

the judicial supremacy of the Roman see. According to the canonists, the pope's office made him chief judge of Christendom—a judge able, according to Innocent III in the decretal *Novit*, to correct any negligent or unjust judge. Likewise the Roman pontiff had broad authority to decide all difficult cases involving questions of proper Christian conduct, a spiritual power wielded for the good of the faithful.[48] Like Innocent IV, Turrecremata also assigned to the papacy certain specific cases that did not involve spiritual maters, for example, cases usually reserved to the emperor, when the imperial throne was vacant.[49]

As chief judge, the pope could impose severe penalties on princes, particularly excommunication. If an erring prince remained unmoved, as had Frederick II,[50] other measures could be taken. Although the pope did not create kingdoms or kings, he could, as we have noted, depose rulers guilty of heresy, tyranny, or incompetence. Moverover, he could release the subjects of erring princes from their oaths of allegiance. (In fact, a heretic king could be deposed by his subjects even without papal approval.)[51] The pope could even alter the ordering of temporal governments, Turrecremata wrote in his peculiar account of the translation of the empire. Because the Byzantine emperors did not defend Rome against the Lombards, Pope Stephen deprived the Greeks of the imperial dignity and bestowed it on the Germans, thus changing the mode of imperial election from popular acclamation to the vote of a college of electors. In this one passage, Turrecremata conflated the annointing of Pippin the Short, the coronation of Charlemagne, and later constitutional developments. Following *Venerabilem*, moreover, he described imperial election in terms of episcopal election, arguing that papal confirmation of the election bestowed the fullness of imperial dignity and power.[52] Turrecremata believed that the pope could make further changes in the secular order but did not consider this the ordinary function of the apostolic see. Nor did this power, which was to be used for the good of Christendom, imply that the pope bestowed temporal power on princes.[53]

Clearly, Turrecremata's doctrine of papal temporal power was an adjunct to his ideas about papal responsibility for the welfare of Christian souls. The pope could guide princes, punish them, and even alter their regimes for the good of Christendom and not because of worldly ambition. This was no theory of direct papal power over temporal affairs,[54] nor was it some new doctrine replacing the theory of papal hierocracy.[55] Rather, Turrecremata drew heavily on Aquinas and on canon law[56] to create a synthesis of the more moderate papalist ideas on the temporal aspects and effects of the plenitude of power. His synthesis, presented in a framework which Petrus de Palude had adapted from the works of John of Paris, did not win universal acceptance but did have a strong impact on later theologians like Cajetan, Vitoria, and Suarez.[57] Bellarmine dubbed this doctrine the theory of indirect papal temporal power, a term borrowed from Innocent IV. Under that name it has endured to the present day, being adopted by Jacques Maritain as a guide to the proper relationship of Church and State.[58]

Lay Intervention in Ecclesiastical Affairs

By contrast to the Dominican cardinal's enduring doctrine of indirect papal power in temporal affairs, his opinions on the reverse question remained a fragmented response to increasing lay intervention in the ecclesiastical affairs of his age.

Long before Turrecremata's time, papal pretensions to temporal power had begun to ring hollow. Boniface VIII was humiliated by Philip the Fair, while Clement V seemed subservient to him. John XXII and Benedict XII waged a long, largely fruitless campaign against Louis of Bavaria.[59] In the conciliar epoch, princes made new advances in the control of the clergy. After the wars and internal chaos of the fourteenth century, strong dynastic governments reappeared, "new monarchs"[60] which resumed the efforts of earlier kings to dominate local ecclesiastical patronage and to tax the clergy. Thus, Charles VII, taking advantage of the conciliar crisis, issued the Pragmatic Sanction of Bourges (1438), which implemented the Basel reform decrees for the monarchy's benefit but avoided open support of conciliarist ideas. Frederick III, king of the Romans, and other princes as well, sold Eugenius IV and Nicholas V their allegiances in return for rights of patronage granted them in concordats.[61]

Turrecremata realized that the Church faced a serious problem. One of his reasons for opposing the French demands for a third council site was the likelihood that participants would obey their princes and ignore higher considerations. This could be a disaster for the papacy and a threat to the liberty of the Church.[62] However, Turrecremata did not advocate a new bar to lay encroachment on ecclesiastical liberties in the manner of the Investiture Controversy, since his concept of Christendom was oriented toward cooperation between the two powers.[63] Only by cooperation could peace be maintained. For this reason, excommunication of princes and peoples was to be avoided because of its grave temporal and spiritual consequences, namely, disrupting the peace and scandalizing the faithful.[64]

Writers on Turrecremata's thought ordinarily ignore his comments on lay intervention in ecclesiastical affairs. But an examination of the relevant passages reveals his ambivalent and expedient attitude: a denial of lay rights in theory coupled with an acceptance of them in practice to avoid scandal and strife. The temporal power certainly could not judge the spiritual: as proof, Turrecremata cited all the old arguments about the greater dignity of the Church, including Hostiensis's contention that the spiritual power was as much greater than the temporal, as the sun (by Ptolemy's estimate) was greater than the moon.[65] Even the emperor, the greatest layman, could not control the Church, judge the pope, pretend to be the founder of papal power, or, through the Donation of Constantine, claim to be feudal lord of the Roman see; the emperor was primarily the chief defender of Christendom, guided in his actions by papal commands.[66]

Turrecremata nevertheless allowed the emperor, and other princes, a fairly large role in ecclesiastical affairs. Imperial laws that favored the Church could be accepted into canon law, as had been necessary when rulers like Charlemagne were much more feared than the pope.[67] Princes had no real right to confer benefices—this was a spiritual matter beyond lay competence.[68] But Turrecremata advised acceptance of any worthy nominee presented by a prince, out of respect, to avoid scandal, and to prevent disruption of the peace by angry lay patrons.[69] In the bull *Etsi de statu* Boniface VIII had conceded to Philip the Fair a discretionary right to tax the clergy for the defense of the realm. Although Turrecremata did not believe princes could do this by right, he cited Christ and Peter, who had humbly submitted to lesser authorities by paying tribute to Rome, as giving examples which permitted taxation of the clergy for the purpose of maintaining peace and order.[70]

Conversely, Turrecremata recognized certain duties of ecclesiastics towards lay authorities. As we have seen, he defended the Church's possession of temporal goods and employment of temporal power, which, if not abused, were useful to the Church;[71] however, possession of temporalities created certain obligations. The Gregorian reformers had deemphasized the feudal obligations of the clergy; Turrecremata accepted them, with some reservations. For example, he said that a bishop could place his feudal duties ahead of such ecclesiastical business as the attendance of synods, unless the synod was called by the pope.[72]

In the matter of councils and possible schisms, finally, Turrecremata did allow for an imperial role—a clear reaction to his own experiences in a troubled era. During the Schism, intellectual currents favorable to lay power over the Church had been much strengthened. Conciliar theorists like Dietrich of Niem and Zabarella had urged the emperor and other princes to convoke a council, citing the example of Constantine, who had assembled the Council of Nicaea. Sigismund of Luxemburg had fulfilled their expectations by helping to compel John XXIII to call the Council of Constance and by playing a role in the early sessions of the Council of Basel.[73] Turrecremata's own presence at Constance, where the Schism was effectively terminated, had been a side effect of Sigismund's successful effort to bring Spanish representatives to Constance. It is thus no surprise that Turrecremata granted the emperor a key role in the convocation of a council, one which—like Constantine's!—derived from a papal mandate; if the emperor tried to call a council without papal authorization, the resulting assembly was illegal.[74] However, if during a vacancy or a crisis caused by an erring pope the cardinals refused to call a needed general council, this duty devolved upon the emperor and other Christian princes as the Church's temporal guardians.[75] In the *Summa de ecclesia* Turrecremata went a step further, making his greatest concession to temporal power. Any major clerical threat to peace other than schism could be handled by the pope; but when the papacy was at the heart of the problem, the emperor, as the guardian of peace, could call a council to end the schism.[76] Furthermore, at any council the emperor and other princes were present as chief officers of the Church's secular arm, to deal with heretics and other malefactors. This role was so important that the emperor could attend a council even if the pope did not invite him.[77] On a similar basis, the princes could employ force against an antipope or coerce an evil pope to amend his life. And if the pope fell from his see through heresy, he could be seized by the princes.[78]

All in all, Turrecremata's doctrine of lay intervention was admirably suited to an age in which the papacy followed Petrus de Monte's advice to Eugenius IV to "cede a little" to the princes to keep their loyalty.[79] Yet, concessions only whetted the appetites of the more potent princes, whose powers over the clergy increased, and the popes concentrated more and more on local Italian poltics. This contributed in turn to the discontents of lesser princes, who received no concessions, and to the alienation of northern Europe from what seemed to be an increasingly distant and worldly Roman court. In the long run this dual trend harmed Europe in general and the papacy in particular, for reformers found a ready audience among the discontented as well as ready support among the German princelings, the Swiss cities, and the king of the North. The great princes, who had won much of what they wanted, were reluctant to embrace the Reformation, but their realms, too, were troubled by religious controversy. So, the fabric of Christendom was torn apart, leaving the popes with a stronger position in central Italy and a set of hollow claims to broader temporal power.[80]

CONCLUSION

A delayed impact of Johannes de Turrecremata's thought on posterity can be discerned from the differing circulation and audience of his varied works. In his own lifetime, his devotional writings and polemical tracts were widely circulated in manuscript and, by his command, in print. Then and in the following decades, Turrecremata's major ecclesiological works, the *Summa de ecclesia* and *Commentaria super Decreto*, reached a far smaller public. Copies were transcribed for curialists like Nicholas Palmericus and Francesco della Rovere (Sixtus IV), while others made their way into the Vatican Library or into the hands of a few influential professors. Both of these works, which must have been expensive due to their bulk, only reached a wider audience in their sixteenth-century printed editions. In fact, an edition of the *Summa* was circulated by the Counter-Reformation papacy as a counterweight to the polemics of Protestant reformers.[1]

Yet despite their initial limited circulation, Turrecremata's major works had a profound impact on the study of ecclesiology, the theory of the nature and government of the Church. Throughout the Middle Ages that branch of theology had been an ill-defined pursuit; most writings on the subject were scattered comments by canonists on legal texts or polemical tracts by such diverse figures as Moneta of Cremona, James of Viterbo, William of Ockham,

121

Marsilius of Padua, John Wycliff, Stanislav of Znojmno, and John Hus. (One wonders how well these authors, many of whom were extremists, reflected the ecclesiological ideas of their less adventurous brethren.) In Turrecremata's day, an authoritative synthesis of ecclesiological materials was much needed. The conciliar movement had raised a challenge to papal supremacy at the very time when the Hussites rejected the fundamental principles of the medieval Church: obedience to all prelates, particularly the pope; the automatic nature of holy orders; and membership of sinners in the Church. John of Ragusa did write on these subjects, but his conciliarist leanings may have lost his works any chance of reaching a wide audience.[2] Thus, the role of synthesizer fell to Turrecremata, a papalist and reformer. Though not a brilliant thinker like Cusa, Turrecremata was an able polemicist and well versed in theology and law, with a reputation for probity and a zeal for orthodoxy. Turrecremata's critiques of conciliarism and Hussitism, contained in expositions of basic doctrines acceptable to Rome, were very thorough, the most complete papalist polemics of the Conciliar Crisis.[3]

Turrecremata's authority was first cited by Laurentius Aretinus, who noted the appearance of the tract *Flores sententiarum*. The younger generation of papalists, whether reformers like Dominicus de Dominicis or extremists like Arévalo,[4] looked to Turrecremata with respect. Canonists like Felinus Sandaeus and Johannes Antonius de Sancto Georgio, reform-minded curialists like Jacobazzi and Gozzandini, Dominicans like Cajetan all carried Turrecremata's name and influence down to the Reformation era.[5] North of the Alps, the most extreme papalists, men like Albertus Pighius, lost sight of Turrecremata's interest in reform, using his authority to butress papalist arguments that many Germans must have thought were out of place when they looked at the career of a pontiff like Alexander VI.[6] When the Reformation crisis erupted, the chief foes of Luther—Eck, Prierias, Politus, and Cajetan—all made use of Turrecremata's works in their apologetic writings, although only Cajetan showed any real comprehension of the issues involved. But Turrecremata's influence was not wholly negative, contributing as it did to the reform proposals presented to Paul III by Bartolomeo Guidiccioni.[7]

The impact of Turrecremata's thought proved far more creative in Spain than in Italy or Germany. The Spanish Dominicans, for whose reform Turrecremata had long labored, contributed to the Golden Age a vigorous Thomist school interested in practical as well as speculative questions whose leader, Francisco de Vitoria, educated such luminaries as Domingo de Soto, Melchior Cano, and Domingo Bañez.[8] Bartolomé de las Casas found a place in their ranks, a secure place from which to continue his struggle in the defense of the rights of the American Indians. All of these luminaries made use of Turrecremata's major works without falling into slavish dependence. Their works, and those of the Augustinian theologian Alonso de la Vera Cruz, carried Turrecremata's fame to the New World.[9] The Dominican cardinal's authority was also cited by Spanish jurists, including the polymath Antonio Augustín.[10] The newborn Jesuit order adopted Turrecremata's works as part of its apologetic arsenal. Among his most zealous admirers were the second general of the Society of Jesus, Lainez, and the great theologian Suárez.[11] Turrecremata's name was involked frequently at the Council of Trent by Soto, Politus, and others; Lainez even made a vain effort to persuade the council that Turrecremata's version of the mendicant doctrine of jurisdiction should be transformed into defined dogma. Indeed, the Tridentine coupling of zeal for orthodoxy with zeal for the reform of abuses may be seen, at least in part, as the fruit of Turrecremata's arduous labors.[12]

Turrecremata's ideas remained popular among the polemicists of the Counter-Reformation, the foremost of whom, Bellarmine, helped create the new theological science of ecclesiology.[13] Parallel to this stream of his influence was one of criticism by Protestants and Gallican Catholics, Bishop Bossuet and Jean de Launoy among the most vocal critics.[14]

In a later age, when the First Vatican Council debated the possibility of defining the doctrine of papal infallibility, Turrecremata's name was invoked frequently in both affirmative and negative arguments. The first modern study of Turrecremata's life and works, Lederer's biography, was an offshoot of these arguments.[15] Turrecremata's ideas also attracted the attention of the Anglican divine Edward

Pusey, who cited Turrecremata's rejection of the doctrine of the Immaculate Conception in attacking Pius IX's definition of that doctrine as an obstacle to Christian unity.[16] Given all this impact during a span of four centuries, it is no more than justice to conclude that Turrecremata's zeal, probity, and unremitting labors have earned him a permanent place among the worthies of the Order of Preachers.[17]

But what of Turrecremata's reputation in our own century? Particularly, what is the lasting contribution of that first complete analysis of ecclesiology? In recent years, the Dominican cardinal's ecclesiology, with its strongly monarchic and juridical biases, has fallen into disfavor among Catholic theologians. Nonetheless, the study of his doctrines has remained a vital part of the present, lively inquiry into the historical roots of Roman Catholic ecclesiology.[18] And now, in the closing decades of the present millenium, when the world of *"Pacem in terris"* is swept by new political, economic, social, and cultural changes—when tensions within the institutional church in the aftermath of the Second Vatican Council, and the relations of the ecclesiastical to the temporal sphere, have once again become matters of public interest, when the value of terms like indefectibility and infallibility is openly debated by theologians and historians, theology and ecclesiology have come into an arena wider than the scholar's study—there may be an unexpected relevance in seeing how Johannes de Turrecremata synthesized a coherent ecclesiology amid the problems of the turbulent conciliar age.

NOTES

Preface

1. The cardinals created by Felix V are assigned perjorative mottoes by Giovanni Palazzi, *Fasti Cardinalium Ommnium Sanctae Romanae Ecclesiae* (Venice, 1703), vol. 2, cols. 259–76. Philip Hughes, *The Church in Crisis* (New York, 1961), pp. 260–86.

2. Jacques Quétif and Jacques Echard, *Scriptores Ordinis Praedicatorum* (Paris, 1719) 1:837–43; Georg Joseph Eggs, *Purpura docta* (Munich, 1714) 2:125–29; Stephan Lederer, *De spanische Cardinal Johann von Torquemada: Sein Leben und seine Schriften* (Frieburg, 1879).

3. Paul de Vooght, "Le concile oecuménique de Constance et le conciliarisme," *Istina* 9 (1963): 56–86; idem, *Les pouvoirs du concile et l'autorité du pape* (Paris, 1965), pp. 137–61.

4. Particularly useful are the works of Karl Binder and Vicente Beltran de Heredia.

5. Johannes Baptista Bičiunas, *Doctrina Ecclesiologica S. Roberti Bellarmini cum illa Joannis Card. de Turrecremata comparata* (Rome, 1963) is composed of seriatim, undocumented statements.

6. WE; Karl Binder, *Konzilsgedanken bei Kardinal Juan de Torquemada O.P.* (Vienna, 1976), as criticized by Ulrich Horst in *Annuarium historiae conciliorum* 9 (1977): 223–25.

7. The problem of the erring pope is mentioned only in an epilog to MC (135–38), despite the importance of the problem in the Conciliar Crisis.

8. Gerhard Henning, *Cajetan und Luther* (Stuttgart, 1966); Hubert Jedin, "Concilio e riforma nel pensiero del cardinal Bartolomeo Guidiccioni," *Revista di storia della chiesa in Italia* 2 (1948): 33–60.

NOTA BENE: The following works came to hand too late for inclusion in this book: Ernesto Zaragoza Pascual, *Los priores de la*

Congregacion de S. Benito de Valladolid (Silos, 1973); Stefano Orlandi, *Beato Angelico* (Florence, 1964); José Luis de Orella y Unzue, *Partidos politicos en el primer Renacimiento (1300–1450)* (Madrid, 1976); Gerald Christianson, *Cesarini: The Conciliar Cardinal* (St. Ottilien, 1979); Joachim W. Stieber, *Pope Eugenius IV: The Council of Basel and the Secular and Ecclesiastical Authorities in the Empire* (Leiden, 1978). This last is interesting because of its partly successful defense of the Council of Basel.

Chapter 1

1. Jacques Quétif and Jacques Echard, *Scriptores Ordinis Praedicatorum* (Paris, 1719), vol. 1, pt. 2, pp. 789–90.

2. Stephan Lederer, *Der spanische Cardinal Johann von Torquemada: Sein Leben und seine Schriften* (Freiburg, 1879), pp. 14–15; Johannes Franciscus Robertus Stockmann, *Joannes de Turrecremata OP: vita eiusque doctrina de corpore Christi mystico* (Bologna, 1951), p. 15; Quétif et al., *Scriptores*, vol. 1, ft. 2, p. 837. Turrecremata studied at Salamanca according to Vincente Beltran de Heredia, "Noticias y documentos para la biografía de Cardinal Juan de Torquemada," *AFP* 30 (1960): 55.

3. Luis Suarez Fernandez, *Castilla, el cisma y la crisis conciliar (1378–1440)* (Madrid, 1970), pp. 77–95; Lederer, *Torquemada*, pp. 16–21; WE 5.

4. Noel Valois, *La France et la Grande Schisme d'Occident*, 4 vols. (Paris, 1896–1902), 4:227–407; Louise Ropes Loomis, *The Council of Constance*, ed. John Hine Mundy and Kennerly M. Woody (New York, 1961). For the text of *Haec sancta*, see Mansi 27. 590–91.

5. Suarez, *Castilla*, pp. 95–100; José Goñi Gaztambide, *Los Españoles en el Concilio de Constanza* (Madrid, 1966), pp. 145–50, 191–49; Henry Joseph Schroeder, *Disciplinary Decrees of the General Councils* (St. Louis, 1937), pp. 447–55.

6. *Chartularium Universitatis Parisiensis*, ed. Heinrich Denifle (Paris, 1897), 4:677; Karl Binder, "El cardenal Juan de Torquemada y el movimiento de reforma ecclésiastica en el siglo XV," *Revista de teologia* 3 (1953): 46; Jean Kubalic, "Jean de Raguse: Son importance pour l'écclésiologie du xvᵉ siècle," *Revue des sciences religieuses* 41 (1967): 151; Daniel Antoinin Mortier, *Histoire des maîtres généraux de l'ordre des Frères Prêcheurs* (Paris, 1909), 14:301.

7. *Acta Capitulorum Generalium*, ed. Benedictus Maria Reichart (Rome, 1900), 3:208; Mortier, *Histoire des maîtres généraux*, 4:280–81. Eugenius IV was once believed to have made Turrecremata master of the Sacred Palace in 1431 and to have sent him to Basel, see Karl Binder, "El magistero del sacro palazzo apostolica del Cardinale di Torquemada," *Memorie Domenicane* 71 (1954):3–24.

8. Noel Valois, *Le pape et le concile 1418–1450* (Paris, 1909), 1:1–93, 110–46; Joseph Gill, *Personalities of the Council of Florence and Other Essays* (Oxford, 1964), pp. 97–98; Walter Brandmüller, *Das Konzil von Pavia-Siena, 1423–1424*, 2 vols. (Münster, 1968–74).

9. Valois, *Le pape et le concile*, 1:199; Vicente Beltran de Heredia, "La embayado de Castilla en el Concilio de Basilea y su discussion con los Ingleses acerca la precedencia," *Hispania sacra* 10 (1957):5–27; idem, "Noticias y documentos," 57–58; Lederer, *Torquemada*, pp. 31, 34; Haller 2:203. A full Castilian embassy arrived in 1433; Turrecremata assisted it as late as May 11, 1435, see Haller 3:193, 4:131.

10. Schroeder, *Disciplinary Decrees*, pp. 460–61; Binder, "El cardenal Torquemada," p. 52.

11. Johannes de Segovia, *Historia gestorum generalis synodi Basiliensis*, 2 vols., ed. Wiener Akademie (Vienna, 1878–1935), 1:696, 809–10; Stockmann, *De corpore mystico*, p. 21; Haller 3:234, 304, 350, 513.

12. Johannes de Turrecremata (JDT), "*Sermo de Sancto Ambrosio*," Palat. lat. 976 fols. 24v–30r. Binder, "El cardenal Torquemada," p. 51; Vicente Proaño Gil, "Doctrina de Juan de Torquemada sobre el concilio," *Burgense* 1 (1960):74.

13. Johannes de Ragusio, *Tractatus de reductione Bohemorum*, ed. Wiener Akademie (Vienna, 1857), p. 279. Ernest Fraser Jacob, "The Bohemians at the Council of Basel, 1433," in *Prague Essays*, ed. Richard William Seton-Watson (Oxford, 1949), pp. 81–123; Lederer, *Torquemada*, pp. 29–31.

14. Lederer, *Torquemada*, pp. 43–44; Binder, "El cardenal Torquemada," p. 52; Haller 2:422–23. Dionysius was either Denis du Moulin, the titular Patriarch of Antioch, later one of Felix V's cardinals, or the theologian Denis de Sabrevoys, see Noel Valois, *Le crise conciliaire*, 2:241.

15. Edmund Bursche, *Die Reformarbeiten des Basler Konzils* (Lodz, 1921), pp. 59–61. Turrecremata's *Tractatus contra decretum irritans* is printed as *Solemnis tractatus in favorem Eugenii papae IV*, in Mansi 30. 550–90.

16. Valois, *Le pape et le concile*, 1:215–310.

17. Johannes de Segovia, *Historia*, 1:614; Valois, *Le pape et le concile*, 1:311–30.

18. WE 18; Binder, "Il magistero," pp. 12–14, 25; Raymond Creytens, "Le *Studium Romanae Curiae* et le Maître du Sacré Palais," *AFP* 12 (1942):5–83. Turrecremata was allowed to hold this office *in absentia*, see *Bullarium Ordinis Fratrum Praedicatorum*, ed. Antoninus Bremond (Rome, 1731), 3:81.

19. Lederer, *Torquemada*, pp. 72–75; WE 17–18; Hans Cnattingius, *Studies in the Order of St. Bridget of Sweden* (Stockholm, 1963), pp. 169–75. In 1446 Turrecremata sent a copy of his treatise to Vadstena, see Beltran, "Noticias y documentos," pp. 64–65. For an imperfect edition of the work, see JdT, *Defensiones quorundam articulorum rubrorum revelationum Sanctae Brigittae factae in concilio Basiliensi*, Mansi 30 cols. 699–814.

20. JdT, *Repetitions super quibusdam propositionibus Augustini de Roma*, Mansi 30 cols. 979–1034. Haller 2:415–16; Binder, "Il magistero," p. 11; Lederer, *Torquemada*, pp. 90, 108; Stockmann, *De corpore mystico*, pp. 21, 65–66. For a rehabilitation of Favaroni,

see Gino Ciolini, *Agostino de Roma (Favaroni d. 1443) e la sua Cristologia* (Florence, 1944).

21. JdT, *Tractatus de veritate conceptionis beatissime virginis*, ed. Edward Bouverie Pusey (Brussells, 1966). Johannes de Segovia, *Historia*, 1:846–96; WE 19–20. Turrecremata's opposition to this doctrine was termed reactionary by José Martin Palma, "Maria y la Iglesia segun Juan de Segovia y Juan de Torquemada," *Estudios marianos* 18 (1957): 207–30.

22. Jacob, "Bohemians," pp. 117–23; William R. Cook, "John Wyclif and Hussite Theology, 1415–1436," *Church History* 42 (1973): 347–49.

23. JdT, *Tractatus de sacramento eucharistie*, Vat. lat. 976 fols. 131v–162r.

24. Johannes de Segovia, *Historia*, 1:927; WE 19–21. This is the likely date of JdT, *Tractatus de aqua benedica*, Vat. lat. 976 fols. 97r–101r.

25. Schroeder, *Disciplinary Decrees*, pp. 464–66, 473–79; Ernest Frasar Jacob, *Essays in Later Medieval History* (Manchester, 1968), pp. 121–23.

26. JdT, *Tractatus contra advisamentum quod non liceat appellare de concilio ad papam*, Mansi 30 cols. 1072–94. Johannes de Segovia, *Historia*, 2:821–28; Lederer, *Torquemada*, p. 110; WE 18.

27. JdT, *Votum super advisamento quod papa debeat iurare servire decreta de conciliis generalibus*, Mansi 30 cols. 590–606. Lederer, *Torquemada*, pp. 115–18; Valois, *Le pape et le concile*, 2:23–24; WE 18–19.

28. Johannes de Segovia, *Historia*, 1:839; Haller 4:158, 201; Gilles Meersseman, *Giovanni da Montenero O.P. Difensore dei Mendicati* (Rome, 1936).

29. Haller 4:350.

30. Joseph Gill, *Eugenius IV: Pope of Christian Unity* (Westminster, Md., 1961), pp. 91–108; Valois, *Le pape et le concile*, 2:35–81; WE 20–21; Beltran, "Noticias y documentos," p. 68; Lederer, *Torquemada*, p. 81.

31. JdT, *"Flores sententiarum de auctoritate summi pontificis,"* Vat. lat 2580 fols. 87v–93v. Turrecremata influenced Cesarini as early as 1434 according to Vicente Proaño Gil, "Doctrina sobre el concilio," p. 77, n. 16.

32. Suarez, *Castilla*, pp. 132–37, 386–99; Beltran, "Noticias y documentos," pp. 68–72; Lederer, *Torquemada*, p. 21.

33. JdT, *"Latinorum responsio ad libellum a Graecis exhibitum circa Purgatorium,"* in *De Purgatorio Disputationes*, ed. Louis Petit and Georg Hofmann (Rome, 1969), pp. 32–59. Joseph Gill, *The Council of Florence* (Cambridge, 1959), pp. 85–130.

34. *RTA* 13:826–27; Johannes de Segovia, *Historia*, 2:174–85; Georg Hofmann, *Papato, conciliarismo, patriarchato (1438–1439)* (Rome, 1940), pp. 11–14; Valois, *Le pape et le concile*, 2:146–48. On October 2, 1438, Eugenius named Turrecremata archdeacon of Cagliari, see *Bullarium Ordinis Fratrum Praedicatorum*, 3:88–89.

35. JdT *Propositio ad dietam Norimbergensis* is printed in Mansi

31A cols. 41–62 as an oration at the meeting in Mainz, see Hofmann, *Papato*, pp. 10, 15–21; Binder, "Il magistero," pp. 17–22.

36. JdT, *Propositio ad dietam Maguntinam*, in app. 4 of Pacifico Massi, *Il Magistero Infallibile de Papa nella Teologia di Giovanni Torquemada* (Turin, 1957). 14:94–154; Edmund Vansteenbergehn, *Le Cardinal Nicholas de Cuse (1401–1464)* (Paris, 1920), pp. 67–68, 232, n. 5; Hofmann, *Papato*, pp. 22–23.

37. Gill, *Council of Florence*, pp. 180–269; idem, *Personalities*, pp. 104–24.

38. JdT, *Disputatio de azymo et fermentato, et de transubstantione*, Mansi 31B cols. 1651–74; idem, *Turrecremata demonstrat veritatem formae transubstantiationis*, Mansi 31B cols. 1863–86. Andreas de Sancta Croce, *Acta Latina Concilii Florentini*, ed. Georg Hofmann (Rome, 1955), pp. 236–39, 353; Lederer, *Torquemada*, pp. 141–45; Gill, *Council of Florence*, pp. 280–83; Hofmann, *Papato*, pp. 38–58; Martin Anton Schmidt, "The Problem of Papal Primacy at the Council of Florence," *Church History* 30 (1961): 35–49. According to Turrecremata, Patriarch Joseph II left a deathbed testament that urged reunion with Rome; see Gill, *Personalities*, pp. 27–29.

39. Aeneas Silvius Piccolomini (Pius II), *De gestis concilii Basilensis* ed. Denys Hay and W. K. Smith (Oxford, 1967). Gill, *Council of Florence*, pp. 310–13; Antony Black, "The Universities and the Council of Basel: Ecclesiology and Tactics," *Annuarium historiae conciliorum* 6 (1974): 341–51.

40. JdT, *Oratio synodalis de primatu*, ed. Emmanuel Candal (Rome, 1954). Beltran, "Noticias y documentos," p. 80. Turrecremata described this incident in *SE* 2.100 239r.

41. Conradus Eubel, *Hierarchia Medievalia* (Münster, 1901), 2:8. For Turrecremata's arms, a burning tower on a golden field, set in a blue shield with gold fleurs-de-lis, see Vat. lat. 2580 fols. lr.

42. Beltran, "Noticias y documentos," p. 81; *Bullarium Ordinis Fratrum Praedicatorum*, 3:111.

43. JdT, *Responsio in blasphemam invectivam ad sanctissimum canonem iustissime condemnationis damnatissimae congregationis Basiliensium*, Mansi 31A cols. 63–127. WE 26; Johannes de Segovia, *Historia*, 2:504; Valois, *Le pape et le concile*, 2:224–29.

44. Gaston du Fresne de Beaucourt, *Histoire de Charles VII* (Paris, 1885) 3:371–73; Beltran, "Noticias y documentos," pp. 82–83; WE 85–129.

45. JdT, *Super petitione domini regis Franciae, ut alius tertium celebraretur universale concilium*, Mansi 35 cols. 43–56; WE 26; du Fresne, *Charles VII*, pp. 376–77; Remigius Baümer, "Eugen IV und der Plan eines 'Dritten Konzils' zur Beilegung des Basler Schismas," in *Reformata Reformada: Festagabe für Hubert Jedin*, ed. Erwin Iserloh and Konrad Repsen (Münster, 1965), 1:87–128. Cardinals Albergati, Le Jeune, and Turrecramata served as commissioners for German affairs according to Valois, *Le Pape et le concile*, 2:252, n. 2.

46. JdT, *Apparatus super decretum unionis Grecorum*, ed. Emmanuel Candal (Rome, 1942).

47. Flavio Biondo, *Scritti inediti e rari di Biondo Flavio*, ed. Bartolomeo Nogara (Rome, 1927), pp. xli, 21–22; Gill, *Council of Florence*, p. 325.

48. JdT, *"Reprobations trigintaocto articulorum quos tenent heretici Usiti de Maldevis,"* Vat. lat. 974 fols. 71r–94v. WE 27–28; Gill, *Personalities*, pp. 101–2; Thaddeus V. Tuleja, "Eugenius IV and the Crusade of Varna," *The Catholic Historical Review* 35 (1949): 257–75.

49. Hubert Jedin, *A History of the Council of Trent*, trans. Ernest Graf (London, 1949–57), 1:29–30.

50. "Me assumptum ad cardinalatum per sancte memorie dominum Eugenium qui me dispensavit ut continuarem officium ordinis predicatorum," CSD D91 ante cl.q17 (1:498). Binder, "El cardenal Torquemada," p. 45.

51. JdT, *"Expositio Regulae Sancti Benedicti,"* Chigi lat. D.VI.91–94. Turrecremata's authorship of this work, questioned by Lederer (*Torquemada*, pp. 171–73), was upheld by Chrysostomus Gremper, "Des Kardinals Johann von Torquemada Kommentur zur Regel des heiligen Benedikt," *Studien und Mittelungen zur Geschichte des Benedikinerordens* 45 (1927): 223–82.

52. JdT, *"Impugnationes quorundam propositionum quas quidam Alphonsus de Matricali possuit et asseruit,"* Vat. lat. 976 fols. 118r–131v. Augustin de Asis, *Ideas Sociopoliticas de Alonso Polo (El Tostado)* (Seville, 1955), pp. 1–8; 61–63; WE 28.

53. Piccolomini, *De gestis*, p. xx; Suarez, *Castilla*, p. 137–41.

54. In the same year Turrecremata served as chamberlain of the Sacred College, see Eubel, *Hierarchia Medievalia*, 2:8, 30.

55. Cecilia Mary Ady, *Pius II* (London, 1913), p. 95; Paolo Rotta, *Il Cardinale Nicolo di Cusa* (Milan, 1928), pp. 66–72; Aeneas Silvius Piccolomini (Pius II), *Der Briefswechsel des Eneas Silvius Piccolomini*, ed. Rudolf Wolkan (Vienna, 1912), 2:219, 242–43; Lino Gomez Canedo, *Don Juan de Carvajal* (Madrid, 1947), pp. 63–99.

56. Gomez, *Carvajal*, pp. 99–126.

57. Salo Wittmeyer Baron, *A Social and Economic History of the Jews* (New York, 1969), 13:22–24. The *Conversos* were sincere Christians according to Benzion Netanyahu, *The Maranos of Spain from the Late Fourteenth to the Early Fifteenth Century* (New York, 1966). For Turrecremata's deciding vote, see Piccolomini, *Briefswechsel*, 2:275.

58. JdT, *Tractatus contra Madianitas et Ismaelitas*, ed. Nicolas Lopez Martinez and Vicente Proaño Gil (Burgos, 1957). Vicente Beltran de Heredia, "Las Bulas de Nicholas V acerca de los conversos de Castilla," *Sefarad* 21 (1961): 22–47.

59. Fernando Pulgar, *Claros varones de Castilla*, ed. Robert Brian Tate (Oxford, 1971), pp. 57–59; Nicolas Lopez Martinez, *Los judaizantes Castellanos y la inquisition en tiempo de Isabel la Catholica* (Burgos, 1954), pp. 389–90. Baron, *History of the Jews*, 13:315, n. 23 offers the undocumented theory that Turrecremata's mother was a New Christian. For a Dominican denial, see Quétif et al., *Scriptores*, 1:842.

60. "Ratio tanto eius commentatores in pluribus passibus mihi non placuisset," *CSD*, ad De Consecratione dedicatio ad Nicholaum V (4:3).

61. Thomas M. Izbicki, "Johannnes de Turrecremata: Two Questions on Law," *Tidjschrift voor Rechtsgeschiednis* 43 (1975): 91–94; *WE* 29. Turrecremata was the first papalist canonist after the Schism according to Walter Ullmann, *Principles of Government and Politics in the Middle Ages*, 2nd ed. (London, 1968), p. 106, n. 1.

62. JdT, *Gratiani Decretorum libri quinque secundum Gregorianus Decretalium libros titulosque distincti*, 2 vols. (Rome, 1726). Turrecremata's authorship was questioned by Georg Hänel, "Ueber die *Nova Ordinatio*," *Berichte über der Verhandlungen der K. sächsichen Geselschaft der Wissenschaft zu Leipzig*, Phil. Hist. Klasse 8 (1855): 111–42. For a refutation, see Karl Binder, "Kardinal Juan de Torquemada Verfasser der *Nova Ordinatio Decreti Gratiani*," *AFP* 22 (1952): 268–93.

63. Binder, "Verfasser," pp. 280–85; Jedin, *Trent*, 1:127; Stockmann, *De corpore mystico*, p. 46; Izbicki, "Two Questions on Law." The earliest tract on the Church, composed in the thirteenth century, is Moneta Cremonensis, *Adversus Catharos et Waldenses* (Ridgewood, N.J., 1964).

64. *SE* 2.71 198v, 2.75 217v–218, 2.100 240r.

65. Vicente Beltran de Heredia, "Colección de documentos inéditos para illustrar la vida del Cardenal Juan de Torquemada O.P.," *AFP* 7 (1937): 210–45. By contrast, Nicholas of Cusa's reforming efforts failed, see Donald Sullivan, "Nicholas de Cusa as Reformer," *Medieval Studies* 36 (1974): 382–428.

66. Beltran, "Collección de documentos," p. 213; idem, "The Beginnings of Dominican Reform in Castille," in *Spain in the Fifteenth Century*, ed. John Roger Highfield (London, 1972), pp. 226–47.

67. Mortier, *Histoire des maîtres généreaux*, 4:455; Binder, "El cardenal Torquemada," p. 61; Raymond Creytens, "La déposition de Maître Martial Auribelli O.P. par Pie II (1462)," *AFP* 45 (1975): 153, 159, 185. Turrecremata worked for the canonizations of Catherine of Siena and Vincent Ferrer, besides supporting the Dominicans against the Franciscans in the Precious Blood controversy, a quarrel stilled by the command of Pius II, according to Stockmann, *De corpore mystico*, pp. 29, 31–32.

68. Binder, "El cardenal Torquemada," p. 59; Beltran, "Noticias y documentos," pp. 107, 130. For Turrecremata's letter confirming the Pontebuono decrees, dated Mantua, July 29, 1459, see Vat. lat. 13690 fols. 77vb–99ra.

69. Gill, *Council of Florence*, pp. 348–411; Steven Runciman, *The Fall of Constantinople, 1453* (Cambridge, 1965).

70. Karl Binder, "Martino Gazati, Verfasser der Kardinal Juan de Torquemada O.P. zugeschreiben *Centum quaestiones de coetu et auctoritate dominorum cardinalium* in Codex Barberini 1192 und 1552," *Angelicum* 28 (1951): 139–51; Thomas M. Izbicki, "Notes

on Late Medieval Jurists," *Bulletin of Medieval Canon Law* 4 (1974): 52.

71. Turrecremata's exalted conception of the cardinalate contributed to this opposition according to Jedin, *Trent* 1:82–83.

72. Beltran, "Noticias y documentos," p. 94.

73. Aeneas Silvius Piccolomini (Pius II), *The Commentaries of Pius II*, ed. Leona Gabel (Northampton, Mass., 1936–47), pp. 461–64; Binder, "El cardenal Torquemada," p. 54; Beltran, "Noticias y documentos," pp. 93, 122–26.

74. *CSD* ad D. dedicatio (1:314). For a cross reference to *SE*, see *CSD* D22.cl.ql (1:206).

75. Gaspar da Verona, *De Gestis Pauli Secundi*, ed. Giuseppe Zippel (Città di Castello, 1904), p. 36.

76. Piccolomini, *Commentaries*, pp. 93–107; Ludwig Pastor, *The History of the Popes from the Close of the Middle Ages* (St. Louis, 1902), 3:7–13; Beltran, "Noticias y documentos," p. 108; Eugenio Garin, *Portraits from the Quattrocento* (New York, 1972), pp. 31–33.

77. Turrecremata's ready collaboration with Pius II is illustrated by the former's readiness to accept new cardinals created by the latter, see Piccolomini, *Commentaries*, p. 497.

78. Beltran, "Noticias y documentos," pp. 129–30.

79. JdT, *"Tractatus contra principales errores perfidi Machometti et Turcorum sive Sarracenorum,"* Vat. lat. 974 fols. 18r–55r. Norman Daniel, *Islam and the West* (Edinburgh, 1966), pp. 276, 278; Enrico Cerulli, *Nuove ricerche sul Libro della Scalla e la conoscenza dell'Islam in Occidente* (Vatican City, 1972), pp. 78–80, 82–83.

80. Richard William Southern, *Western Views of Islam in the Middle Ages* (Cambridge, Mass., 1962), pp. 83–98; Dario Cabalenas, "Juan de Segovia y el Primer Alcoran Trilingue," *al-Andalus* 14 (1949): 149–73.

81. Piccolomini, *Commentaries*, pp. 186–297; Lederer, *Torquemada*, p. 268.

82. Heiko Obermann, Daniel E. Zerfoss, and William J. Courtenay, eds., *Defensorium obedientiae apostolicae et alia documenta* (Cambridge, Mass., 1968), pp. 18–41, 224–27; Pardon Tillinghast, "An Aborted Reformation: Germans and the Papacy in the Mid-Fifteenth Century," *Journal of Medieval History* 2 (1976): 57–79.

83. Philip James Jones, *The Malatesta of Rimini and the Papal State* (Cambridge, 1974), pp. 176–239.

84. Hans Pfeffermann, *Die Zussamenarbeit der Renaissancepäpste mit der Türken* (Berne, 1946), pp. 77–81; Southern, *Western Views of Islam*, pp. 98–103; Franz Babinger, "Pio II e l'Oriente maomettano," in *Enea Silvio Piccolomini, Papa Pio II*, ed. Domenico Maffei (Siena, 1968), pp. 1–13; Franco Gaeta, "Alcune osservatione sulla prima redazione della lettera a Maometto," in ibid., pp. 177–87.

85. Eubel, *Hierarchia Medievalia*, 2:32; Piccolomini, *Commentaries*, pp. 531–32; Hubert Jedin, *Studien über Domenico de' Domenichi* (Wiesbaden, 1959), p. 187. Turrecremata made his will in 1460, see Beltran, "Noticias y documentos," p. 131.

86. Beltran, "Noticias y documentos," pp. 95, 137–40; idem, "Colección de documentos," pp. 227–28, 242–43; Eubel, *Herarchia Medievalia*, 2:111–12, 173.

87. JdT, *Symbolum pro informatione Manichaeorum*, ed. Nicolas Lopez Martinez and Vicente Proaño Gil (Burgos, 1958). Franje Rački, "Kardinal Ivana Torquemada razprava proto bosanskum Paternom," *Starine ne sviet izdaje Jugoslavenska Akademya Znanosti i idnyetnosti* 14 (1882): 1–21; Dragutin Kamber, "Kardinal Torquemada i Tri Bosanska Bogomila (1461)," *Croatia sacra* 3 (1932):27–93; Silvio Furlani, "Giovanni da Torquemada e il suo Tratado contro i Bogomili," *Ricerche religiose* 18: (1947) 164–77.

88. Frederick Heymann, *George of Bohemia, King of Heretics* (Princeton, 1965), pp. 230–383; Gomez, *Carvajal*, pp. 234–40.

89. Vicente Beltran de Heredia, *Historia de la Reforma de la Provincia de España (1450–1550)* (Rome, 1939), pp. 3–10; idem, "Colección de documentos," pp. 213–16, 231–33; Mortier, *Histoire des maîtres généreaux*, 4:455–57; Beltran, "Beginnings of Dominican Reform," p. 238; Jésus Maria Palomares Ibánez, "Aspectos de la historia del convento de San Pablo de Valladolid," AFP 43 (1973): 91–135.

90. Beltran, *La Reforma*, pp. 6–8; idem, "Colección de documentos," pp. 212–13, Lederer, *Torquemada*, p. 270.

91. Binder, "El cardenal Torquemada,' 60; Mortier, *Histoire des maîtres généreaux*, 4:381; Beltran, *La Reforma*, p. 6; idem, "Noticias y documentos," pp. 133–34; Creytens, "La déposition," pp. 171–72.

92. The choir was completed by Paul II in 1469; the last debts for the cloister were paid by Sixtus IV in 1474, see da Verona, *De Gestis Pauli Secundi*, pp. 36, n. 7, 53–54.

93. Victor Scholderer, *Printers and Readers in Italy in the Fifteenth Century* (London, 1949), pp. 2–3. Uncertainty whether Turrecremata had invited these printers to Italy was expressed by Renzo Frattarolo, *La stampa in Italia fra Quattro- et Cinquecento ed altri saggi* (Rome, 1967), pp. 31–39.

94. JdT, *Meditationes*, ed. Heinz Zirnbauer *(Wiesbaden, 1968)*. *Charles Marie Daley, Dominican Incunabula in the Library of Congress* (Washington, D.C., 1932), pp. 15, 17–18.

95. Pastor, *History of the Popes* (St. Louis, 1902), 4:6–7.

97. Ibid., 4:12; Stockmann, *De corpore mystico*, p. 133.

98. WE 31; Lederer, *Torquemada*, p. 174, 263–65; Stockmann, *De corpore mystico*, pp. 42–43. For an illustration of Turrecremata, old and gaunt, presenting this portion of the *Commentaria* to Paul II, see Vat. lat. 2269 fol. 1r.

99. JdT, *"Libellus velociter compositus et editus contra certos hereticos noviter impugnantes paupertatem Christi et suorum apostolorum,"* Vat. lat. 974 fols. 55v–62r; idem, *Novus tractatus super paupertatem Christi*, Vat. lat. fols. 62v–63r; idem, *De paupertate et perfectione*, Vat. lat. fols. 63r–65r. These tracts are wrongly described by Pastor (*History of the Popes*, 4:116) as directed against the Fraticelli. Palmericus, it is interesting to note, owned a copy of Turrecre-

mata's *Summa*, codex Vat. lat. 2701.

100. JdT, *Opusculum de honore Romani imperii*, in Hubert Jedin, "Juan de Torquemada und das Imperium Romanum," *AFP* 12 (1942): 274–78. Richard Trame, *Rodrigo Sanchez de Arévalo, 1404–1470* (Washington, D.C., 1958), pp. 148–49, 154–58. This dispute echoes the earlier controversy aroused by Antonio Roselli's *Monarchia*, see John A.F. Thomson, "Papalism and Conciliarism in Antonio Roselli's *Monarchia*," *Medieval Studies* 37 (1975): 445–58; Karla Eckermann, *Studien zur Geschichte der monarchischen Gedankens im 15. Jahrhunderts* (Berlin, 1933).

101. JdT, *Questiones evangeliorum de tempore et de sanctis et Flos theologie* (Basel, 1484); idem, *"Libellus de nuptis spiritualibus,"* Vat. lat. 974 fols. 68r–74r.

102. Eubel, *Hierarchia Medievalia*, 2:39; Gilles Meersseman, "La Bibliotheque des Frères Prêcheurs de la Minerve à la fin du xvᵉ siècle," in *Mélanges August Pelzer* (Louvain, 1947), pp. 605–34. In 1469 Paul II gave Pedro de Torquemada 2,000 ducats to help him find brides for his sons, the cardinal's nephews, see da Verona, *De Gestis Pauli Secundi*, p. 54.

103. Pastor, *History of the Popes*, 2:8–9, 4:408–09; *Pius II*, p. 71; da Verona, *De Gestis Pauli Secundi*, pp. 36–37, 53–54.

104. Stockmann, *De corpore mystico*, pp. 33–43; Lederer, *Torquemada*, p. 270; Pastor, *History of the Popes*, 2:353–54; Beltran, "Noticias y documentos," pp. 89–110; Raoul Morçay, *Saint Antonin* (Tours, 1914), p. 384. Pope Eugenius IV and Turrecremata helped Antoninus found the convent of San Marco in Florence according to Carlo Celso Calzolai, *Frate Antonino Pierozzi* (Rome, 1960), pp. 63–73.

105. Noel Valois, *Fra Angelico et le Cardinal Jean de Torquemada* (Paris, 1904); John Pope-Hennessy, *Fra Angelico* (New York, 1952), pp. 30, 196; Beltran, "Noticias y documentos," pp. 94–95, 103–4, 108, 116; Gomez, *Carvajal*, p. 297; Nicolas Antonio, *Bibliotheca Hispana Vetus* (Madrid, 1788) vol. 2, fol. 287r; Vicente Beltran de Heredia, "Nuevos Documentos inéditos sobre el poeta Juan de Mena," *Salmanticensis* 3 (1956): 502–8.

106. Beltran, "Colección de documentos," pp. 219–20; idem, "Noticias y docuementos," pp. 90–105.

107. Piccolomini, *Commentaries*, pp. 497–99.

108. Jedin, *Trent*, 1:88.

109. Piccolomini, *Commentaries*, p. 553.

Chapter 2

1. Johannes de Ragusio, *"Tractatus de ecclesia,"* Basel Univ. Bibl. A.I. 29 fols. 303v5431r. Karl Binder, "Der *Tractatus de ecclesia* Johannes von Ragusa und die Verhandlungen des Konzils von Basel mit dem Hussiten," *Angelicum* 28 (1951): 30–54; idem, "Zum Schriftbeweis in der Kirchentheologie des Kardinals Juan de Torquemada O.P.," in *Warheit und Verkündigung: Michael Schmaus zum*

70 Gebrutstag, ed. Leo Scheffczyk, Werner Dettloff, and Richard Heinzmann (Munich, 1967), 525–26; Franz Xaver Seibel, "Die Kirche als Lehrautoritat nach dem *Doctrinale antiquitatem fidei catholicae ecclesiae* des Thomas Waldensis," *Carmelus* 16 (1969): 3–69.

2. J.F.R. Stockmann, *Johannes de Turrecremata O.P. vita eiusque doctrina de corpore Christi mystico* (Freiburg, 1951), pp. 53–56; Scott H. Hendrix, *Ecclesia in Via* (Leiden, 1974), pp. 15–16.

3. Hendrix, *Ecclesia in Via*, pp. 17–42; Robert F. Evans, *One and Holy: The Church in Latin Patristic Thought* (London, 1972), pp. 154–60; Yves Congar, *L'eglise de S. Agustin á l'époque moderne* (Paris, 1970), pp. 11–24.

4. Hendrix, *Ecclesia in Via*, pp. 42–72; Achilles Darquennes, "La définition de l'eglise d'après Saint Thomas d'Aquin," *L'organization corporative du Moyen Age à la fin de l'Ancien Regime* 7 (1943): 1–53.

' 5. Brian Tierney, *Foundations of the Conciliar Theory* (Cambridge, 1955), pp. 3–6, 23–25, 87–153; Matthew Spinka, *John Hus' Concept of the Church* (Princeton, 1966), pp. 172–208; Howard Kaminsky, *A History of the Hussite Revolution* (Berkeley, 1967), pp. 29–31, 40–48; Louis B. Pascoe, *Jean Gerson: Principles of Church Reform* (Leiden, 1973), pp. 49–79.

6. Francis Oakley, *Council Over Pope?* (New York, 1969), pp. 56–77.

7. *SE* 1.2 3r. The multiple meanings of *ecclesia* were much discussed by Hus and his foes, see WE 41.

8. "Est enim catholicorum sive fidelium collectio. . . . Sive Ecclesia est universitatis fidelium quae unius veri dei cultu unius fidei professione conveniunt . . . Ecclesia est convocatio multorum ad unius dei cultum," SE 1.1.2v. The same doctrine, found in the works of Aquinas, the publicists, and the canonists, was taught by John of Ragusa and Andreas Escobar, see Congar, *L'église*, pp. 340–41; WE 41–42; Paul Ourliac, "L'église et les laiques à la fin du Moyen Age: Etude de droit canonique," in *Mélanges offerts au Professeur Louis Falletti* (Paris, 1971), pp. 473–85.

9. *SE* 1.21.23v–25r. Stockmann, *De corpore mystico*, pp. 85–100.

10. "Manifestum est qui extra unitatem fidei sunt quam universalis ecclesia credit et praedicat salvari non posse," SE 121.24r. This maxim, derived from Origen, was employed by Innocent III and Boniface VIII, see Stockmann, *De corpore mystico*, pp. 89–92; James Muldoon, "*Extra ecclesiam non est imperium:* The Canonists and the Legitimacy of the Secular Power," *Studia Gratiana* 9 (1966): 553–83.

11. "*Ecclesiae enim.* id est. religio christiana una dicitur hoc modo, quia omnes fideles cum unius fidei professione confromitatem sive communionem in eisdem habent sacramenta quot notat Apostolus dicens unum baptisma," *CSD* C24.ql.c18 (3:2974) See *SE*1.8 .10v, 4(pt.2) 22.397v–398r. Like Aquinas, Turrecremata rejected any forced conversion of infidels; however, conversion and the consequent profession of faith obliged the believer to remain orthodox, see *CSD* D45.c5.ql (1:371). Elphége Vacan-

dard, *L'Inquisition* (Paris, 1907), pp. 190–217.

12. Stockmann, *De corpore mystico,* pp. 68–70; Scott H. Hendrix, "In quest of the *Vera Ecclesia:* The Crises of Late Medieval Ecclesiology," *Viator* 7 (1976): 347–78.

13. "Primo quiden cuius fide sine operibus mortua sit. Iac. 11 tamquam arida et mortua membra . . . Illi qui in ecclesia continentur per fidem solam informem de ecclesia in comparatione iustorum quasi numero solo esse dicuntur, qui vero per unitatem fidei, que per dilectionem operatur, in ecclesia sunt numero et merito ad ecclesiam pertinere iudicantur," SE 1.5.6v–7r. Binder, "Zum Schriftbeweis," pp. 532–34; Yves Congar, *The Mystery of the Church* (Baltimore, 1960), pp. 111–13; Hendrix, *Ecclesia in Via,* pp. 72–74.

14. *SE* 1.8.10v; *CSD* D11.c6 (1:108); Johannes de Turrecremata (JdT) *"De sacramento Eucharistie,"* Vat. lat. 976 fols. 131v–162r at 142v; idem, *Symbolum pro informatione Manicheorum,* ed. Nicolas Lopez Martinez and Vicente Proaño Gil (Burgos, 1958), pp. 92–94. Turrecremata was restating standard scholastic sacramental doctrines, see *WE* 110–11.

15. Stanislaus J. Grabowski, *The Church: An Introduction to the Theology of Saint Augustine* (St. Louis, 1957), pp. 200–205, 451.

16. Similarly, Nicholas of Cusa so valued unity that he rejected the divisive Council of Basel in favor of Eugenius IV, who worked for Christian unity, see Paul Sigmund, *Nicholas of Cusa and Medieval Political Thought* (Cambridge, Mass., 1963), pp. 242, 306; Gerd Heinz-Mohr, *Unitas Christiana* (Trier, 1958), pp. 74–139.

17. "Credo unam sanctam catholicam et apostolicam, ubi quattuor de ecclesia sancti patres tradunt docent et praedicant. . . . Circa quod notandum quod unitas ecclesie colligitur ex multis. Primo ex unitate principis seu capitis quo regitur et gubernatur, qui unius est, scilicet Christus dominus deus noster, quem pater dedit caput super omnem ecclesiam quae est corpus ejus ad Ephaes. 1. Secundo ecclesia dicitur una ex unitate fidei qua illustrat et in qua fundatur . . . Tertia unitate baptisme . . . quia ianua sacramentorum est, intelligitur unitas aliorum sacramentorum . . . Quarto ecclesia dicitur una ab unitate spei. . . . Quinta . . . unitate charitatis que connecitur et vivificatur. . . . Sexto . . . unitate spiritus vivificantis . . . scilicet sanctus tanquam ultima et principalis perfectio corporis mistici quasi anima in corpore et in omnibus membris ecclesie dividens singulos ut vult, divisiones gratiarum sunt . . . Septima unitate ultimi finis. . . . Octavo . . . unitate unius praesidentis rectoris et gubernatoris visibiliter conversantis cum ea. . . . Hic autem unus praesidens pastor rector et gubernator in tota universali via Christi gerens rector et gubernator summus pontifex est," SE 1.6.7v58v. Nicolas Lopez Martinez, "El cardenal Torquemada y la unidad de la Iglesia," Burgense 1 (1960): 45–71.

18. "Ideo specialiter potestatem ligandi, solvendique Petro concessit, ut ad unitatem nos invitaret; ideo enim eum principem Apostolorum constituit, ut Ecclesia unum haberet et principalem

Vicarium, ad quem diversa membra Ecclesia recurrerent, si forte inter se dissentirent, quod si diversa capita capita assent in Ecclesia, unitatis vincula rumperentur," SE 2.25.139v. On the error of the Greeks, see JdT, *Apparatus super decretum unionis Grecorum*, ed. Emmanuel Candal (Rome, 1942), pp. 26–27. In a tract denouncing German neutrality, Arévalo argued that refusal to obey the pope was tantamount to heresy, see Richard Trame, *Rodrigo Sánchez de Arévalo, 1404–1470*. (Washington, D.C., 1958), pp. 44–47.

19. Marsilius of Padua, *The Defender of Peace*, trans. Alan Gewirth (New York, 1956), pp. 267–73; Johannes Hus, *Tractatus de ecclesia*, ed. Samuel Harrison Thomson (Cambridge, 1956), pp. 70–72, 104; Spinka, *Hus' Concept*, pp. 223–24, 274–75; Hendrix, *"Vera Ecclesia,"* p. 355.

20. "Qui deserit cathedram Petri deserit ecclesiam Christi. Est sic, qui extra ecclesiam Petri est, que est ecclesia Christi, non est in Ecclesia," CSD D93.c3(1:68). Bonifacius VIII, *Unam sanctam* (Extrav. Commun. 1.8.1), Friedberg 2.1245–46. 21. SE 1.19.12r–13r. WE 70–82.

22. Spinka, *John Hus' Concept*, pp. 387–88; Hendrix, *"Vera Ecclesia,"* pp. 348–53, 356, 371–74.

23. SE 1.11.15r–v; JdT, *Tractatus de veritate conceptionis beatissime virginis*, ed. Edward Bouverie Pusey (Brussels, 1966), p. 528. These distinctions, inherent in Augustine's works, were most clearly formulated by Thomas Netter, see Grabowski, *Church*, pp. 465–69.

24. SE 1.13.16v–18r, 1.19r; *CSD* ad De Cons. D1.c8.q3 (4:10–11). This was also the doctrine of John of Ragusa and Andreas Escobar, see WE 88–93.

25. "Post ascensionem domini, apostoli in fide et sancta doctrina verbo praedicationis miraculis sanctitatis exemplis fundarunt, et robarunt ecclesiam . . . quia apostolorum fidem, praedicationem documenta atque auctoritatem retinet semper et observat. Retinet quidem potestatem in clavibus, sententiarum in verbo et vitam in exemplo," SE 1.18.20v–21r. The Protestant Reformers rejected the Medieval emphasis on apostolicity of ministry, according to Yves Congar, "Apostolicité de ministère et apostolicité de doctrine: Reaction protestante et tradition catholique" in *Volk Gottes: Festgabe für Joseph Höfer*, ed. Remigius Bäumer and Heimo Dolch (Freiberug, 1967), pp. 106–7.

26. Kaminsky, *Hussite Revolution*, pp. 39–51; Louis B. Pascoe, "Jean Gerson: the *Ecclesia Primitiva* and Reform," *Traditio* 30 (1974): 379–409; idem, *Jean Gerson*, pp. 50–58.

27. "Absque dubio omnes ordines fuerunt in primitiva ecclesia et a christo instituti: sed dupliciter conferebatur ordo. scilicet. coniunctis alli ordini et disiunctis, in primitiva enim ecclesia propter paucitatem ministrorum et magnum idoneitatem suscipientium, quia omnes excellentes fuerunt sanctitatis: omnes ordines conferebantur ordine diaconorum," CSD D2 ante c1 (1:15). On the later separation of ecclesiastical titles and offices, see CSD

D93.c24 (2:623–27). *SE* 1.1 2r–3r, 1.28.32v–34r, 1.58.58v; CSD D45.c3 (1:369–70). Stockmann, *De corpore mystico,* pp. 97–100; William Edward Maguire, *John of Torquemanda O.P.: The Antiquity of the Church* (Washington, D.C., 1957); WE 107–25; Gordon Leff, "The Making of the Myth of a True Church in the Later Middle Ages," *Journal of Medieval and Renaissance Studies* 1(1971): 1–15.

28. "Cause vero efficiens ecclesiae duplex distinguitur, una principaliter, et alia instrumentalis. Principalis est ipse Christus qui plantator est et fundator ecclesie. . . . Causae vero instrumentalis ecclesiae dicuntur ipsa sacramenta quae a Christi passione habentia virtutem tamquam instrumenti divine pietatis disponunt et operatur ad edificationem et formationem corporis ecclesie," SE 1.1.12v. JdT, *Repetitiones super quibusdam propositionibus Augustini de Roma,* Mansi 30.979–1034 at 1012–13. This Thomistic argument was much used in anti-Hussite polemics, see WE 39–43.

29. "Causa autem materialis sunt ipsi fideles, quam apostolus tangit in nomine ecclesie dicens . . . collectio fidelium est," SE 1.1.3r. Stockmann, *De corpore mystico,* p. 92.

30. "Causa vero formalis est unitas corporis mistici cum Christo," *SE* 1.1.3r. See JdT, *Repetitiones,* col. 1012. Lopez, "La unidad," p. 52.

31. "Finis autem ecclesie duplex est, unus in vita praesenti. scilicet. sanctitas animarum; alius. scilicet ultimus. est futurae gloriae adeptio," JdT, *Repetitiones,* col. 1012; "Ceterum falsum dicunt quod ecclesia sit obiectum finale potestatis papalis. quoniam licet potestas papalis sit ei data in aedificatione ecclesiae: non tamem ipsa ecclesia dicitur finis ultimus potestatis eius: sed ipsa beatitudo ad cuius pascua ipsa universalis ecclesia per pastorem suum atque rectorem qui est papa," SE 2.7.192v–193r. Turrecremata and John of Ragusa both rejected, in their interpretations of the Nicene Creed, the idea that one believed "in," rather than through, the Church, see Johannes Brinkstrine, "Zu dem neuntem Glaubensartikel *et unam sanctam catholicam et apostolicam ecclesiam,*" *Catholica* 12 (1958): 141–43.

32. *SE* 1.31–41.35v–49v. Binder, "Zum Schriftbeweis," pp. 525–45; WE 126–50.

33. Henri de Lubac, *Corpus Mysticum,* 2nd ed. (Paris, 1949), pp. 13–19, 116–35.

34. Darquennes, "L'Eglise d'après Saint Thomas," pp. 30–49; Ernst Kantorowicz, *The King's Two Bodies* (Princeton, 1957), pp. 194–97, 201–5; WE 151–53; Roy C. Petry, "Unitive Reform Principles of the Late Medieval Conciliarists," *Church History* 31 (1962): 164–81.

35. Spinka, *Hus' Concept of the Church,* p. 196. Hus thought predestination the only sure guarantee of ecclesiastical unity according to Paul de Vooght, "Eglise et corps mystique: Les erreurs de Jean Hus sur les prédestinés," *Irenikon* 26 (1953): 250.

36. JdT, *Repetitiones,* cols. 991–93. WE 117; Binder, "Zum Schriftbeweis," p. 537. For a more favorable view of Favaroni, see

Gino Ciolini, *Agostino da Roma (Favaroni d.1443) e la sua Cristologia* (Florence, 1944), pp. 43–47. The Dominican theologian Henry Kalteisen, who participated in the debates with the Hussites, also played a key role in the proceedings against Favaroni, see Hendrix, *"Vera Ecclesia,"* pp. 368–70.

37. *SE* 1.43.50r, 1.63.70r; JdT, *Repetitiones,* cols. 1004–5. Stockmann, *De corpore mystico,* pp. 200–202.

38. *SE* 1.44.51r, 1.43.56v, 1.50.58v, 1.52.65r; 1.68.82v. Turrecremata drew on the works of Aquinas and Duns Scotus, see Stockmann, *De corpore mystico,* pp. 128–30. See also Andreas Escobar, *Tractatus polemico-theologicus de Graecis errantibus,* ed. Emmanuel Candal (Madrid, 1952), p. 48.

39. "Quia talis natura conformitas communis est bonis, et malis praescitis, et praedestinatis, omnes plane homines unum specie cum homine Christo," *SE* 1.51.60r. Turrecremata also used Innocent V's argument that Christ's humanity was a part of the Mystical Body, of which his divinity was head, see *SE* 1.47.55v–56r. WE 163–64. The Thomist idea that all men were potential members of the Mystical Body was quite important in the Spanish Indies Debate, see André Vincent, "L'Intuition fondamentale de Las Casas et la doctrine de Saint Thomas," *Nouvelle revue théologique* 96 (1974): 944–52.

40. *SE* 1.60.72v–73v; JdT, *Repetitiones,* col. 1023. WE 185. See Pascoe, *Jean Gerson,* p. 73.

41. WE 172–79; Mark John Farrelly, *Predestination, Grace, and Free Will* (Westminster, Md., 1964), pp. 109–51.

42. Spinka, *Hus' Concept,* p. 295; Paul de Vooght, *Hussiana* (Louvain, 1960), pp. 58–65.

43. "Denominatio simpliciter filiorum Dei, et membrorum Christi presentem iustitiam accipienda sit et non secundum divinam praedestinationem quae quorum sit ignotum nobis, est ergo fundamentum illorum falsum," *SE* 1.55.64v; "Si enim soli praedestinati et in Christi charitate existentes ad ecclesiam pertinere dicentur, cum ignotum esset qui tales essent, non dubium quoniam inter fideles multa schismata et scissure plurime orierentur sicut experientia cognoscimus eo tempore haereticorum [Hussites], quo dogma hoc pestiferum decurrebat. . . . Si autem ecclesia in solis praedestinatis consisteret, eadem incertitudinis vacillaret pontificium clavium ecclesiae, quia apud non infirma est certitudo praedestinorum," JdT, *Repetitiones,* cols. 1019–20. Spinka, *Hus' Concept,* pp. 172–208; Vooght, *Hussiana,* pp. 124–58.

44. *SE* 1.57.68v–69v.

45. Ibid. 1.55.67v. Hendrix, *"Vera Ecclesia,"* pp. 371–73.

46. Paul de Vooght "Le Cardinal Cesarini et le Concile de Constance," in *Das Konzil von Konstanz,* ed. August Franzen and Wolfgang Miller (Freiburg, 1964), pp. 357–80.

47. Paul Lazarus, *Das Basler Konzil* (Lübeck, 1965); Ernest Fraser Jacob, *Essays in Later Medieval History* (Manchester, 1968), p. 140.

48. MC 85–129.

49. "Ubi non parum admirandum adversarius Basilien. tanta calignine mentis involutus. et execatos malitia, ut in materiis fidei diffiniendis, et declarandis maluerunt sequi homines ab ecclesia Deo in doctrine sue damnatos: sicut fuit Marsilius de padua Ocham cum complicibus suis, ex quoniam doctrina extracta sunt pro magna parte decreti illa praefata Basilien," SE 2.100.240r. Paul de Vooght, *Les pouvoirs du concile et l'autorité du pape* (Paris, 1965), pp. 137–62; John Neville Figgis, *Studies of Political Thought from Gerson to Grotius* (Cambridge, 1956), pp. 31–54.

50. Brian Tierney, "Ockham, the Conciliar Theory, and the Canonists," *Journal of the History of Ideas* 15 (1954): 40–70; Hendrix, *"Vera Ecclesia,"* pp. 359–63.

51. Marsilius of Padua, *Defender of Peace*, pp. 299–364. Paul Sigmund, "The Influence of Marsilius of Padua on Fifteenth Century Conciliarism," *Journal of the History of Ideas* 13 (1962): 392–402; Oakley, *Council Over Pope?* p. 59.

52. Tierney, *Foundations*, pp. 23–105, 132–98; idem, "Pope and Council: Some New Decretist Texts," *Medieval Studies* 19 (1957): 197–218; Antony Black, "The Council of Basel and the Second Vatican Council," *Studies in Church History* 7 (1971), pp. 229–34. Conciliarism also included elements of episcopalism and of the idea that the cardinals shared supreme power with the pope, see Oakley, *Council Over Pope?* pp. 63–67. A limited influence of Marsilius and Ockham is suggested by August Franzen, "The Council of Constance: Present State of the Problem," *Concilium* 7 (1957): 46.

53. Petry, "Unitive Reform Principles," pp. 164–68; Congar, *L'Eglise*, pp. 309–10.

54. Oakley, *Council Over Pope?* pp. 61–74.

55. Tierney, *Foundations*, pp. 220–37.

56. Augustin de Asis, *Ideas sociopoliticas de Alonso de Polo (El Tostado)* (Seville, 1955), pp. 61–63; Congar, *L'Eglise*, pp. 328–30, 335.

57. Ernest Fraser Jacob, "Panormitanus and the Council of Basel," in *Proceedings of the Third International Congress of Medieval Canon Law*, ed. Stephan Kuttner (Vatican City, 1971), pp. 205–15; Knut Wolfgang Nörr, *Kirche und Konzil bei Nicolaus de Tudeschis (Panormitanus)* (Cologne, 1964).

58. Heinz-Mohr, *Unitas Christiana*, pp. 57–72, 118–68; Sigmund, *Cusa*, idem, "Cusanus' *Concordantia:* A Reinterpretation," *Political Studies* 10 (1960): 180–97.

59. Nicolai Rubenstein, "Marsilius of Padua and Italian Political Thought of His Time," in *Europe in the Late Middle Ages*, ed. John Rigby Hale, John Roger Highfield, and Beryl Smalley (Evanston, Ind., 1965), pp. 44–75. Even Panormitanus used this form of argument, see MC 35.

60. Gundisalvo Vera-Fajardo, *La Ecclesiologia de Juan de Segovia* (Vitoria, 1968); Jacob, *Essays in Later Medieval History*, pp. 129–33.

61. Antoninus de Florentia, *Summa Theologica* (Graz, 1959), 3.1190, 1274–76; Rodrigo Sánchez de Arévalo, *"Dialogus de re-*

mediis schismatis," Vat. lat. 4002 fols. 21v–22v; Petrus de Monte, *De primatu pape* in Rocaberti 18:100–41 at 102, 120–21.

62. Petrus de Monte, *De primatu papae,* p. 121; Rodrigo Sánchez de Arévalo, *"Contra tres propositiones concilii Basiliensis,"* Vat. lat. 4154.

63. Thomas M. Izbicki, "The Manuscript Library of Cardinal Johannes de Turrecremata O.P.," *Scriptorium* (in press).

64. "Si hoc ergo in ecclesia sit, Petrus, quando claves accepit ecclesiam sanctam significavit," c. Quodcumque (C24.ql.c6), Friedberg 1.967. Tierney, *Foundations,* pp. 23–46, 200–237; Nörr, *Panormitanus,* pp. 36–38, 129; MC 24–29.

65. "Si Petrus solus ut procurator nomine ecclesiae claves accepit, nihil potestatis acquisitus esset sibi quando claves sibi datae sunt, sed solum universitate ecclesiae . . . secundum quae Petrus non pontifex, non primus, non caput, non pastor, non princeps dicendus veniret ecclesiae, sed potius ecclesia Petri," JdT, *Propositio ad dietam Norimbergis,* Mansi 31A.41–62 at 49.

66. *"Excommunicat ecclesia.* id est. auctoritas ecclesiae. Si ergo ecclesiam sanctam significavit non ut quidem male exponunt. id est. sub signo et nomine ecclesiae tamquam syndicus, aut procurator ecclesiae, haec expositio est falsissima, quoniam sic nomine ecclesiae sequerentur multi errores. primo quod nulla dignitas aut authoritas ex collatione esset Petro acquista, sed solum ecclesiae, sicut procurator nihil sibi acquirit, sed ei cuius est procurator in suscipiendo aliquid nomine eius, sed hoc est falsissimum, quia Petro Christus inquit 'beatus etc. tibi dabo etc.' Secundo requeretur, quod nomen principatus aut pastoris aut capitis ecclesiae non veraciter diceretur de Petro, sed de ecclesia. cuius nomine recepisset clavium principatum ille, qui nomine alicuius recepit possessionem regni, aut episcopatus, non ipse sed cuius nomine accepit dicitur rex aut episcopus. Tertio sequeretur, quod potestas clavium data esset communitati ecclesiae universalis, quod non alius ostendimus de clavibus que proprie dicuntur regni coelorum esse impossibile," CSD C24.ql.c6 (3:267–68).

67. Possibly Turrecremata thought this doctrine was Marsilius's legacy, see MC 54–55.

68. "De plenitudine potestatis possumus loqui dupliciter. Uno modo prout plenitudine potestatis includit tam potestatem ordinis quam potestatem iurisdictionis. Alio modo prout solum includit potestatem iurisdictionis," SE 2.71.195v. This crucial chapter was printed in mutilated form by Black MC 169–70); Ewart Lewis, *Medieval Political Ideas* (New York, 1954), 2:425–29. Orders, jurisdiction, and plenitude of power will be discussed in chapter 3.

69. "Nulla communitas ut sic potest sacerdotibus consecratione esse subiectum ergo nec potestas clavium," *CSD* ad De Poen. D1.c51.q2 (5:42); *SE* 2.72.199v.

70. "Universitas non habet animam glo. super ca. Romana § in universitate," SE 2.71.195v. On the Mystical Body, see SE 2.26.139r–140r. MC 54–55.

71. *SE* 2.71.196v, 198v.

72. "Nulla universitas potest dici veritate habere perfecte aut plane aliquam potestatem in cuius exercitium numquam per se potest exire," SE 2.71.196r. On the exercise of the power of orders, see SE 2.71.196r–v.

73. SE 2.71.196v; CSD ad De Poen. D1.c51.q2 (5:42).

74. Tierney, *Foundations*, pp. 106–53.

75. "Nulla potestas potest convenire alicui universitate sive in omnibus membris eius simul ad quam est inhabilis magna pars illius universitatis sed ad potestatem iurisdictionis ecclesiastice sive in foro conscientiae sive exterioris iudicii magna pars universitatis ecclesie est inhabilis nec est capax illius. ergo talis potestas non potest dici convenire universitati ecclesiae . . . laicis personis nulla facultas data est disponendis ecclesiasticis officiis . . . mulier enim non est subiectum idoneum principatus, sed magis subiectionis," SE 2.71.197r. See Antoninus, *Summa Theologica*, vol. 3, col. 1190; Arévalo, *Dialogus*, fols. 21v–22r. Antony Black, "The Political Ideas of Conciliarism and Papalism, 1430–1450," *Journal of Ecclesiastical History* 20 (1969): 57.

76. "Si universitati ecclesiae in communi, ut universitati data esset potestas clavium iurisdictionis sequeretur quod nec papa, nec ecclesiae praelati possint exire in actum sive exercitium potestatis, nisi ad minus convocatis omnibus fidelibus tam laicis quam clericis, sed hoc est falsum," SE 2.71.197r. Turrecremata also used this argument to refute the conciliarist contention that Christ intended the general council to hear, as representative of the Church, denunciations of obstinate sinners, see JdT, *Oratio synodalis de primatu*, ed. Emmanuel Candal (Rome, 1954), pp. 28–29. This line of argument was also employed by the humanist Poggio Bracciolini, see MC 55–56.

77. "Talis potestatis plenitudo non potest esse subiective, et formaliter in universitati Ecclesiae, sed solum in Romano pontifice et per consequens . . . non potest esse excellentiori modo in universitate ecclesiae quam in Romano Pontifice," SE 2.71.198r.

78. *SE* 2.65.189r. Brian Tierney, " 'Divided Sovereignty' at Constance: A Problem of Medieval and Early Modern Political Theory," *Annuarium historiae conciliorum* 7 (1975): 251–52.

79. Nörr, *Panormitanus*, pp. 16–17, 85.

80. *SE* 3.38.320r. This argument first appeared in JdT, *Tractatus contra advisamentum quod non liceat appellare de concilio ad papam*, Mansi 30.1072–94 at 1083. Lopez, "La unidad," pp. 57–58. Similarly see Antoninus, *Summa Theologica*, vol. 3, cols. 1274–76.

81. "Significare autem ecclesiam hoc modo, sicut Augustinus ait, non est idem quod accipere nomine ecclesiae potestatem, sicut procurator, aut sinducus, aut servus vice aut nomine Domine suscipiat aliquid ab aliquo; cum Petrus caput et rector loco Christi Constitutus sit ecclesiae et illum locum habet quem Christus habebat; clarum est quod Christus non erat sindicus et servus ecclesiae. . . . Petrus quandoque suscipiat claves ecclesiam significavit, quia non solum pro persona sua suscepit claves; sed pro suis successoribus in ecclesia," JdT, *Tractatus contra advisamentum*, cols.

1086–87. *Oratio synodalis*, pp. 41–42; *SE* 2.72.199r–200r. See also Petrus de Palude, *Tractatus de potestate papae*, ed. Petrus Thomas Stella (Zürich, 1966), p. 186; Arévalo, *Dialogus*, fols. 21r, 22v.

82. "Universitas importa nomine universae ecclesiae non est universitas membrorum ecclesiae, aut pro ipsa communitate fidelium, quoniam . . . impossible est quod qua Petro dicta sunt de clavibus ecclesiae sive divisim sive coniunctim consideratis conveniat, sed est universitas locorum, et successionis sive decursus aetatis ecclesiae. Unde est sensus, quod quando Petrus accepit, accepisse designatur etiam pro omnibus seccessoribus suis, et aliis ecclesiae Prelatis, non tamen in uno loco, aut Provincia una, aut unto tempore, sed in universe Orbe, et per totam aetatem, Ecclesiae, scilicet usque in finem seculi, et hoc est universam figurare Ecclesiam," SE 2.75.205v.

83. *SE* 2.72.200r.

84. Otto Gierke, *Political Theories of the Middle Ages* (Cambridge, 1900), pp. 97–100; Francis Oakley, "From Constance to 1688 Revisited," *Journal of the History of Ideas* 17 (1966): 429–32; idem, "Almain and Major: Conciliar Theory on the Eve of the Reformation," *American Historical Review* 70 (1965): 673–90; MC 54–55.

85. "Grex est non pastor," *SE* 2.73.200v. Lewis, *Medieval Political Ideas*, 2:378–79.

Chapter 3

1. CSD D11.c11.ql (1:49), D23 ante c21.q2 (1:233), D89.c1.q1 (1:580); *SE* 1.96.111r. WE 45; Hugh of St. Victor, *On the Sacraments of the Christian Faith*, trans. Roy Joseph Deferari (Cambridge, Mass., 1951), p. 255.

2. Matthew Spinka, *John Hus' Concept of the Church* (Princeton, 1966), pp. 232–33; Gordon Leff, *Heresy in the Later Middle Ages* (Manchester, 1967), 2:1516–45; William R. Cook, "John Wycliff and Hussite Theology, 1415–1436," *Church History* 42 (1973): 335–49.

3. Turrecremata's belief that conciliarism was created by Marsilius and Ockham has endured to the present day, see August Franzen, "The Council of Constance: Present State of the Problem," *Concilium* 7 (1965): 19–68.

4. Donald Edward Heintschel, *The Medieval Concept of an Ecclesiastical Office* (Washington, D.C., 1956): Martinen van der Kerckhove, *La notion de juridiction dans la doctrine des Décretistes et les premiers Décrétalistes* (Assisi, 1937); Robert Benson, *The Bishop-Elect* (Princeton, 1968), pp. 23–149.

5. Geoffrey Grimshaw Willis, *Saint Augustine and the Donatist Controversy* (London, 1950), pp. 145–68; Hugh of St. Victor, *On the Sacraments*, pp. 259–432; Malcolm Donald Lambert, *Medieval Heresy* (London, 1977), pp. 76–81.

6. "Si enim malitia hominis impedire posset actum clavium sive effectum sacramenti non posset homo habere fiduciam certam

de sua salute aut conscientia sua libera maneret a peccato," SE
1.99.113v–114r. See SE 1.101.114v; CSD D21.c1.q5 (1:189–92),
D36.c1.q2 (1:330), C25.q1.c31 (3:280). Turrecremata also specifically attacked Hussite euchraistic and penitential doctrine, see
SE 1.95.108v, 1.93.105v; CSD De poen. D1.c51 (5:40–41). Spinka,
Hus' Concept, pp. 321–23; Paul de Vooght, *Hussiana* (Louvain,
1960), pp. 102–85. See also Ulrich Horst, "Papst, Bischofe, und
Konzil nach Antonin von Florenz," *Recherches de théologie ancienne
et médievale* 3 (1965): 83–84. Arévalo quickly withdrew a suggestion that refusal to obey the pope could cost a priest his power
of orders, see Richard Trame, *Rodrigo Sánchez de Arévalo* (Washington, D.C., 1958), pp. 47–48.

7. "In comparations ad corpus christi mysticum maior est in
episcopo. quam in simplici sacerdote: cum simplex sacerdos non
valeat omnia sacramenta conferre," CSD D21 ante c1.q2 (1:184);
D21 ante c1.q3 (1:185–86), D23.c7.q1 (1:223–26). Hugh of St.
Victor, *On the Sacraments*, p. 269; Marsilius of Padua, *The Defender
of Peace*, trans. Alan Gewirth (New York, 1956), pp. 233–53;
Spinka, *Hus' Concept*, pp. 270–89; Vooght, *Hussiana*, pp. 45–58;
J. Lécuyer, "Aux origines de la théologie thomiste de l'episcopat,"
Gregorianum 35 (1954): 56–81; Robert P. Stenger, "The Episco-
pacy as an *Ordo* According to the Medieval Canonists," *Medieval
Studies* 29 (1967): 67–112.

8. Alfonso Maria Stickler, "Alanus Anglicus als Verteidiger des
Monarchischen Papsttums," *Salesianum* 21 (1959): 346–406; Brian
Tierney, "From Thomas of York to William of Ockham: The
Franciscans and the Papal *solicitudo omnium ecclesiarum*, 1250–1350,"
Communio 13 (1972): 607–58; Michael Wilks, "*Papa est nomen iur-
isdictionis:* Augustinus Triumphus and the Papal Vicariate of
Christ," *Journal of Theological Studies* n.s. 8 (1957) 71–91, 256–71;
Antony Black, "The Council of Basel and the Second Vatican
Council," *Studies in Church History* 7 (1971): 230–32; Charles
Abraham Zuckermann, "Dominican Theories of Papal Primacy,
1250–1320" (Ph.D. diss., Cornell University, 1971).

9. "Ad regendum populum Christianum secundum legem divinam," *SE* 1.93.104c; "Potestas iurisdictionis, qua aliquis potest
absolvere et ligare, dicitur relative ad subditum," Johannes de
Turrecremata (JdT), *Oratio synodalis de primatu*, ed. Emmanuel
Candal (Rome, 1954), p. 20.

10. "Potestas spiritualis ecclesie duplex est quaedam scilicet
ordinis sive sacramentalis, et quaedum iurisdictionis. Potestas autem ordinis sive sacramentalis dicitur quae per aliquam consecrationem conferatus ad confectionem, et administrationem per
consecrationem sed simplici iniunctione Dei aut hominis confer-
tur . . . utraque potestas spiritualis excedit totam facultatem naturae, ergo necesse est dicere ut a Deo qui auctor naturae est
originem traxerit," SE 1.93.104v. For the attack on the Hussites,
see SE 2.85.217v; CSD C25.q1.c31 (3:280). Howard Kaminsky,
A History of the Hussite Revolution (Berkeley, 1967), pp. 38–39.

11. CSD C25.q1.c31 (3:280), D21.c6 (1200–201).

12. "Potestas iurisdictionis ordinatur ad potestatem consecrationis," CSD D21 ante c1.q2 (1:184). Benson, *The Bishop-Elect*, pp. 383–84; Ludwig Hödl, "*Lex et sacramentum* in scholastischen Verstädnis der Weihsakraments unter besonder Berückssichtigung der Zeit Bonifaz VIII (1294–1303)," in *Lex et sacramentum im Mittelalter*, ed. Albert Zimmermann (Berlin, 1969), pp. 1–30.

13. CSD D21.c4.q3 (1:198–99). Ludwig Hödl, *Die Geschichte der Scholastischen Litteratur und der Theologie der Schlüsselgewalt* (Münster, 1960), 1:376–78; Brian Tierney, *Origins of Papal Infallibility, 1150–1350* (Leiden, 1972), pp. 82–86; Zuckermann, *Dominican Theories*, p. 37.

14. "Potestas iurisdictionis est duplex secundum quod duplex distinguitur forum scilicet conscientiae, et forum causarum. Patet quoniam quaedam est potestas iurisdictionis in foro conscientiae quam habet curam animarum, secundum quam potest absolvendos per imperium ad aliquid faciendum ligare. Alia est potestas iurisdictionis in foro causarum, per quam aliquis in negociis et causis diffiniendis qua vertuntur inter hominem, et hominem habet facultatem diffiniendi, et ius etiam invitum dicendi de qua habetur dist. 10 cap. 1 ubi dicitur aliud est terminum causis imponere, alius est scripturas sacras diligenter exponere. Per hanc potestatem potest quis ad correctionem aliquam ab ecclesia per excommunicationem separari. . . . Quia potestas iurisdictionis in foro causarum dicitur potestas coertiva iurisdictionis, quia fieri potest inviti enim. potestas vero in foro conscientiae dicitur potestas iurisdictionis non coertive, quoniam in hoc foro nullus invitus absolvitur vel ligatur," SE 1.96.109v–110r. Zuckermann, "Dominican Theories," p. 37.

15. "De necessitate huius sacramenti est non solum quod minister habeat ordinis potestatem sed etiam quod habeat potestatem iurisdictionis," SE 1.96.100r. See CSD De poen. D1.c21.q5 (5:44), C13.q1 ante c1 (3:3), C24.q1 post c4 (3:266–67); SE 1.98.112r–v, 1.78.90v, 1.95.108v, 2.55.172v, 2.77.211v, 2.101.241v. Turrecremata did not, however, conclude that the Greeks lost the power of the keys when they had broken with Rome, see JdT, *Apparatus super decretum unionis Grecorum*, ed. Emmanuel Candal (Rome, 1942), pp. 16–17. See also Horst, "Antonin," pp. 85–86; Knut Wolfgang Nörr, *Kirche und Konzil bei Nicolaus de Tudeschis (Panormitanus)* (Cologne, 1964), p. 38. Benson, *The Bishop-Elect*, p. 375; Hödl, *Schlüsselgewalt*, pp. 383–84; Johannes Parisiensis, *De confessionibus audiendis*, ed. Ludwig Hödl (Munich, 1962); Wilks, "*Papa est nomen jurisdictionis*," 83, 87–88.

16. "Claves enim quibus prelati ligant et solvunt arma sunt spiritualia ecclesiae," CSD C2.q7 ante c42 (2:213). See CSD C24.q1 post c4 (3:266); SE 1.90.101v, 1.96.110v.

17. CSD D21.c4 (1:199), C11.q3.c4 (2:405–6), C11.q3.c1 (2:403–4); SE 1.8.10r.

18. SE 1.96.110r; CSD D91.c1.q2 (1:599–600), D32.c6, pt. 1 (1:299), D21.c4.q1 (1:199). Turrecremata, like Augustinus Triumphus, thought jurisdiction in the external forum was sep-

arable from the sacramental power of orders. This doctrine, rooted in canon law, was attacked by the critics of the canonists from Peter the Chanter to Jean Gerson, see Hödl, *Schlüsselgewalt,* pp. 3, 6–8; Jean Gerson, *De potestae ecclesiastica,* in *Oeuvres complétes,* ed. Palémon Glorieux (Paris, 1965), 7:227.

19. Yves Congar, "Aspects ecclésiologiques de la querelle entre mendiants et séculiers dans la seconde moitié du xiiie siècle et le début du xive," *Archives d'histoire doctrinale et littéraire* 38 (1961): 35–151; Jeffrey Garrett Sikes, "John de Pouilli and Peter de la Palu," *English Historical Review* 49 (1934): 219–40; Herveus Natalis, *De iurisdictione,* ed. Ludwig Hödl (Munich, 1959).

20. Roy C. Petry, "Unitive Reform Principles in the Late Medieval Conciliarists," *Church History* 31 (1962): 164–81; Antoninus de Florentia, *Summa theologica* (Verona, 1740), vol. 3, cols. 1274–76; Rodrigo Sánchez de Arévalo, *"Dialogus de remediis schismatis,"* Vat. lat. 4002 fols. 1r–70r; Petrus de Monte, *De primatu papae* in Rocaberti 18:102, 120–21; Paul Sigmund, "Cusanus' *Concordiantia*: A Reinterpretation," *Political Studies* 109 (1960) 187–91.

21. "Ordo qui est inter Romanam ecclesiam et alias ecclesias sive inter Romanum pontificem, et alios prelatos, est secundum influentiam prout unus movet alium ad actus Hierarchicos. ergo potestas iurisdictionis omnium praelatorum ecclesiae derivatur a Romano pontifice," SE 2.55.171v.

22. "Licet a papa in alios non diffunditur Spiritus vitalis, nec gratia, sed a Deo solo. Nihilominus diffunditur ab eo potestas iurisdictionis in alios, sive motus directionis et gubernationis ecclesiae, in praelatos, et rectores, et hoc sufficit ad rationem capitis," CSD D12.c1.q1 (1:112). The theory of Black (MC 6) that the Eugenians thought jurisdiction a "unique type of grace" fails when compared with this quotation.

23. "Manifeste colligitur pertinere ad unitatem ecclesiae, quod a Romano pontifice omnium aliorum praelatorum derivetur auctoritas. . . . Ex quibus videtur quod negare potestatem iurisdictionis inferiorum praelatorum in ecclesia a Romano pontifice immediate non dependere, non solum praeiudicet primatu apostolicae sedis sed etiam unitati universalis ecclesiae," SE 2.55.173r–v. Nicholas Lopez Martinez, "El cardenal Torquemada y la unidad de la Iglesia," *Burgense* I (1960): 45–71.

24. "Si aliis apostolis data fuisset potestas in ea plenitudine, qua Petro data est, Petrus nec maior nec superior nec princeps nec caput fuisset apostoiorum," JdT, *Oratio synodalis,* p. 21. See *SE* 2.32.144v. Bañez thought it sufficient to argue that the Apostles could not bestow on others the jurisdiction that Christ had given to them, see Mario Midali, *Corpus Christi mysticum apud Dominicum Bañez eiusque fontes* (Rome, 1962), pp. 222–23.

25. "Primo quidem est illud Matth. XVIII. quecumque ligaveritis, sed per illud non sunt facti episcopi. propter tria. Primo quia Petrus per similia verba et maiora Mat. XVI. quodcumque ligaveris etc. non fuit factus episcopus. Secundo quia ipsi nondum erant sacerdotes. et ideo per consequens non poterant episcopi.

Tertia quia illud fuit promissio non alicmius potestatis: nec sac-
erdotalis collatio. ergo etc. Secundum est illud Luc. XXII. hoc
facite in meam commemorationem: sed non per hoc facti sunt
episcopi. quia per verba consecrationis non efficitur plus quam
per illa verba significetur. nisi propter naturalem concomiten-
tiam: et inseparabilem significationem vel accesoriam: sed potestas pontificalis non est necessaria: nec concomittans ad
sacerdotalem. . . . Tertia est illud quod dicitur Jo. XX. quorum
remiseritis etc. . . . dicitur communiter omni illi qui ordinatur in
simplicem sacerdotem," CSD D21.c2.q1 (1:193). Wilks, *"Papa est
nomen iurisdictionis,"* pp. 84–86; Nicholas de Lyre, *Postilla litteralis
super totam bibliam* (Lyons, 1545) ad Matt. 16:19 (vol. 5, fol. 52va);
Tierney, *Origins*, pp. 31–32, 82–86; Walter Ullmann, *The Growth
of Papal Government in the Middle Ages*, 2nd ed. (London, 1962),
pp. 7–9, 447–57.

26. *"Tu es petrus* per hoc verba bene Petrus fuit designatus et
ordinatus fidelium futurus pastor: et rector: scilicet non actu constitutus: nisi per illa verba pasce oves meas," CSD D21.c3 (1:197).
On Christ as bishop, see *SE* 2.31.144r. Herveus Natalis, *De iurisdictione*, p. 22; Nicholas de Lyre, *Postilla litteralis* ad Matt. 16:19
(vol. 5, fol. 52va); Brian Tierney, *Foundations of the Conciliar Theory*
(Cambridge, 1955), pp. 25–36; Wilks, *"Papa est nomen iurisdictionis,"* pp. 84–88.

27. "Beati Petri pontificatus fuit datus a christo actu post resurrectionem: et non ante. que conclusio inde patet: quia eo tempore quo salvator noster corporaliter homines visibilis conversabitur
per seipsum rexit ecclesiam . . . post resurrectionem praesentiam
suam corporalem visibilem esset ab ecclesia subtracturus unde
beatus petrus factus est christo pastor: princeps: et episcopus
universalis. quia post ressurectionem ascensurus in celum numquam
unde ad conversationem mortaliter. noster recursus inquit petro.
Simon Ioannis diligis me plus his. pasce oves meas . . . verbo pasce
oves meas factus est petrus princeps ecclesie," CSD D21.c3.q2
(1:193–94). See *SE* 2.31.143v. See also Herveus Natalis, *De iurisdictione*, pp. 19–20; Horst, "Antonin," 94–99; Johannes de Montenegro, *Commento alla formola di unione sul primato 16: giugno 1439,*
in Georg Hofmann, *Papato, conciliarismo, patriarchato (1438–1439)*
(Rome, 1940), p. 45. The Johannine passage could also be understood as a reference to cure of souls, see Nicholas de Lyre, *Postilla
litteralis* ad Io. 21:15–17 (vol. 5, fol. 243rb–va); Wilks, *"Papa est
nomen iurisdictionis,"* pp. 87–88.

28. JdT, *Oratio synodalis*, p. 41; "Nihil iurisdictionis contulit sed
Petro soli pro se et suis successoribus totam potestatem iurisdictionis ecclesiae distribuendum episcopis et curatis et aliis sicut
expediens iudicaret," SE 2.63.187r; SE 2.32.144r–146r, 2.34.147v,
3.4.329v. This argument is misstated as allowing an *electus* partial
jurisdiction before confirmation in A. Langhorst, "Der Cardinal
Turrecremata und das Vaticanum über die Jurisdiktionsgewalt
der Bischöfe," *Stimmen aus Maria-Laach* 17 (1879): 460–62. Cardinal Jacobazzi accepted this doctrine, but it was rejected by

Suarez, see Giuseppe Alberigo, *Lo sviluppo della dottrina sui poteri nella chiesa universale* (Rome, 1964), p. 182, n. 4.

29. Tierney, *Origins*, pp. 159–65; Congar, "Aspects ecclésiologiques," pp. 58–66.

30. *SE* 2.61.179r–180v, 2.63.186r. See Herveus Natalis, *De iurisdictione*, p. 26.

31. "Episcopus summus non habet plenitudinem potestatis per relationem ad corpus verum. sed per relationem ad corpus christi mysticum," CSD D95.c1 (1:629). For the denial of plenitude of power to the whole Church, see chap. 2, above.

32. "Plenitudo vero potestatis est tantum apud illum cuius regimini ipsa tota universalis ecclesia tota orbe diffusa commissa est, qui est Romanus pontifex," SE 2.76.207r; "Plenitudo potestatis data sit in uno membro tantum scilicet principatu quod est caput in corpore: quod est Romanus pontifex," SE 2.72.199v. On the scope of this power, see SE 2.63.186r–v. See also Herveus Natalis, *De iurisdictione*, pp. 10, 17–28. Augustinus Triumphus used the curious phrase *plenitudo deitatis*, see Wilks, *"Papa est nomen iurisdictionis,"* p. 90. Zabarella used *plenitudo potestatis* to designate the pope as rector of the ecclesiastical corporation, see Tierney, *Foundations*, pp. 142–49. Gaines Post, *Studies in Medieval Legal Thought* (Princeton, 1964), pp. 91–162; Robert Benson, *"Plenitudo potestatis:* Evolution of a Formula from Gregory IV to Gratian," *Studia Gratiana* 14 (1967): 193–217; John Antony Watt, "The Use of the Term *plenitudo potestatis* by Hostiensis," in *Proceedings of the Second International Congress of Medieval Canon Law*, ed. Stephan Kuttner (Vatican City, 1965), pp. 161–87.

33. "Papa cui a Christo omnium fidelium cura commissa est omnibus aliis committit vices suas, et impartitur partem sollicitudinis suae in his que exesquantur pertinentia ad regimen ecclesia," SE 2.55.173r; "Authoritas vero aliorum praelatorum, cum sit minor continet praeceptum, et observantiae necessitatem, sed non generaliter, quia non in plenitudine potestatis vocati sunt, CSD D11.c2 (1:105). Innocent III adopted the term *in partem sollicitudinis* for official use, but critics of the curia thought that God, not the pope, called prelates to their share of ecclesiastical government, see Jean Rivière, *"In partem sollicitudinis:* Evolution d'une formule pontificale," *Revue des sciences religieuses* 5 (1925): 210–31; Benson, *The Bishop-Elect*, pp. 172–73.

34. *SE* 2.63.186v, 3.24.299r; CSD D93 ante c1.q2 (1:616). Turrecremata cited Huguccio's theory that Apollos was bishop of Corinth and Paul his metropolitan, to demonstrate the antiquity of the hierarchy of jurisdiction, see CSD C9.q3 post c3 (2:364). This hierarchy was more clearly defined in the North than in Italy, see Robert Brentano, *Two Churches* (Princeton, 1968), pp. 62–173.

35. "Per solam electionem ante confirmationem apostolicae sedis immediate vel mediate non acquiritur potestas iurisdictionis," CSD D63.c10 (1:474). See CSD D18.c7 (1:160), D83.c1 (1:44–45), D61.c6 (1:463), D100 ante c1 (1:653–54); C9.q3.c10

(2:366–67), C25.q1.c2 (3:273); *SE* 2.56.173v–174r. A patriarch, primate, or metropolitan received his power of jurisdiction, including a delegated power to confirm elections, when he received the pallium from the pope, see JdT, *Apparatus*, p. 114. Hofmann, *Papato*, pp. 69–73.

36. *SE* 1.96.110r; CSD D61.c6 (1:463), D80.c2.q2 (1:529–30), D82.c5 (1:541–42), D84 ante c1 (1:549–50), C13.q2 ante c1 (3:5), C25.q1 post c37 (3:282). Turrecremata believed that curates had jurisdiction in apostolic succession from the Disciples as bishops had it from the Apostles, by papal commission, see *SE* 2.63.184r–v. Congar, "Aspects ecclésiologiques," pp. 59–62; Tierney, *Foundations*, pp. 106–31.

37. CSD C13.q2 post c6 (3:182), D12.c13 (1:116–17); "Episcopus non est archiepiscopi vicarius," CSD C9.q3.c7 (2:345). See Nicholas de Tudeschis (Panormitanus), *Consilia* (Venice, 1621), Consilium 37, fol. 26ra. Benson, *The Bishop-Elect*, pp. 189–200.

38. "Papa et alii ministerii eclesiae quantum ad hunc influxum non videtur habere ministerium nisi quantum ad dispositionem subiecti per dispensationem sacramentorum," SE 2.62.183r.

39. *SE* 1.98.113r.

40. Tierney, *Foundations*, pp. 36–46; idem, *Origins*, pp. 14–57. See, however, the controversy between Alfonso Maria Stickler and Brian Tierney in *Catholic Historical Review* 60 (1974): 427–41, 61 (1975): 265–79.

41. Tierney, *Origins*, pp. 115–30; Michele Maccarone, "Una questione inedita dell'Olivi sull'infallibilità del papa," *Rivista di storia della chiesa in Italia* 3 (1949): 307–43.

42. Tierney, *Origins*, pp. 171–237; idem, "Ockham, the Conciliar Theory, and the Canonists," *Journal of the History of Ideas* 15 (1954): 40–70. But see Scott H. Hendrix, "In Quest of the *Vera Ecclesia*: The Crisis of Late Medieval Ecclesiology," *Viator* 7 (1976): 359–65.

43. Some of these mendicant discussions of infallibility may have arisen from curial inquiries into Olivi's orthodoxy held before the Michaelists broke with the pope, see Tierney, *Origins*, pp. 146–64, 171–267.

44. Guido Terreni, *Quaestio de magisterio infallibili Romani pontificis*, ed. Bartolomé Maria Xiberta (Münster, 1926); Thomas Peter Turley, "Infallibilists in the Curia of Pope John XXII," *Journal of Medieval History* 1 (1975): 71–101; Thomas M. Izbicki, "Infallibility and the Erring Pope: Guido Terreni and Johannes de Turrecremata," in *Law, Church, and Society: Essays in Honor of Stephan Kuttner*, ed. Kenneth Pennington and Robert Somerville (Philadelphia, 1977), pp. 100–03.

45. Petry, "Unitive Reform Principles," pp. 168–69; Herman Schüssler, "The Canonist Panormitanus and the Problem of Scriptural Authority," *Concordia Theological Monthly* 38 (1967): 234–41; Paul Sigmund, *Nicholas of Cusa and Medieval Political Thought* (Cambridge, Mass., 1963), pp. 169–72.

46. Remigius Bäumer, "Luthers Ansichten über die Irrt-

umsfähigkeit des Konzils und ihre theologischen Grundlagen," in *Wahrheit und Verküdigung: Michael Schaus zum 70. Geburtstag*, ed. Leo Scheffczyk, Werner Dettloff, and Richard Heinzmann (Munich, 1967), pp. 1000–1001.

47. "Sine fide impossibile est placere Deo, Circa ea vero quae sunt fidei contingit quaestiones moveri. per diversitatem autem sententiarum divideretur ecclesia nisi in unitate per unius sententiam conservaretur," SE 2.2.117r. "Una fides debet esse tocius ecclesiae secundum illud I. Corin. 1. Idipsum dicatis omnes et non sint in vobis scismatis hoc autem servari non posset nisi quaestio fidei exorta determinaretur tenenda per unum qui toti ecclesiae praeest, ut sic eius sententia a tota ecclesia firmiter teneatur," SE 2.107.248v. On the dissensions of the Hussites, see JdT, *Repetitiones super quibusdam propositionibus Augustini de Roma*, Mansi 30.970–1034 at 1019–20.

48. "Licet enim sacerdotibus in collatione ordinis conferatur potestas praedicandi verbum, sicut absolvendi in foro poenitentiae; illam tamen potestatem exercere non debent, nec digne possunt sine speciali licentia superioris, quia precise ex collatione ordinis non subicitur eis," JdT, *Defensiones quorundam articulorum rubrorum revelationum S. Brigittae factae in concilio Basiliensi*, Mansi 30.699–814 at 748.

49. CSD D20.c2 (1:181), D96.c4 (1:636–37); *SE* 4, pt. 2, 17.388v–390r.

50. JdT, *Apparatus*, p. 62. Hermann Schüssler, *Der Primat der heiligen Schrift im Mittelalter* (Leiden, 1977), p. 220. This papalist idea was rejected by Hus, see Spinka, *Hus' Concept*, pp. 96–98.

51. "In causarum decisione non solum est necessaria scientia: qua pollent doctores scripturarum: sed etiam potestas under christus dicturus petro. Quodcunque ligaveris etc," CSD D20 ante c1.q1 (1:177); "Quae apostolica ecclesia docuit, scilicet diffinitione iudiciale esse credenda," *SE* 4, pt. 2, 9.382v; CSD D1.c5 (1:158), C24.q1.c2 (3:266); JdT, *Questiones evangeliorum de tempore et de sanctis* (Basel, 1484), in Dominica quinta post pentecostem q. 2. For a similar discussion of the interpretation of laws, see *SE* 3.53.337v. Tierney, *Foundations*, pp. 36–37; idem, " 'Only the Truth Has Authority': The Problem of 'Reception' in the Decretists and in Johannes de Turrecremata," in *Law, Church, and Society*, pp. 83–84.

52. "Licet divinarum scripturarum excellentissimi doctores scientia pontificibus Romanis forte praeemineant, et dicimus forte, quia potest esse ita dictus Romanus pontifex. quod nullo suo tempore sit par ei . . . nihilominus in causarum sive dubiorum diffinitionis in dispensatione canonum aut mutatione etiam statutorum praedecessorum suorum quae omnia respiciunt auctoritatem merito pontifices praeferentur," SE 3.51.344r. Turrecremata emphasized the role of papal *magisterium* in the preservation of ecclesiastical unity, see, e.g., SE 2.107 .249r, 250r. Tierney, " 'Only the Truth Has Authority,' " pp. 86–87; Heiko Obermann, *The Harvest of Medieval Theology* (Cambridge, Mass., 1963), p. 367.

53. *SE* 2.110 .256r–v, 2.107 .250r

54. "Alias questiones circa fidem determinare, et in lucem veritatis dicere, hoc soli Petro suisque successoribus relinquintur infra eodem quoties. unde Lucae 22. ait dominus Petro Petre ego rogavi pro te ut non deficiat fides tua," CSD C24.q1.c7.q1 (3:268). Turrecremata distinguished between Peter's *magisterium* and Paul's special gift of inspiration, see *SE* 2.107 .294r–v.

55. JdT, *Apparatus*, pp. 64–65; *SE* 4, pt. 2, 3 .377v, 2.107 .250r Joseph Gill, *The Council of Florence* (Cambridge, 1959), pp. 147–62.

56. *SE* 2.52 .168r–v. In the mid-thirteenth century the papacy controlled canonization, see Eric Waldram Kemp, *Canonization and Authority in the Western Church* (Oxford, 1948), pp. 82–140.

57. *SE* 2.107 .250r–v; CSD D15.c3.q2 (1:139); JdT, *"Flores sententiarum de auctoritate summi pontificis,"* Vat. lat. 2580 fols. 87v–93v. at 90v. Aquinas, one of Turrecremata's chief sources, was a central figure in that controversy, see Decima Douie, *The Conflict Between Seculars and Mendicants at the University of Paris in the Thirteenth Century* (London, 1954).

58. Paul de Vooght, "L'évolution du rapport église-écriture du xiiie au xve siècle," *Ephemerides theologiae Lovanienses* 38 (1962): 71–85; Georges Henri Tavard, *Holy Writ or Holy Church?* (London, 1959), pp. 22–51; Tierney, *Origins*, pp. 133–40; Michael Hurley, *"Scriptura sola:* Wycliff and his Critics," *Traditio* 16 (1960): 275–352.

59. Matthew Spinka, *John Hus at the Council of Constance* (New York, 1965), pp. 36–37; Ernest Fraser Jacob, "The Bohemians at the Council of Basel, 1433," in *Prague Essays,* ed. Richard William Seton-Watson (Oxford, 1949), p. 84.

60. Heiko Obermann, *Forerunners of the Reformation* (New York, 1966), pp. 51–120; Henri Holstein, *"Traditio et Scriptura in patristica occidentali,"* in *De Scriptura et Traditione,* ed. Karlo Balić (Rome, 1963), pp. 205–33; Louis B. Pascoe, *Jean Gerson: Principles of Church Reform* (Leiden, 1973), pp. 49–79.

61. Eduardus Stakemeier, *"Traditio et Scriptura iuxta Reformatores,"* in *De Scriptura et Traditione,* pp. 505–26.

62. *SE* 4, pt. 2, 8 .381r; CSD D11.c8 (1:110).

63. "Nihil utiliter ad salutem spiritualem praedicamus quod sacra scriptura spiritus sancti miraculo foecunditate non protulerat aut in se non teneat," SE 1.13.17v; "Sed et quicunque aliter scripturam sanctam intelligit quam spiritus sanctus sensus efflagitat a quo scripta est, licet de ecclesia non recesserit, tamen haereticus appelari potest teste Aug," SE 4, pt. 2, 34.406r. For a defense of the Old Testament, see JdT, *Symbolum pro informatione Manichaeorum,* ed. Nicolas Lopez Martinez and Vincente Proaño Gil (Burgos, 1958), pp. 57–65.

64. "Tum quia constat quod auctoritate ecclesiae capite et principale collate est libri canonis habent robur," *SE* 2.112 .258r; "Illi libri non auctoritatem ab ecclesia, sed a Deo, a quo editi sunt. Et ideo beatus Augustinus dicit quod non crederem evangelio etc. hoc dicit pro tanto, non quod evangelium habet authoritatem ab

ecclesia, sed quia sibi ignotum esset, utrum istud evangelium pertineret ad scripturam sanctam, vel non, nisi ecclesia instinctu spiritu sancto hoc declarasset," CSD C25.q1.c6 (3:316). Similarly, the Church accepted the Apostles' Creed as an expression of fundamental truths, see CSD D15.c1q3 (1:126). The doctrines of Gerson and Biel were similar, see Obermann, *Harvest*, pp. 385–87, 393–408. Terreni, sometimes thought to have made Scripture the pope's creature (Tavard, *Holy Writ or Holy Church?* pp. 31–34), simply thought that the pope determined the canon of Scripture, see Bartolomé Maria Xiberta, "Scriptura, Traditio, et magisterium iuxta antiquos auctores ordinis Carmelitarum," in *De Scriptura et Traditione*, p. 262. Schüssler, *Primat der heiligen Schrift*, pp. 219–21.

65. Tierney, *Origins*, pp. 22–25; *Glossa ordinaria*, D20.c3.

66. Brian Tierney, "*Sola scriptura* and the Canonists," *Studia Gratiana* 11 (1976): 345–66; Tavard, *Holy Writ or Holy Church?* pp. 31–34, 47–51; Hurley, "*Scriptura sola*"; Kaminsky, *Hussite Revolution*, pp. 261, 287, 337, 419, 489–90; Yves Congar, *Tradition and Traditions*, trans. Michael Naseby and Thomas Rainborough (London, 1966), pp. 97–99.

67. Hendrix, "*Vera Ecclesia*," pp. 359–63; Guilelmus ab Ockham, *Dialogues de potestate papae et imperatoris* (Turin, 1966), pp. 415–16.

68. Tierney, *Origins*, pp. 72–82, 218–26; Obermann, *Harvest*, pp. 361–69, 375–82; Francis Oakley, "The *Tractatus de fide et ecclesia, Romano pontifice, et concilio generali* of Johannes Breviscoxe," *Annuarium historiae conciliorum* 10 (1978): 107–8, 121–23.

69. See chap. 1 above.

70. "Omnes enim universarum suarum diffinitionem principia et fundamenta ab ipso sacrae scripture fonte et rupe sumpserunt, sicut exemplariter patet in primis quatuor conciliis universalibus. . . . Ex quo manifestum est ex ipsa institutione divina, quod in tribunali ecclesiae lex divina et scriptura debet esse mensura et regula principalis judiciorum et causarum fidei," JdT, *Tractatus de veritate conceptionis beatissime virginis*, ed. Edward Bouverie Pusey (Brussels, 1966), p. 6; see pp. 15–21. CSD D9.c3 (1:88), D9.c8 (1:93). Obermann, *Harvest*, pp. 285, 387; Tavard, *Holy Writ or Holy Church?* p. 60. Turrecremata's cautious statement (*Defensiones quorundam articulorum rubrorum revelationum Sanctae Brigittae factae in concilio Basiliensi*, Mansi 30.699–814 at 721) that the pope could sanction private revelations that conformed with sound doctrine was a far cry from the Joachite fantasies of such Franciscans as Gerard of Borgo San Donino, see Marjorie Reeves, *The Influence of Prophecy in the Later Middle Ages* (Oxford, 1969), pp. 187–90.

71. Obermann, *Harvest*, pp. 361–422. For a different approach, see Congar, *Tradition and Traditions*.

72. *SE* 2.37 .318v.

73. Turrecremata cited Huguccio's list in CSD D20.c3 (1:182). Congar, *Tradition and Traditions*, p. 96, n. 5 unjustly suggests that Turrecremata thought that the Church, guided by the Spirit, was virtually an end in itself.

74. *SE* 4, pt. 2, 9 .381v–383r, 4, pt. 2, 34 .460r; CSD D20.c3 (1:182). Schässler, *Primat der heiligen Schrift*, pp. 217–19; Tavard, *Holy Writ or Holy Church?* pp. 59–61.

75. "Secundum est eorum que ab apostolis ad nos per succedentium relationem vel scripturas fidelium pervenirent: licet in scripturas sacras non inveniatur," CSD D20.c3 (1:182). In *SE* 4, pt. 2, 9 .381v–382r, Turrecremata cited John 21:25, "Jesus did many other things, etc.," a favorite text of the Franciscans, see, e.g., Nicholas de Lyre, *Postilla litteralis* ad Jo. 21:25 (vol. 5, fol. 244rb).

76. "Apostoli nihil ad salutem humanum necessarium docuerunt, quod non ab evangelio sive a Christo didicerunt," SE 1.19.22.

77. *SE* 4, pt. 2, 9 .382r–v.

78. CSD D20.c3 (1:182), D15.c3.q2 (1:140), *SE* 4, pt. 2, 9 .382v–383r.

79. Friedberg 1.35–36: D15.c2.

80. Aeneas Silvius Piccolomini (Pius II), *De gestis concilii Basiliensis*, ed. Denys Hay and W.K. Smith (Oxford, 1967), pp. 54–56, 114–16.

81. "Aut potest intelligi quod hoc competat illis quatuor conciliis non inquantum concilia sunt, sed inquantum de tali materia sunt scilicet de veritate articulorum fidei, et sic dicimus quod hoc competat illis quatuor conciliis quod revocari non possunt propter hoc scilicet quod non fuerunt nisi declarativa articulorum fidei," SE 3.57.342v. See CSD D15.c1.q1, pt. 2 (1:128), D15.c2 (1:137). See also Johannes de Carvajal, *Contra los apellantes al futuro concilio*, app., in Lino Gomez Canedo, *Don Juan de Carvajal* (Madrid, 1947), p. 338.

82. Tavard, *Holy Writ or Holy Church?* pp. 12–26, 59–61, 244–46; Obermann, *Harvest*, 371–75, 389–93; Congar, *Tradition and Traditions*, p. 111–16.

83. See chapter 3, note 40 above.

84. JdT, *Contra decretum irritans*, Mansi 30.550–90 at 579–80; idem, *Propositio ad dietam Maguntinam*, in Pacifico Massi, *Il magistero infallibile del papa nella teologia di Giovanni da Torquemada* (Turin, 1957). Nicholas of Cusa underwent a similar change of opinion on infallibility, see Sigmund, *Cusa*, pp. 169–72, 238–40, 264, 272–37, 306.

85. "Ecce quod licet beatissima Virgo Maria mater dei, sponsa Christi, regina mundi et angelorum domina, gracia plena et in fide semper immobilis fuerit, non tamen arguitur inde quod·pocior fuerit potestate clavium ipso Petro," JdT, *Oratio synodalis*, p. 55. This Marian doctrine was employed by Ockham, see Hendrix, "Vera Ecclesia," 361–63; Yves Congar, "Incidence ecclésiologique d'une thème de dévotion mariale," *Mélanges de science religeuse* 7 (1950):277–92.

86. "In his que fidei sunt hominumque necessaria saluti, ab ipso omnium auctore Deo, cuius providencia in sui dispositione non fallitur, hoc preclaro infallibilitas munere iudicii donaretur,"

JdT, *Propositio ad dietam Maguntinam,* p. 165. Massi, *Il magistero,* pp. 81–83.

87. *SE* 2.110 .254r–255v; CSD C24.q1.c14 (3:271); see Johannes de Carvajal, *Contra impugnantes responsum sanctissimi domini nostri Eugenii papae divina providencia quarti,* in Gomez, *Carvajal,*pp. 282–83.

88. Tierney, *Foundations,* pp. 41–46; idem, *Origins,* pp. 31–39, 226–37.

89. "Papa qui caput est ecclesiae et magister et dux populi Christiani, non potest errare in his, que de fide tenenda et credenda apostolus sui officio publicae Christiano populo decerneret, sive diffineret esse, credenda, et tenenda, sive quod apostolicae sedis iudicium in his que fidei sunt est indefectibile, quod idem est," CSD C24.q1.c4 (3:270–71); "Illius sedis iudicium quod nunquam in fide defecit nec defectuosum est videtur esse indefectibile iudicium in his quae fidei sunt, sed sedis apostolicae iudicium nunquam in fide deficit nec defectuosum est. ergo sedis apostolicae iudicium indefectibile est in his quae fidei sunt," SE 2.110.254v. Massi, *Il magistero,* p. 78.

90. "Licet tota universalis ecclesia non possit a recta fide, de ea tamen non est hic sermo, sed de ecclesia romana, quae dicitur mater omnium ecclesiarum et caput et magister. Clavium est autem, quod huiusmodi non est ecclesia universalis, quae dicitur congregatio omnium fidelium," CSD C24.q1.c9 (3:268). Paul de Vooght, "Esquisse d'un enquêt sur le mot infaillabilité durant la période scholastique," in *L'infaillabilité de l'Eglise* (Chevetogne, 1963), pp. 100–103. For Turrecremata's discussion of Augustine's dictum *in figura ecclesiae,* see chap. 2 above.

91. "Ecclesia universalis que errare non potest dicit congregacionem distinctam. aut separatum Romano pontifice, cum illa dicatur collectio omnium fidelium," JdT, *Oratio synodalis,* p. 54. Vooght, "Esquisse," p. 137.

92. "Tu es Petrus et super hanc petram aedificabo ecclesiam meam. Quam Christi promissiones de firmitate fidei apostolicae sedis accipiendum esse sancti doctores in religione et sapientia clarissimi contestantur. Manifestum est quod nec adversus Petrum. nec adversus ecclesiam portae praevalebunt infernorum," SE 2.109.252; "Item idem Apostolicae sedis privilegium patet ex illa promissione Christi, qua Petro pro sua sede loquens ait Lucae 22. Ego pro te rogavi, ut non deficiat fides tua, et tu aliquando conversus confirma fratres tuos," CSD C24.q1.c9 (3:268). For a similar use of these arguments, see Terreni, *Quaestio,* pp. 10, 21, 25. However, there is no trace of this line of reasoning in Nicholas de Lyre, *Postilla litteralis* ad Luc. 22:32 (Vol. 9, fol. 177va–b). For canonistic exegesis of the Lucan text, see Brian Tierney, "A Scriptural Text in the Decretals and in Saint Thomas: Canonistic Exegesis of Luke 22:32," *Studia Gratiana* 20 (1976): 361–77.

93. CSD D50.c54 (1:425).

94. *SE* 2.102 .258v; CSD D21 ante c1 (1:182–86).

95. Piccolomini, *De gestis,* pp. 62, 132.

96. CSD C24.q1.c14 (3:271), C2.q7.c33 (2:207). See Terreni,*Questio*, pp. 29–31.

97. "Non permitteret eum dominus determinare haeresim aut errorem contra fidem sed prohiberet aliquo dictorum modorum," *SE* 2.112 .260r. The suggested interventions, derived from Terreni's *quaestio*, ran the gamut from sudden conversion to sudden death. The pope was supposed to guard against error by consulting the cardinals and other learned men before making a doctrinal pronouncement.

98. "Assistentia spiritus sancti permissa a Christo non respicit personam papae, sed officium seu sedem. Et ideo cum opinari sit personae iudicare vero sit officii, licet esset possibile, papam male opinari, errare tamen sententiando in iudicio de his quae sunt fidei non est possibile stante divina promissione," CSD C24.q1.c14 (3:271). *See* 2.112 .259v. On Huguccio, see Tierney, *Foundations*, pp. 58–65. The same opinion was advanced by Augustinus Triumphus, Herveus Natalis, Antoninus of Florence, and Arévalo, see Michael Wilks, *The Problem of Sovereignty in the Later Middle Ages* (Cambridge, 1963), p. 500, n. 2; Tierney, *Origins*, pp. 146–64; Trame, *Arévalo*, p. 41, n. 51.

99. "Si Romanus pontifex efficitur haereticus ipso facto quo cadit a cathedra, et sede Petri, et per consequens iudicium quod faceret talis haereticus non esset iudicium apostolicae sedis immo nec iudicium alicuius auctoritatis est dicendum aut momenti, quia cum per heresim cadisset a praelatione per consequens auctoritate iudicande privatus esset," SE 2.112.260v. Tierney, *Foundations*, pp. 58–67; Tierney, " 'Only the Truth Has Authority,' " pp. 75–76.

100. "Rationem assignat quidem dicentes, quia 'deus non permitteret eum diffinire haeresim, aut aliquid contra fidem, sed prohibet eum aut per mortem, aut per aliam fidelium resistentiam, aut per aliorum instrucionem, aut per internam inspirationem, aut per alios modos secundum quos Dei ecclesie sancte, et fidei unitati multipliciter provideri potest' [Terreni, *Quaestio*, p. 26]. Nos vero aliam rationem damus, quare neganda est illa minor. videlicet quia si Romanus pontifex incideret in haeresim damnatum, et ita effectus haereticus, ipso facto quo cadat a fide Petri, cadit a cathedra et sede Petri, et per consequens iudicium quod faceret talis hereticus, non esset iudicium apostolicae sedis. Immo nec iudicium alicuius authoritatis esset dicendum, aut momenti; quia cum per haeresim cecedisset a prelatione, per consequens autoritate iudicandi privatus esset," CSD C24.q1.c14 (3:271). Turrecremata criticized Terreni for trying to exculpate Anastasius II, see CSD D19.c9 (1:174–67). Izbicki, "Infallibility and the Erring Pope."

101. Stephan Lederer, *Der spanische Cardinal Johann von Torquemada: Sein Leben und seine Schriften* (Freiburg, 1879), pp. 199–205, 239; Johannes Baptista Bičiunas, *Doctrina ecclesiologica S. Robert i Bellarmini cum illa Joannis Card. de Turrecremata comparata* (Rome, 1963), p. 48. Candal [JdT, *Oratio synodalis*, pp. 31, 69–70] confused *ipso facto* deposition with providential acts, despite the

exclusion of deposition from the list of such acts in *SE* 2.112.260r.

102. Massi, *Il magistero*, pp. 101, 104; John Fenton, "The Theology of the General Council," in *The General Council*, ed. William Joseph McDonald (Washington, D.C., 1962), pp. 159–60. See Schüssler, *Primat der heiligen Schrift*, p. 215.

103. *De summi pontificis infallibilitate personali* (Naples, 1870), p. 8.

104. Ibid.

105. Hödl, *Schlüsselgewalt* 1:116–217, 376; Tierney, *Origins*, pp. 39–45, 139, 171–237.

106. "Iste due claves ordinis. scilicet. scientia discernendi et potentia dignos recipiendi et indigno excludendi a regno non distinguitur in essentia auctoritatis, sed una et eadem per essentiam potestatis sive auctoritatis solumque distinguitur per comparationem ad actus quorum unus praesupponit alium. Clavis. enim. quae dicitur potestas ligandi et solvendi est quae immediate rerum peccati removendo coelum aperit," SE 1.93.106r. *Ibid.* I c.95 fol.109r "Si scientia quae dicitur habitus sive infusus diceretur hic clavis, hoc non est verum, sed scientiae quae hic dicitur clavis est auctoritas exercendi autem scientiae quae auctoritas quandoque sine scientia est quandoque scientia sine ipsa sicut patet etiam in iudicibus secularibus," SE 1.95.109r. See CSD De poen. D1.c51.q5 (5:44), C24.q1 post c4 (3:266–67); *SE* 2.71 .196v. Zuckermann, "Dominican Theories," p. 111; *"Papa est nomen iurisdictionis,"* p. 85, n. 1.

107. JdT, *Tractatus contra advisamentum quod non liceat appellare de concilio ad papam*, Mansi 30. 1072–94 at 1090; idem, *Oratio synodalis*, p. 55. In *Tractatus de veritate conceptionis beatissime virginis*, 510, Turrecremata noted that the council defined rather than created truth. Fenton, "Theology of the General Council," pp. 171–73; Ulrich Horst, "Grenzen der päpstlichen Autorität: Konziliare Elemente in der Ekklesiologie des Johannes Torquemada," *Freiburger Zeitschrift für Philosophie und Theologie* 19 (1972): 363.

108. *SE* 3.49 .335r–v. For Cajetan's use of this argument, see Bäumer, "Luthers Ansichten," pp. 1001–2.

109. CSD D19.c8 (1:174–76). Antoninus, Pornaxio, and Petrus de Monte taught similar doctrines, see Bäumer, "Luthers Ansichten," pp. 1000–1001.

110. "Quod Christus promittendo beato Petro quod fides eius in ecclesia sua et sede numquam esset defectiva Luc. 22 ut dictum est in concilio plenario Romanus pontifex intelligitur ut caput et magister ac diffinitor ex consequenti promisso illa extenditur ad concilium universale plenarium quod et auctoritate et approbatione apostolicae sedis fulcitur," SE 3.60.347v. See CSD C24.q1.c14 (3:270–72). Vooght, "Esquisse," p. 137.

111. *SE* 3:58 .344v–345r, 3.60 .347r.

112. "Illa congregatio in diffinitione unanimi sua in his quae fidei sunt credenda est non errare cuius diffinitionis opponitur tenentes sunt haeretici," SE 3.58.345v. Massi, *Il magistero*, p. 112; Vooght, "Esquisse," p. 141; Schüssler, *Primat der heiligen Schrift*,

pp. 215–17. See Sigmund, *Cusa*, pp. 145, 171–74, 264–65; Horst, "Antonin," p. 108.

113. For a more favorable opinion, see Vooght "Esquisse," pp. 140–41.

114. *"Archipresbyter* . . . hic subest archidiacono in administratione temporalium: sed ei preest ratione ordinis qua ratione presbyter maior est diacono," CSD D25.c1, pt. 2 (1:244). Heintschel, *Ecclesiastical Office*, pp. 49–51, 62–66.

115. *Extrav. Commun.* 1.8.1: Friedberg 2.12, 45–46.

116. CSD C2.q7.c34.q2 (2:208–9).

117. Denys Rutledge, *Cosmic Theology* (London, 1964).

117. "Unde si omnes sacerdotes essent equales sicut prefati heretici menciuntur status ecclesiae non esset ordinatus sed confusus quod nephas esset dicere cum a sapientissimo sit disposita. . . . Ordo autem attenditur secundum praelationem. et subiectorum. prelatio autem attenditur secundum ascensum et descensum. non secundum equalitatem et nascendo superiue est et reductio ad unum," JdT, *"Reprobationes trigintaocto articulorum quos tenent heretici Usiti de Maldevis,"* Vat. lat. 974 fols. 71r–94v at 87v. Kaminsky, *Hussite Revolution*, pp. 361–433.

119. JdT, *Symbolum*, p. 110; *SE* 1.71 .85r; CSD D21 ante c1.q2 (1:183–84). MC 57–62.

120. "In triumphante ecclesia unus praesidet . . . ergo in militante debet unus praesidens," SE 2.2.117r; "Sed sic est quod in angelica hierarchia nulla potestas ad actos hierarchicos perficiendos tribuitur desuper a deo persone. vel ordine, aut toti ierarchie, que non tribuatur mediante primo illius ierarchie. ergo pari modo nulla potestas a Christo ipsi ecclesiastice ierarchie, aut universali concilio illam representanti tribuitur, que non conferatur mediante Romano pontifice qui est primus in tota ierarchia," JdT, *Oratio synodalis*, p. 17.

121. "Ordo ecclesiasticae hierarchie non est necessarius sed voluntarius. et per consequens potest mutare placet capiti totius ordinis scilicet summo pontifici . . . ideo cum angelorum natura sit immutabilis ordo inter eos habet immutabilem quam, quae in Hierarchia Ecclesiastica non est," SE 2.67.190v. The episcopalists thought the exact arrangement of the ecclesiastical hierarchy was immutable, see Congar, "Aspects ecclésiologiques," pp. 120–23. Black (MC 59–60) ignored the above when he claimed that Turrecremata neglected Aquinas's distinction between nature and grace.

122. MC 61.

123. Walter Ullmann, *Principles of Government and Politics in the Middle Ages*, 2nd ed. (London, 1966); Wilks, *Problem of Sovereignty*. For a criticism, see Francis Oakley, "Celestial Hierarchies Revisited: Walter Ullmann's Vision of Medieval Politics," *Past and Present* 60 (1973): 1–48; Charles Abraham Zuckermann, "The Relationship of Universals to Theories of Church Government," *Journal of the History of Ideas* 35 (1975): 579–94.

124. MC 59–60.

125. Hofmann, *Papato*, p. 16; MC 56–58, where argument by analogy is described as the Eugenian contribution to political theory.

126. The problem of the heretic pope is relegated to an epilog by Black (MC 135–38) and to an incomprehensible deviation from monarchism by Wilks (*Problem of Sovereignty*, pp. 488–523).

127. *SE* 4, pt. 2, 9 .382r–383r; CSD D20.c3 (1:182), D15.c3 (1:140).

128. Sigmund, *Cusa*, pp. 49–51; Congar, "Aspects ecclésiologiques," pp. 114–45; Sikes, "John de Pouilli" 232–33; Pascoe, *Jean Gerson*, (Leiden, 1973), pp. 17–48, 206–8; idem, "Jean Gerson: Mysticism, Conciliarism, and Reform," *Annuarium historiae conciliorum* 6 (1974): 135–53.

129. Sigmund, *Cusa*, pp. 129–30, 301–2. Neoplatonism inspired Cusa's change of allegiance according to Black (MC 64).

130. See, respectively, Ewart Lewis, *Medieval Political Ideas* (New York, 1954), 1:239 and MC 54.

131. Corporate theory, as an ascending theory, is stressed by Black (MC 7–52); episcopalism, as a descending theory, by Ullmann (*Principles*, pp. 313–15).

132. MC 108–12 on John of Segovia.

133. Paul de Vooght, *Les pouvoirs du concile et l'autorité du pape* (Paris, 1965), pp. 137–62; Noel Valois, *Le pape et le concile (1418–1450)* (Paris, 1909), 1:218–28, 2:106–71, 277–79; Antonio Domingo de Sousa Costa, *Mestre André Dias de Escobar* (Rome, 1967), p. 67, criticizing editorial comments in Andreas Escobar, *Tractatus polemico-theologicus de Graecis errantibus*, ed. Emmanuel Candal (Madrid, 1952), p. 67.

Chapter 4

1. Johannes Hus, *Tractatus de ecclesia*, ed. Samuel Harrison Thomson (Cambridge, 1956), pp. 20–21, 64–66, 107; Paul de Vooght, *L'hérésie de Jean Hus* (Louvain, 1960), pp. 466–81; Ernest Fraser Jacob, "The Bohemians at the Council of Basel, 1433," in *Prague Essays,* ed. Richard William Seton-Watson (Oxford, 1949), pp. 81–123.

2. John B. Morrall, *Gerson and the Great Schism* (Manchester, 1960), p. 105; Louis B. Pascoe, *Jean Gerson: Principles of Church Reform* (Leiden, 1973), p. 210; Paul Sigmund, *Nicholas of Cusa and Medieval Political Thought* (Cambridge, Mass., 1963), p. 181; Knut Wolfgang Nörr, *Kirche und Konzil bei Nicolaus de Tudeschis (Panormitanus)* (Cologne, 1964), pp. 81–84; Paul Lazarus, *Das Basler Konzil* (Lübeck, 1965).

3. Some less responsible papalists, Raphael de Pornaxio among them, thought safeguards against papal error unimportant, even unnecessary, see Jeffrey A. Mirus, "On the Deposition of the Pope for Heresy," *Archivum historiae pontificiae* 13 (1975): 244–48.

4. Hus, *Tractatus de ecclesia* pp. 43–52; Paul de Vooght, *Hussiana*

(Louvain, 1960), pp. 45–53, 124–58; Matthew Spinka *John Hus' Concept of the Church* (Princeton, 1966), pp. 151–289.

5. *SE* 2.112 .259v. Brian Tierney, *Foundations of the Conciliar Theory* (Cambridge, 1955), pp. 36–46, 220–37.

6. Aeneas Silvius Piccolomini (Pius II), *De gestis concilii Basiliensis*, ed. Denys Hay and W.K. Smith (Oxford, 1967), p. 27; Tierney, *Foundations*, p. 41.

7. "In ecclesia romana omnes fundavit dignitates ecclesie," Johannes de Turrecremata (JdT), *Questiones evangeliorum de tempore et de sanctis et Flos theologie* (Basel, 1484), in festo beati Petri q. 1. These attributes are detailed in idem, *Apparatus super decretum unionis Grecorum*, ed. Emmanuel Candal (Rome, 1942), p. 66; idem, *Symbolum pro informatione Manichaeorum*, ed. Nicolas Lopez Martinez and Vicente Proaño Gil (Burgos, 1958), pp. 60–61.

8. "Omnes alii ecclesiae per orbem diffuse sunt a Romana ecclesia instituta et fundata: ergo omnis iurisdictionis ecclesiasticae auctoritas aliorum praelatorum derivatur a papa sive a Romano pontifice," SE 2.55.172v; see Petrus de Palude, *Tractatus de potestate papae*, ed. Petrus Thomas Stella (Zürich, 1966), pp. 179, 182.

9. "Potestas episcoporum, aut curatorum non sit a papa, sicut a causa in esse considerata persona sua. A sede autem papali sit sicut a causa communi quae semper permanet fundata super firmam petram," SE 2.64.187r. On the pope's being virtually the Church, see CSD 1.17 .20r, 2.83 .216r. The distinction between office and person was an important factor in the papalist tradition, see Walter Ullmann, *Principles of Government and Politics in the Middle Ages*, 2nd ed. (London, 1966), pp. 488–523.

10. CSD D11.c3 (1:106).

11. "Romanus pontifex [et per consequens ecclesia romana] primatum et principatum quem habet super omnes ecclesias sive omnes fideles: non habet ab homine: sed a christo," CSD D22.c2 (1:211); see D12.c1.q2 (1:112–13). Yves Congar, *L'ecclésiologie du Haut Moyen Age de Saint Grégoire le Grand à la désunion entre Byzance et Rome* (Paris, 1968), pp. 149–62; James Thomson Shotwell, ed., *The See of Rome* (New York, 1927).

12. CSD C2.q7.c37 (2:210). Giuseppe Alberigo, *Cardinalato e collegialità* (Florence, 1969), pp. 72–84. In *SE* 2.36.150r, Turrecremata attacked those who thought Peter never was bishop of Rome, an argument used by the cardinal's whipping boys Marsilius and Ockham, see Guilelmus ab Ockham, *Dialogus de potestate papae et imperatoris* (1614; rpt. Turin, 1966), pp. 486–87; Marsilius of Padua, *The Defender of Peace*, trans. Alan Gewirth (New York, 1956), pp. 249–53. Antoninus of Florence thought the presence of the papacy in Rome necessary for the welfare of the Church, see Ulrich Horst, "Papst, Bischofe, und Konzil nach Antonin von Florenz," *Recherches de théologie ancienne et médievale* 32 (1965): 96.

13. CSD C24.q1.c15 (3:273). On papal peregrinations, see Guillaume Mollat, *The Popes at Avignon, 1305–1378*, trans. Janet Love (New York, 1965), pp. xi–xiv.

14. Stephan Kuttner, *"Cardinalis:* The History of a Canonical

Con⁻ept," *Traditio* 3 (1945): 129–214; Mollat, *Popes at Avignon*, pp. 30͜ˎ '0; Carl Gerold Fürst, *Cardinalis* (Munich, 1967).

15. Kuttner, "*Cardinalis*," pp. 174–77; Giuseppe Albergio, "Le origini della dottrina sullo *ius divinum* del cardinalato, 1053–1087," in *Reformata reformada: Festgabe für Hubert Jedin*, ed. Erwin Iserloh and Konrad Repgen (Münster, 1965), pp. 39–58.

16. Tierney, *Foundations*, pp. 68–84, 149–53; Alberigo, *Cardinalato e collegialità*, pp. 97–109. This interpretation of Hostiensis has been questioned by John Andrew Watt, "The Constitutional Law of the College of Cardinals: Hostiensis to Johannes Andreae," *Medieval Studies* 33 (1971): 121–51.

17. Tierney, *Foundations*, pp. 180–90; Alberigo, *Cardinalato e collegialità*, pp. 144–57.

18. Tierney, *Foundations*, pp. 220–37; Alberigo, *Cardinalato e collegialità*, pp. 159–85.

19. Francis Oakley, *The Political Thought of Pierre d'Ailly* (New Haven, 1964), pp. 124–28, 146–50, 216–17; Alberigo, *Cardinalato e collegialità*, pp. 112–35.

20. Alberigo, *Cardinalato e collegialità*; these pretensions were denied by John of Paris and Alvarus Pelagius, see pp. 135–44.

21. Francis Oakley, *Council Over Pope?* (New York, 1969), pp. 61–74; John Kennerly Woody, "The Organization of the Council," in Louise Ropes Loomis, *The Council of Constance*, ed. John Hine Mundy and Kennerly M. Woody (New York, 1961), pp. 52–65.

22. Walter Ulmann, "Eugenius IV, Cardinal Kemp, and Archbishop Chichele," in *Medieval Studies Presented to Aubrey Gwynn S.J.*, ed. John Andrew Watt, John B. Morrall, and Francis X. Martin (Dublin, 1961), pp. 359–83.

23. Dominicus de Dominicis, "*Consilium in materia creationis cardinalium ad petitionem summi domini Pii secundi*," Barb. lat. 1487 fols. 301r–312v; Hubert Jedin, *Studien über Domenico de' Domenichi (1416–1478)* (Wiesbaden, 1957), pp. 67, 80, 86–87; idem, *History of the Council of Trent*, trans. Ernest Graf (London, 1957), 1:76–86; Sigmund, *Cusa* pp. 294–300; Walter Ullmann, "The Legal Validity of Papal Electoral Pacts," *Ephemerides iuris canonici* 12 (1956): 256–60, 265; Alberigo, *Cardinalato e collegialità*, p. 195.

24. Jedin, *Trent*, 1:82; Oakley, *Council Over Pope?* pp. 86–87; Alberigo, *Cardinalato e collegialità*, pp. 125, 187.

25. "Cardinalatum status intelligitur institum a deo cum immediate succedat statu apostolico," CSD C2.q7.c34.q2 (2:208); SE 1.80.92v, 1.83.94v, 2.36.149v. Turrecremata also said that the cardinals succeeded the elders who assisted Moses, see Alberigo, *Cardinalato e collegialità*, p. 80; Manuel Garcia Miralles, "El cardenalato de institucion divino y el episcopado en el problema de la succession apostolica según Juan de Torquemada," in *XVI semaña española de teologia* (Madrid, 1957), pp. 256, 263, 266–69; see also Jedin, *Domenichi*, p. 79.

26. *SE* 1.80 .92r–93r, 1.81 .93v, 2.75.203v; see Jedin, *Domenichi*, p. 80. For a more juridical idea of the cardinals' senatorial status, see Sigmund, *Cusa*, pp. 105–6.

27. Tierney, *Foundations*, pp. 234–37; Nörr, *Panormitanus*, pp. 151–58.

28. CSD D23.c1.q2 (1:214), D79.c10.q1 (1:528), D79.c9.q2 (1:527), D79.c10.q4 (1:528–29). Objections to any candidate, except a heretic, could be lodged only before the process of election was completed, see CSD D79.c9q1 (1:527). Cardinals were best qualified to become pope, see CSD D23.c1q2 (1:214).

29. CSD D23.c1 (1:212). Robert L. Benson, *The Bishop-Elect* (Princeton, 1968), pp. 160–67; Jean Gerson, *De potestate ecclesiastica*, in *Oeuvres complètes*, ed. Palémon Glorieux (Paris, 1965), 7:227; F. Wasner, "De consecratione, inthronizatione, coronatione Summi Pontificis," *Apollinaris* 8 (1935): 86–125, 249–81, 428–43; Michael Wilks, *The Problem of Sovereignty in the Later Middle Ages* (Cambridge, 1963), pp. 389–90.

30. JdT, *Contra decretum irritans*, Mansi 30.550–90 at 587. Walter Ullmann, "Medieval Views Concerning Papal Abdication," *Irish Ecclesiastical Record* 71 (1949): 125–33; Livario Oliger, "Petri Iohannis Olivi: *De Renuntiatione Papae Coelestini V Questio et Epistola*," *Archivum Franciscanum historicum* 10 (1918): 309–73.

31. SE 4 (pt. 1) c10 .368r. "Quia sic essent iudices in proprio facto," "Quia vero continget possit discordia inter Cardinales, ideo ut non omnes simul concurrent ad aliquem unum eligendum, ordinatum est in concilio universalis ecclesiae," SE 2.51.165r; see Nörr, *Panormitanus*, pp. 157–58.

32. "Domini enim cardinales eligendo bene determinat personam non tamen dant ipsi dignitatem, sive potestatem papalem. Aliud enim est conferre potestatem determinatae personam quae ex collatione iam facto assequatur talem potestatem," SE 2.43.155v–156r; "Videtur distrahere potestate et auctoritate papae, non potest poni in forma electionis, quia sicut nec ecclesia dat papae potestatem, ita nec formam electionis potest dare, per quam arctaretur potestas data a Christo summis pontificibus—duo, quod electores dando vocem ei, ecclesia consentit in eum, et ipso assentiente electioni immediate consequitur potestatem datam Petro ab ipso Deo," JdT, *Votum super advisamento, quod papa debet iurare servare decreta de conciliis generalibus*, Mansi 30.590–606 at 605. See Horst, "Antonin," pp. 76–79; Jedin, *Domenichi*, p. 86. Cusa thought the Church's consent was a precondition for this divine grant, see Sigmund, *Cusa*, pp. 143–44.

33. John Andrew Watt, "The Early Medieval Canonists and the Formation of Conciliar Theory," *Irish Theological Quarterly* 24 (1957): 13–31; Spinka, *Hus' Concept*, pp. 172–289.

34. Charles Lefebvre, "L'enseignement de Nicolas de Tudeschis et l'autorité pontificale," *Ephemerides iuris canonici* 14 (1958): 331.

35. "Vacante sed nullus dicitur succedere Romano pontefice in plenitudine potestatis ita nec per consequens in exercitio aut administratione plena illius quemadmodum nec capitulum succedit vacante sede episcopo in his que ad solum episcopum pertnent," SE 3.41.322v; "sedes vacare id est carere administratore," SE 2.79.212r. On the immortality of the papal office, see SE 2.112

.259r.

36. "Cardinales non possunt creare cardinalem. . . . Cuius etiam dictum recitate Hostiensis licet qui dixerant cardinales tunc posse creare cardinalem cum possunt tunc papa creare quod plus est. Sed ratio non procedit quia capitulum creat episcopum nec tamen confert beneficia ad illius collationem expectatum," CSD D79.c14 (1:525). Turrecremata obviously thought Hostiensis more of an oligarch than does Watt, "Constitutional Law," pp. 131–33. Lorenzo Spinelli, *La Vacanza della sede apostolica dalle origini al concilio Tridentino* (Milan, 1955), pp. 172–73.

37. *SE* 2.64 .187r, 2.79 .211v–212r. This was, essentially, the doctrine of Augustine Triumphus, see Spinelli, *La Vacanza*, pp. 172–73.

38. "Praeterea corpus ecclesiae pro illo tempore vacantis licet careat capite visibilis gubernatore: nicholominus cardinales vicem capitis," CSD D79.c7.q2 (1:526); CSD 18.c4 (1:158), *SE* 2.79 .212r; JdT, *Oratio synodalis de primatu*, ed. Emmanuel Candal (Rome, 1954), p. 77. The cardinals represented the Holy See in much the same way as did papal legates, see *SE* 2.75 .203v–204r.

39. Tierney, *Foundations*, pp. 149–53, 179–92; Watt, "Constitutional Law," pp. 134–37. Cardinalatial consent to key papal decisions was demanded by Nicholas of Cusa, see Sigmund, *Cusa*, pp. 134–37.

40. CSD D23.c1q2 (1:214); CSD C2.q7 c.34 q2 (2:208–9).

41. "A summo pontifice Christo vicario assumuntur ad assistentiam sibi et cooperandum in regimine rei publice Christianae," CSD D2.q7.c34.q2 (2:208); "Cum habeat plenitudinem potestatis, ut quicquid authoritatis sit apud dominos Cardinales totum emanat ab ipsa sede," CSD D43 ante c3.q2 (1:63). Foreign to Turrecremata was Hostiensis's distinction between papal plenitude of power in act and cardinalatial plenitude of power in potential, see Watt, "Constitutional Law," pp. 131–34.

42. "Papa potest sine Cardinalium quicquid cum Cardinalibus potest. Honestissimum tamen est, et reipublicae Christianae saluberrimum, ut ardua negotia sine eorum concilio non ageret, cum etiam hoc plurimum authoritatis confert rebus agendi," CSD D4 ante c3.q2 (1:63). See *SE* 3.46 .333r. Turrecremata used cardinalatial prestige to defend Eugenius IV's transfer of the Council of Basel to Ferrara, a decision which had the consent of almost all the members of the Sacred College, see JdT, *Apparatus*, p. 18. Nörr, *Panormitanus*, pp. 87–89.

43. Miralles, "El cardenalato," pp. 268–69. In contrast to this doctrine, Arévalo termed the cardinals the pope's creatures, see Richard Trame, *Rodrigo Sánchez de Arévalo, 1404–1470* (Washington, D.C., 1958), pp. 127–28.

44. Michele Maccarone, *Vicarius Christi* (Rome, 1952); Wilks, *Problem of Sovereignty*, pp. 464–73; Charles Abraham Zuckermann, "Dominican Theories of Papal Primacy, 1250–1320" (Ph.D. Diss., Cornell University, 1971); Walter Ullmann, *Medieval Papalism* (London, 1949), pp. 76–113; Tierney, *Foundations*, pp. 68–92.

The title *Vicarius Christi* was the capstone of the papalist edifice according to Walter Ullmann, *The Growth of Papal Government in the Middle Ages*, 2nd ed. (London, 1962), pp. 447–51.

45. Hus, *Tractatus de ecclesia*, pp. 70–72, 82, 112–13; Spinka, *Hus' Concept*, pp. 167–68.

46. JdT, *Apparatus*, p. 103. For a similar use of the title "patriarch," see CSD D99.c4 (1:652).

47. JdT, *Oratio synodalis*, p. 11, 28. For similar interpretations of the titles "ministerial head," "shephered," "rector," and "prelate," even "bridegroom," see *SE* 2.20 .134v, 2.27 .141r, 2.53 .169r, 2.65 .189r, 2.71 .198r. WE 69–70, 145. John of Segovia thought the head subject to the whole body, see Uta Fromherz, *Johannes von Segovia als Geschichtsschreiber des Konzils von Basel* (Basel, 1960), p. 141.

48. "Regimen ecclesia est a Deo institutum monarchium . . . patet; quoniam hoc regimen est nobilius reputatum tam a philosophis ut patet. 8. Eth. et 3. poli. quam a theologis, et credendum est quod Deus instituit regimen ecclesiae suae in nobiliori specie regiminis," *SE* 2.71.197v. *SE* 2.2 .117r. Thomas Aquinas, *On the Governance of Rulers*, trans. Gerald B. Phelan (Toronto, 1935). MC 62–67. For Thomists who preferred some form of polity, see Nicolai Rubinstein, "Marsilius of Padua and Italian Political Thought of His Time," in *Europe in the Later Middle Ages*, ed. John Rigby Hale, John Roger Highfield, and Beryl Smalley (Evanston, Ind., 1965), pp. 144–75; see also Charles T. Davis, "Roman Patriotism and Republican Propaganda: Ptolemy of Lucca and Pope Nicholas III," *Speculum* 50 (1975): 411–33.

49. *SE* 2.19 .133v–134r; JdT, *Oratio synodalis*, p. 64. This was the Decretist understanding of the *petra* in Matt. 14:16–17, see Tierney, *Foundations*, pp. 25–29. See also John A. F. Thomson, "Papalism and Conciliarism in Antonio Roselli's *Monarchia*," *Medieval Studies* 37 (1975): 447.

50. "Papa tenet in ecclesia locum domini nostri Iesu Christi," *SE* 2.65.189v. In such passages Turrecremata shows the influence of one of his chief sources, Augustinus Triumphus, whose high flown rhetoric easily disguises his more cautious statements, see William D. McCready, "The Papal Sovereign in the Ecclesiology of Augustinian Triumphus," *Medieval Studies* 9 (1977): 177–205. One of the most important purchases Turrecremata made at Basel was a codex which contained Augustinus's *Summa* and works of other leading mendicant publicists such as Petrus de Palude and Herveus Natalis, see Vat. lat. 4109.

51. *SE* 2.4 .118v–121r, 2.23 .136r–137v, 2.6 .177v–181r; see Sigmund, *Cusa*, p. 266, 269–71; Horst, "Antonin," pp. 81–83, 89–91, 96; MC 68–69.

52. *SE* 2.23 .136r–v, 4 (pt. 1) c3.360r.

53. "Quoniam papa non est omnino aliud caput distinctum a capite quod est Christus, sed est eius Vicarius et vicem eius et personam potestatem et auctoritatem representans in terris, et eius iudicium, iudicium Dei reputantur, et sententia eius et con-

sistorium eius consistorium Dei: et ideo non sunt proprie duo capita sed unum," SE 2.c13.139v–140r. Turrecremata warned against too close identification of the pope with Christ in SE 2.79 .211v–212r. Likewise he denied that the pope had supremacy in grace, see SE 2.43 .155v, 2.82.215v; JdT, *"Reprobationes trigintaocto articulorum quos tenent heretici Usiti de Maldevis,"* Vat. lat. 974, fols. 71r–94v at 79r. WE 69–70. Suprahuman status for the papacy, first claimed by Innocent III, was a papalist excess censured by both conciliarists and Hussites, see Wilks, *Problem of Sovereignty,* pp. 164–66, 357–61, 537; Piccolomini, *De gestis,* pp. 66–68; Howard Kaminsky, *A History of the Hussite Revolution* (Berkeley, 1967), pp. 41–42; Gordon Leff, *Heresy in the Later Middle Ages* (Manchester, 1967), 2:663; McCready, "Ecclesiology of Augustinus Triumphus," p. 281.

54. JdT, *Oratio synodalis,* p. 40; CSD D22.c2 (1:210–12); SE 2.38 .152r, 2.71 .195r–199r; "Quod facit praelatus dicitur facere ecclesia," SE 2.92.225v. Turrecremata denied that papal power was conferred by Constantine, see SE 2.46 .158r–159v. He was attacking Marsilius of Padua, *Defender of Peace,* p. 271; Hus, *Tractatus de ecclesia,* p. 119–30.

55. JdT, *Apparatus,* p. 97; SE 3.36 .317v–318r. Turrecremata interpreted the title "servant of the servants of God" in this light, see SE 2.87 .220r. MC 77–78.

56. *S.E.* II c.40 fol.154r, "Impropria locutio est cum dicitur quod Romanus pontifex sit Vicarius beati Petri: cum solius Dei cuius vice gerit in terris Vicarius sit. Petrus . . . cum Vicarius esset Christi. non poterat facere alium Vicarium . . . Vicarius id est successor illius: vel Vicarius id est Vicarium potestatem quam ipse gessit tenens sive exercens," SE 2.40.154r. Maccarone, *Vicarius Christi,* pp. 258–59.

57. "Quia papa non modo urbis est episcopus, sed in toto orbe habet potestatem, et iurisdictionem . . . quia est unum de principalibus fundamentis eorum; qui adversantur principatui romani pontificis," CSD D4 ante c3.q3 (1:62–63). For attacks on the Hussites, with side blows at conciliarism, see SE 2.25 .138r–139r, 2.37 .318v. Hus, *Tractatus de ecclesia,* pp. 47–52.

58. CSD D93 ante c1.q2 (1:616–17), D23.c1q3 (1:113); SE 2.65 .188r–189v, 2.48 .162v, 4 (pt. 1) c1 .358r. Legates implemented this power, see SE 3.14 .290r; CSD D94.c2 (1:628), D97.c3 (1:650). Yves Congar, "Aspects ecclésiologiques de la querelle entre Mendiants et Séculiers dans la seconde moité du XIIIᶜ siècle et le debut du XIVᶜ," *Archives d'histoire doctrinale et littéraire* 38 (1961): 119–38; Jeffrey Garrett Sikes, "John de Pouilli and Peter de Palu," *English Historical Review* 49 (1934): 231–38.

59. SE 2.77 .208r, 2.35 .149r; CSD D87.c3 (1:514–15), D93.c8 (1:619); JdT, *Responsio in blasphemam invectivam ad sanctissimum canonem iustissime condemnationis damnatissime congregationis Basilieensium,* Mansi 31A.63–127 at 114; see Horst, "Antonin," pp. 104–5. Richard Zwölfer, "Die Reform der Kirchenverfassung auf dem Konzil zu Basel," *Basler Zeitschrift für Geschichte und Altertums*

Kunde 28 (1929): 144–247.

60. CSD D85.c1.q2 (1:559–60); *SE* 2.43 .323v; JdT, *Questiones evangeliorum*, in festo beati Petri q. 3. See Dominicus de Dominicis, "*Aparatus sive glose facte ad requisitionem serenissimi domini Frederici Imperatoris dum esset apud eundem imperatorem orator*," Barb. lat. 1487 fols. 157r–161r.

61. "Papa totius ecclesiae princeps solutus sit legibus quoad vim coactivam . . . Lex autem non habet vim coactivam nisi ex principis potestae," JdT, *Propositio ad Dietam Norimbergensis*, Mansi 31A 41–62 at 57; "Cum ergo Romanus pontifex princeps ecclesiae sit nullius ecclesiae legibus coactus sive tenetur obnoxius, notanter dicimus ecclesiae, quia aliud est de legibus iuris divini et naturalis," SE 3.51.336v. See SE 2.64 .187v, 3.36 .318r, 3.49 .333r, 3.51 .336v; CSD C25 q1c6 (3:315). See also Nörr, *Panormitanus*, pp. 46–50; Thomson, "Roselli's *Monarchia*," pp. 448–49. Antony Black, "The Political Ideas of Conciliarism and Papalism, 1430–1450," *Journal of Ecclesiastical History* 20 (1964): 58–59; Brian Tierney, "The Prince Is Not Bound by the Laws: Accursius and the Origins of the Modern State," in *Atti del Convegno Internazionale di studi Accursiani*, ed. Guido Rossi (Milan, 1968), 3:388–400.

62. "His est casus in quo papa papam ligare potest in quo papa in canonem late sententie incidit. Nec huic obviat regula: par parem solvere vel ligare non potest: quia si papa haereticus est in eo quod haereticus est minor quolibet catholico, haec glossa," SE 2.102.241v. See CSD C25.q1.c1 (3:312–13). Tierney, *Foundations*, p. 253.

63. CSD C25.q1.c1 (3:312–13).

64. CSD D17.c4 (1:153), D15.c2.q2 (1:136); *SE* 3.51 .337r. Conciliarists allowed the pope a wide, but not unlimited, power of dispensation, see Nörr, *Panormitanus*, pp. 81–84; Sigmund, *Cusa*, p. 181. For canonistic doctrine on this subject, see Stephan Kuttner, "Pope Lucius III and the Bigamous Archbishop of Palermo," in *Medieval Studies Presented to Aubrey Gwynn S.J.*, ed. John Andrew Watt, John B. Morrall, and Francis X. Martin (Dublin, 1961), pp. 409–50.

65. "Per ly ecclesiam qui tanquam iudicii denunciatio fienda est sive ad fienda est sive ad quem fidelis remittitur, praelatus ecclesiae intelligi debeat sic accipiendus veniat, et non universalis ecclesiae aut per orbem dispersa aut synodaliter congregata . . . non solum Petrum licet ad ipsum specialiter in figure totius ecclesiae directus sit sermo in signum principatus sui ad quem a domino erat electus quam praelatos ad observationem huius praecepti astringere voluit," SE 2.92.225r, 2.c69.191v; CSD D79.c3 (1:524), C13.q2 ante c12 (3:10). Fromherz, *Segovia*, p. 145; Tierney, *Foundations*, pp. 28–29, 57–67.

66. CSD D10.c8 (1:100). This matter will be discussed in chapter 6.

67. JdT, *Responsio in blaspehmam*, cols. 88–89; idem, *Propositio ad dietam Norimbergensis*," cols. 51, 57.

68. "Ubi cum per gladios duos mystice intelligantur duae potestates, spiritualis et temporalis, ut beatus Bernardus lib. de consideratione exponit, quas apud Romanum pontificem aliquo modo residere dicit: manifeste datur intelligi Romanum pontificem ex Christi ordinatione iurisdictionem coactivam quae per gladios designatur habere," SE 2.46.158v. Alfonso Maria Stickler, "De ecclesie potestate coactiva materiali apud magistrum Gratianum," *Salesianum* 4 (1942): 2–23, 97–119.

69. *SE* 4 (pt. 1) c8 .365r, 2.46 .159v; CSD C11q3.c15 (2:411), D93.c1.q3 (1:618). Marsilius of Padua, *Defender of Peace*, pp. 113–26, 364–405; Ewart Lewis, "The 'Positivism' of Marsilius of Padua," *Speculum* 35 (1963): 541–82; Hus, *Tractatus de ecclesia*, pp. 81–87.

70. *SE* 2.52 .168r, 2.89 .220v; 2.113 .264v. Brian Tierney, *Medieval Poor Law* (Berkeley, 1959), pp. 22–44.

71. "Potestatem cuiuscunque Vicarii nemo potest restringere, aut ampliare nisi principalis. Sed papa est Vicarius Iesu Christi . . . ergo huiusmodi Vicarii potestatem nemo nisi Christus . . . potest restringere diminuere mutare aut etiam ampliare, SE 2.44.156v–157r. MC 136; Jedin, *Trent*, 1:85–86; Aegidius Romanus, *De ecclesiastica potestate*, ed. Richard Scholz (1896; rpt. Stuttgart, 1961); Petrus de Palude, *Tractatus de potestate papae*. Antonio Roselli's *Monarchia*, thought extremely papalist at the time of the Council of Basel, was criticized for the opposite reason, conciliar leanings, by later Roman loyalists, see Thomson, "Roselli's *Monarchia*," pp. 456–58. Even conciliarists could attribute wide-ranging powers to the pope, see Nörr, *Panormitanus*, pp. 56–59.

72. *SE* 2.23 .137r–v; JdT, *Apparatus*, p. 9.

73. "Cum ergo solus deus superior sit Romano pontifice, cum illius solius servus sit et vicarius, pertineat eius iudicium in hoc casu," JdT, *Oratio synodalis*, p. 63. See SE 2.93 .226r–227r, 2.98 .233v–234v. James M. Moynihan, *Papal Immunity and Liability in the Writings of the Medieval Canonists* (Rome, 1961); Ulrich Horst, "Grenzen der päpstlichen Autoritat: Konziliare Elemente in der Ekklesiologie des Johannes Torquemada," *Freiburger Zeitschrift für Philosophie und Theologie* 19 (1972): 368.

74. Tierney, *Foundations*, pp. 58–65, 199–219, 248–50; idem, "Pope and Council: Some New Decretist Texts," *Medieval Studies* 19 (1957): 197–218; Moynihan, *Papal Immunity*, pp. 94–102; Wilks, *Problem of Sovereignty*, pp. 502–3; Petrus de Palude, *Tractatus de potestate papae*, p. 194.

75. Ernest F. Jacob, *Essays in Later Medieval History* (Manchester, 1968), pp. 138–40; Sigmund, *Cusa*, p. 150; Jean Fleury, "Le conciliarisme des canonistes au concile de Bâle daprès le Panormitain," in *Mélanges Roger Secretan* (Montreux, 1964): 61–62; Antony Black, "The Universities and the Council of Basel: Ecclesiology and Tactics," *Annuarium historiae conciliorum* 6 (1974): 341–51.

76. "Non potest denunciari praelatus qui superiorem non habet nisi sit late peccatum eius quod a superioritate cadat," SE

2.102.242v, 2.98.234v. MC 70; Hus, *Tractatus de ecclesia*, pp. 149–55.

77. "Inferior non potest aliquid constituere contra determinata per superiorem . . . sed sacra scriptura est inspirata a spiritu sancto . . . interpretari quippe evangeliorum ad sensum bonum et catholicum non contradicendo veritati fidei, et scripturae sanctae, hoc licet summo pontifici, sed per hoc non dispensat in evangelio," CSD C25.q1.c6 (3:315). JdT, *Oratio synodalis*, pp. 58–59.

78. "Si dicitur quae dicantur ad generalem statum ecclesiae pertinere, videtur nobis quod inter alia sunt ista quae omnes fideles tangere possunt, ut sunt illa ex quorum alteratione tota ecclesia turbaretur, sicut ponitur exemplum de depositione omnium episcoporum simul," SE 3.57.342v. Gaines Post, "Copyists' Errors and the Problem of Papal Dispensations *contra statutum generale ecclesiae* or *contra statum generale ecclesiae* According to the Decretists and Decretalists, ca. 1150–1234," *Studia Gratiana* 9 (1966): 359–405; Yves Congar, "Status Ecclesiae," ibid., 15 (1972): 1–31; John H. Hackett, "State of the Church: A Concept of the Medieval Canonists," *Jurist* 23 (1963): 259–90.

79. "Similiter possent ad universalem statum ecclesiae dici pertinere praecepta divina praecepta legis naturalis et omnes tangit universaliter . . . quando papa dispensat aut mutat canones secundum oportunitates temporum et negociorum non facit contra canones aut statuta sanctorum patrum, quia servatur intentio statuentium quae est utilitas ecclesiae," SE 3.57.342v–343v. CSD D95.c1 (1:629). See also Horst, "Antonin," p. 103; Nörr, *Panormitanus*, pp. 76–80.

80. "Papa non potest facere aliquid quod vigat in potestatis suae diminutionem, aut derogationem dignitatis apostolicae suae," SE 2.104.245r. 70; Ullmann, *Principles*, pp. 102–3.

81. JdT, *"Flores sententiarum de auctoritate summi pontificis,"* Vat. lat. 2580 fols. 87v–93v at 93va; idem, *Oratio synodalis*, p. 58; CSD D40.c6 (1:351–53). This last is Turrecremata's comment on the famous dictum *a nemine iudicandus, nisi deprehenditur a fide devius,* see Victor Martin, "Comment s'est formée la doctrine de la superiorité du concile sur le pape" *Revue des sciences religieuses* 17 (1937): 124–30. Paul de Vooght, *Les pouvoirs de concile et l'autorité du pape* (Paris, 1965), pp. 137–45.

82. Piccolomini, *De gestis*, p. 32; Fleury, "Le conciliarisme," pp. 60–62; Fromherz, *Segovia*, p. 146; Sigmund, *Cusa*, p. 178; Philip Hughes, *The Church in Crisis* (New York, 1960), pp. 260–86.

83. "Causa propter quam praelatus haereticus est ipso facto praelatione privatus est, quia haereticus non potest praeesse in spiritualibus catholicis . . . papa et praelatus quique aliis ecclesiasticis factus pertinax haereticus sit praelatione privatus," SE 4 (pt. 2) 20.395r. Turrecremata cited Huguccio in SE 3.8 .282r. Brian Tierney, " 'Only the Truth Has Authority': The Problem of 'Reception' in the Decretists and in Johannes de Turrecremata," in *Law, Church, and Society: Essays in Honor of Stephan Kuttner,* ed. Kenneth Pennington and Robert Somverville (Philadelphia, 1977), p. 87.

168   PROTECTOR OF THE FAITH

84. "Quod cum papa dicitur posse accusari de heresi intelligendum est de heresi et de stricte sumpti: que est contra articula fidei: et qui illis sunt annexa aut necessaria. Et ista conclusio est hu. in presenti c. qui respondeo ad illud quod simonia dicitur heresi dicit sic. Simonia non proprie dicitur heresis. heresis proprie dicitur circa articulos fidei. et de tali soli potest papa accusari," CSD D79.c9.q1 (1:527); "Si Romanus pontifex incideret in heresim damnatum, et ita effectus esset haereticus," CSD C24.q1.c14 (3:271). See *SE* 2.110 .241r. John T. Gilchrist, *"Simonia heresis* and the Problem of Orders from Leo IX to Gratian," in *Proceedings of the Second International Congress of Medieval Canon Law*, ed. Stephan Kuttner (Vatican City, 1965), pp. 209–35.

85. CSD D17 ante c1.q3 (1:149). Charles Lefebvre, "Gratien et les origines de la 'denonciation évangélique': De l'*accusatio* à la *denuntiation*," *Studia Gratiana* 4 (1956): 233–50.

86. CSD D17 ante c1.q3 (1:149), C7.q1.c8.q1 (2:311–12); *SE* 3.8 .282v, 3.46 .331v. In CSD C2.q7.c4 (2:197) Turrecremata criticized Huguccio for allowing the pope to judge himself.

87. "Nolet hoc facere [make a public profession of faith], requirendus esset, ut congregare et concilium universale, aut autoritatem daret congregandi ad inquisitionem veritatis. Si vero hoc etiam nollet facere, tunc iudicio nostro domini cardinales, qui prestantia membra sunt ecclesiae Romanae, quibus potissime incumbit necessitatibus ecclesiae universalis providere, et imminentibus periculis obviare, deberent convocare, et congregare praelatos ecclesiae ad inquirendum de veritate infamiae, an. scilicet. Papa veraciter esset haereticus, an non," CSD D17 ante c1.q3. (1:149); here Turrecremata expressed his faith in the pope's willingness to call a council. Horst, "Konziliare Elemente," p. 371. The need for some responsible authority to call a council explains the tendency of some conciliarists, even those who were not, like Pierre d'Ailly, themselves cardinals, to exalt the authority of the Sacred College, see Alberigo, *Cardinalato e collegialità*, pp. 159–85.

88. CSD D79.c8 (1:197); *SE* 3.31 .309r, 3.14.290r–v.

89. *SE* 3.8 .282r. Some conciliarists extended this power to almost any Christian; see, e.g., Franciscus de Zabarella, *"De schismatibus authoritate imperatoris tollendis,"* in Simon Schard, *De iurisdictione, authoritate et praeeminentia imperiale, ac potestate ecclesiastica* (Basel, 1566), pp. 690–95.

90. "Papa non vult dare autoritatem ipsi congregati, ipsum ius intelligitur dare sibi authoritatem alias frustratoria esset provisio iuris, quae in casu heresis disposuit, quod concilium ponit iudicare Papam haereticum, aut declarare si per negationem Papae pertinaciter in heresi persistentis aufertur. Nam frustra assent iure, nisi eis assignaretur ministri," CSD D17 ante c1.q3 (1:149). Horst, "Konziliare Elemente," p. 373.

91. JdT, *Propositio ad dietam Norembergensis*, cols. 56–57; idem, *Tractatus contra advisamentum quod non liceat appellare de concilio ad papam*, Mansi 30.1072–94 at 1086; idem, *Oratio synodalis*, p. 14; *SE* 3.28 .305r, 3.30 .307r–v, 3.34 .313v, 3.38 .319r. Ewart Lewis,

Medieval Political Ideas (New York, 1954), 2: 527–28; Brian Tierney, "Hermeneutics and History: The Problem of *Haec Sancta*," in *Essays in Medieval History Presented to Bertie Wilkinson,* ed. T.A. Sandquist and Michael R. Powicke (Toronto, 1969), p. 360.

92. "Christus non defecerit in necessariis ecclesie militantis: sequitur quod per ecclesiam militantem papa si efficitur hereticus potest abscindi: et per consequens si fuerit de heresi diffamatus iudicio universalis ecclesie sit subiectus. . . . Hoc autem non possunt inquiere nisi inquirendo: an papa de heresi diffamatus sit catholicus vel hereticus. ergo in hoc casu prelati catholice habent potestatem inquirendo de papa super heresi mendaciter diffamata. licet in rei veritate iurisdictionis non habeant super ipsum: sicut potest quis alium citare: quam iudex non sit," CSD D21.c7.q3 (1:202). See *SE* 3.8 .282v.

93. CSD D17 ante c1.q3 (1:148–49). Horst, "Konziliare Elemente," pp. 382–83.

94. CSD D17 ante c1.q2 (1:148), C2.q7.c33 (2:207); *SE* 2.13.128r.

95. "Si vero hoc papa agere noluet, cum tunc videatur esse pertinax, et incorrigibilis, et haereticus formatus, tunc concilium praelatorum congregatum debet iuris auctoritate procedere ad depositionem illius," CSD D17 ante c1.q3 (1:149); *S.E.* II c.112 fol.260v, "Si Romanus pontifex efficitur haereticus ipso facto quo cadit a fide Petri cadet a cathedra, et sede Petri," SE 2.112.260v; "Claves sunt datae ecclesiae . . . ergo existens extra ecclesiam non habet eas. . . . Haereticus est ab ecclesiae corpore separatus. ergo ipso facto quod est haereticus est privatus honore et potestate ecclesiasticae iurisdictionis," SE 4 (pt. 2) 18 .391v–392r. See SE 4 (pt. 2) 18 .390v, 392v. On occult heresy, see SE 4 (pt. 2) 20. 394r. See also Antoninus de Florentia, *Summa theologica* (Verona, 1740), vol. 3, cols. 1207–9; Mario Midali, *Corpus Christi mysticum apud Dominicum Bañez eiusque fontes* (Rome, 1967), p. 207. A mad pope could be removed as though he were dead, see *SE* 3.8 .283r.

96. See, e.g., *SE* 3.46 .332v: "Falsum est quod concilium universale iure deponat, aut deponere possit Romanum pontificem nisi in casu heresis."

97. "Yunc vero . . . concilium praelatorum debet iuris auctoritate procedere ad depositionem illius ut quibusdam placet vel ut nobis plus gratim est iuxta dicta ad declarationem quod ille non sit amplius papa et quod vocet apostolica sedes, huiusmodi enim criminis proprius iudex est universale concilium," SE 3.8.282v; "Proprie loquendo nec propter haeresim papa deponitur a concilio sed potius declarationem non esse papa cum ostenditur quod in haeresim fuit collapsus et incorrigibilis in ea obstinatus perservarat," SE 2.102.241v. See SE 3.46 .332v, 4 (pt. 2) 20 .395v. Petrus de Monte accepted this line of argument; however, Cajetan later argued that the council had a ministerial power to actually depose the pope, see Horst "Konziliare Elemente," pp. 372, 387–88. Dominicans contemporary with Cajetan followed Turrecremata more closely on papal deposition, see Mirus, "Deposition," pp. 237–43.

98. Nicholas de Tudeschis (Panormitanus), *Consilia, tractatus, questiones, et practica* (Venice, 1621), fol. 4vb.

99. *SE* 2.93 .228r–v; CSD D19.c9 (1:174–76). Turrecremata's critical discussion of the texts concerning papal heresy was not as penetrating as was that of Guido Terreni, see Thomas M. Izbicki, "Infallibility and the Erring Pope: Guido Terreni and Johannes de Turrecremata," in *Law, Church, and Society*, pp. 97–111. However, Turrecremata's arguments had more influence than did Terreni's, see Remigius Bäumer, "Zum Kirchenverstädnis Albert Pigges: Ein Beitrag zur Ekklesiologie der vortridentiner Kontroverstheologie," in *Volk Gottes: Festgabe für Joseph Höfer*, ed. idem (Freiburg, 1967), pp. 314–19; Hans Küng, *Structures of the Church* (London, 1965), pp. 275–76. For Turrecremata's treatment of the case of Honorius I, see Johann Joseph Ignaz von Döllinger, *Fables Respecting the Popes of the Middle Ages*, trans. Alfred Plummer (New York, 1872), pp. 246–48; Georg Kreuzer, *Die Honoriusfrage in Mittelalter und in der Neuzeit* (Stuttgart, 1975), pp. 131–33. See also Thomson, "Roselli's *Monarchia*," p. 449.

100. "Praeterea, cum in depositione omnium Episcoporum simul non possit esse causa iusta, maxime praesumeretur in tali depositione defectas fidei in Papa, et hoc faceret in destructionem fidei, ex quo turbaretur tali Christianitas," SE 3.57.342v.

101. CSD D4 post c3.q1 (1:64), D12 ante c1 (1:111). At Basel Turrecremata said that the council was superior to the pope in matters of reform, see JdT, *Contra advisamentum quod non liceat appelare*, col. 1078. Like Laurentius Aretinus, he probably understood the term "reform" in *Haec sancta* as a reference to *status ecclesiae*, see Karla Eckermann, *Geschichte des monarchisen Gedankens* (Berlin, 1933), pp. 161–68.

102. *SE* 2.104 .244r, 2.105 .245v, 2.106 .246r–247v; CSD D10.c9 (1:101–72). Horst, "Konziliare Elemente," p. 369. See Sigmund, *Cusa*, p. 278.

103. "Papam esse incorrigibilem potest intelligi dupliciter uno modo continuatione criminis . . . . Secundo modo per ipsius criminis pertinacem defensionem ut dicat et defendat tale crimen: quod manifestum circum voluntari habet maliciam non esse pecatum gloss. autem habet locum in secundo modo. . . . Non autem habet locum, et in primo modo incorrigibilitas," CSD D40.c6 (1:353). Horst, "Konziliare Elemente," pp. 368–69. Tierney, *Foundations*, pp. 251–52. See Thomson, "Roselli's *Monarchia*," p. 450.

104. CSD C7.q1.c12.q5 (2:315–26).

105. *SE* 4 (pt. 1) 10 .367–368r, 4 (pt. 1) 19 .373v–374r; CSD D79.c8 (1:526). Horst, "Konziliare Elemente," pp. 373–74.

106. *SE* 4 (pt. 1) 13 .371v. For a contrary opinion, see Thomson "Roselli's *Monarchia*," pp. 450–51. Jean Gerson, "On the Unity of the Church," in Matthew Spinka, ed., *Advocates of Reform from Wycliff to Erasmus* (Philadelphia, 1953), pp. 146–7.

107. *SE* 4 (pt. 1) 9 .367v, 4 (pt. 1) 13 .370v, 371v. Küng, *Structures of the Church*, pp. 273–75.

108. *SE* 4 (pt. 1) 10 368–369r. Henry of Langenstein, "A Letter

on Behalf of a Council of Peace," in Spinka, *Advocates of Reform*, pp. 122–26; Howard Kaminsky, "Cession, Subraction, Deposition: Simon de Cramaud's Formulation of the French Solution to the Schism," *Studia Gratiana* 15 (1972): 295–317; Robert Norman Swanson, "The University of Cologne and the Great Schism," *Journal of Ecclesiastical History* 18 (1977): 1–15.

109. "Cum duo contra fas ordinati sunt de quorum nullius iure habetur certitudo: et nullius eorum est idoneus. Aut esset magnum scandalum si alter eorum maneret tunc enim expulsus et reiectus tertius eligatur," CSD D79.c8 (1:526). See Fleurry, "Le conciliarisme," p. 58.

110. These are, respectively, the opinion of Black (MC 136) and Küng (*Structures of the Church*, pp. 272–73).

111. Henry of Langenstein, "Letter," pp. 130–31; Jacob, *Essays in Later Medieval History*, p. 125. *Epikeia*, an Aristotelean concept popularized by Aquinas, was an important part of conciliar theory, according to Walter Ullmann, *Origins of the Great Schism* (London, 1948), pp. 198–99.

112. Paul de Vooght, "Le conciliarisme aux conciles de Constance et de Bâle," in *Le concile et les conciles* (Chevetogne, 1960), pp. 176–78.

Chapter 5

1. Noel Valois, *Le pape et le concile, 1418–1450* (Paris, 1909), 1:110–46; Aeneas Silvius Piccolomini (Pius II, *De gestis concilii Basiliensis*, ed. Denys Hay and W. K. Smith (Oxford, 1967), pp. 22, 24, 48, 62, 90, 126; Karl Binder, *Konzilsgedanken bei Kardinal Juan de Torquemada O.P.* (Vienna, 1976), pp. 169–74. Thomas E. Morrissey, "The Decree *Haec Sancta* and Cardinal Zabarella," *Annuarium historiae conciliorum* 10 (1978): 145–76. For a reconstruction of Cesarini's speech at Florence on conciliar power, see the first chart appended to Johannes de Turrecremata (JdT), *Oratio synodalis de primatu*, ed. Emmanuel Candal (Rome, 1954).

2. Edward Cuthbert Butler, *The Vatican Council* (London, 1930), 2:287–89; Augustin Renaudet, *Le concile gallican de Pise-Milan* (Paris, 1922); Remigius Bäumer, "Die Konstanzer Dekrete *Haec Sancta* und *Frequens* in Urteil katholischer Kontroverstheologen des 16. Jahrhunderts," in *Von Konstanz nach Trent: Festgabe für August Franzen*, ed. idem (Munich, 1972), pp. 147–74.

3. See, e.g., Philip Hughes, *The Church in Crisis* (New York, 1960), pp. 272–73; Corrado Leonardi, "Per una storia dell'edizione Romana dei concili ecumenici (1608–1612) da Antonio Augstin a Francesco Aduarte," in *Mélanges Eugène Tisserant* (Vatican City, 1964), 6:595, n. 48.

4. Paul de Vooght, "Le Cardinal Cesarini et le Concile de Constance," in *Das Konzil von Konstanz*, ed. August Franzen and Wolfgang Müller (Freiburg, 1964), pp. 357–80; idem, *Les pouvoirs du concile et l'autorité du pape* (Paris, 1965), pp. 185–98.

5. Binder, *Konzilsgedanken*, pp. 229–40; Hans Küng, *Structures of the Church* (London, 1964), pp. 240–85; Joseph Gill, "The Fifth Session of the Council of Constance," *Heythrop Journal* 5 (1964): 131–43; August Franzen, "The Council of Constance: Present State of the Problem," in *Concilium* 7 (1965): 19–68; Hubert Jedin, *Bischöfliches Konzil oder Kirchenparlement?*, 2nd ed. (Basel, 1965); Brian Tierney, "Hermeneutics and History: The Problem of *Haec Sancta*," in *Essays in Medieval History Presented to Bertie Wilkinson*, ed. T.A. Sandquist and Michael R. Powicke (Toronto, 1969), pp. 354–70; Francis Oakley, *Council Over Pope?* (New York, 1969), pp. 105–31.

6. Vooght, *Les pouvoirs*, pp. 137–62; idem, "Le concile oecuménique de Constance et le conciliarisme" *Istina* 9 (1963): 56–86.

7. "Nullum decretum emanabile a concilio potest ligare papam et ejus irritare potestatem, nisi in casibus, in quibus juxta assertionom adversae partis est superius papae scilicet in materia haeresis, in materia, schismatis, et in materia reformationis universalis ecclesiae in capite et in membris, scilicet data, quod in aliquo casu posset per concilium universale decretum irritans poni contra papam; arguo sic, sed quod papa det beneficia, confirmet et dignitates non est primo, secundo aut tertio; ergo in dispositione ecclesiarum concilium non potest decretum irritans contra papam, modo, et forma, ut praetenditur," JdT, *Contra decretum irritans*, Mansi 30.550–90 at 563. Vooght, *Les pouvoirs*, pp. 138–39.

8. JdT, *Tractatus contra advisamentum quod non liceat appellare de concilio ad papam*, Mansi 30.1072–97 at 1077; "concilio Constantiensi, quando fuit ex omnibus tribus obedientiis congregatum, in quo solo tempore tanquam universale concilium fuit generaliter, sed totam ecclesiam habitam, non emanavit tale decretum," idem, *Votum super advisamento quod papa debeat jurare servare decreta de conciliis generalibus*, Mansi 30.590–606 at 604. Vooght, *Les pouvoirs*, pp. 139–45.

9. "Quod vero secundus articulus prefato decreto [*Haec Sancta*] etiam contradicat, patet manifeste: quoniam si a cunctis fidelibus indubita fide credendum est, quod papa canonice electus, habeat supremam potestatem in ecclesia dei, de necessitate sequitur quod concilium universale non habeat potestatem immediate a Christo, cui ipse papa obedire teneatur, cum obedientiam inferiores ex ordine superioribus tantum debeant," JdT, *Oratio synadolis*, p. 11; see pp. 36, 77. Vooght, "Le concile oecuménique," pp. 74–75.

10. Vooght, *Les pouvoirs*, pp. 157–57; Gill, "Fifth Session," pp. 138–39. Arévalo suggested that *Haec sancta* might be heretical, see Richard Trame, *Rodrigo Sánchez de Arévalo, 1404–1470* (Washington, D.C. 1958), pp. 42–43.

11. "Non potest dici ad veritatem catholice pertinere congregationem illam sub obedientia Ioannis Constancie congregatum pro tempore illo prefatum decretum de potestate conciliorum edidit, facere concilium generale et ecclesiam catholicam representare, sine insupportabili scandalo aliarum obedientiarum," JdT, *Oratio synadolis*, p. 6. This argument has been criticized be-

cause the Roman and Avignon claimants had few followers, see Vooght, *Les pouvoirs*, p. 147.

12. JdT, *Responsio in blasphemam invectivam ad sanctissimum canonem justissime condemnationis damnatissime congregationis Basiliensium*, Mansi 31A.63–127 at 71–73.

13. "Pro quo solo tempore convenientibus omnibus simul tribus obedientiis fuit certum dicere quod universalis ecclesia reparesantative congregata esset Constantiae," SE 2.99.236r.

14. "Prefati domini Joannes et Benedictus de papatu contendentes, suspecti de haeresi, et ut tales notorii et incorrigibiles delati fuerunt," JdT, *Responsio in blasphemam*, cols. 72–73. See idem, *Oratio synodalis*, pp. 76–77. The depositions decreed at Pisa were not acts of a legitimate council, see *SE* 4, (pt. 1), 13 .372v. Vooght, *Les pouvoirs*, pp. 147–51, 157. The same argument was later used by Jacobazzi and Cajetan in their discussions of the Council of Pisa, see Remigius Bäumer, "Die Zahl der Allgemeinem Konzilien in der Sicht von Theologen des 15. und 16. Jahrhunderts," *Annuarium historiae conciliorum* 1 (1969): 298–301, 307. In contrast to this attack on the Pisan council and its line of popes, Antonio de Roselli defended both, see John A.F. Thomson, "Papalism and Conciliarism in Antonio de Roselli's *Monarchia*," *Medieval Studies* 37 (1975): 449–51.

15. JdT, *Contra advisamentum quod non liceat appellare*, col. 1091. This argument was used to refute one employed by Cesarini in idem, *Oratio synodalis*, pp. 4–5. Vooght, *Les pouvoirs*, p. 72.

16. "In sessione 36 . . . decrevit quod futurus Romanus pontifex . . . debeat reformare ecclesiam in capite Romane curiae secundum aequitatem et bonum regimen ecclesiae etc. . . . Ecce quod manifeste datur intelligi quod synodus illa hoc discernens non apprbaverit aut mente habuit illa decreta prima Constantie. . . . Clarissimum est autem quoc hi duo articuli per dominum Martinum assentiente et approbante concilio plenario. Constantien. videlicet quod papa sit caput sancte sedis catholice, id est universalis, et quod habeat supremam potestatem in ecclesia Dei: non possunt simul stare cum decreto illo quod Constantiae factum legitur per quosdam obediencia Ioann. Balthasar de superioritate conciliorum supra papam," SE 2.99.237r. See idem, *Responsio in blasphemam*, cols. 69, 63–64; idem, *Oratio synodalis*, pp. 10–11. Vooght, reviving arguments attacked by Turrecremata, has neglected Martin V's reaffirmation of papal power in the bull *Inter cunctas*, which he usually cites to show how the pope upheld the authority of the Council of Constance and of its decrees, see *Les pouvoirs*, pp. 72, 153–56; Martinus V, *Inter cunctas*, Mansi 28.1204–20 at 1212.

17. Richard Trame, "Conciliar Agitation and Rodrigo Sánchez de Arévalo," in *Studies in Medievalia and Americana: Essays in Honor of William Lyle Davis S.J.*, ed. Gerald G. Steckler and Leo Donald Davis (Spokane, Wash., 1973), pp. 89–112; Heiko Obermann et al., eds., *Defensorium Obedientiae Apostolicae et Alia Documenta* (Cambridge, Mass., 1968); Hubert Jedin, "Sánchez de Arévalo und die

Konzilfrage unter Paul II," *Historisches Jahrbuch* 72 (1942): 161–84; Anthony Black, "Henricus de Campo: The Council and History," *Annuarium historiae conciliorum* 2 (1970): 78–86; Paul Sigmund, *Nicholas of Cusa and Medieval Political Thought* (Cambridge, Mass., 1963), pp. 296–97.

18. JdT, *Apparatus super decretum unionis Grecorum*, ed. Emmanuel Candal (Rome, 1942), pp. 19–20; *SE* 3.66 .355r. See Trame, *Arévalo*, pp. 68–110. For a more favorable view of *Frequens*, see Thomson, "Roselli's *Monarchia*," pp. 454–55. This decree was still a focus of debate in the sixteenth century, see Terence Mukerin, "The Fifth Council of the Lateran (1512–1517): A Chapter in the Struggle Against Gallicanism," *St. Meinrad Essays*, vol. 12, no. 4 (1961): 44.

19. JdT, *Contra decretum irritans*, col. 555; SE 2.100 .238r–239v.

20. JdT, *Tractatus de veritate conceptionis beatissime virginis*, ed. Edward Bouverie Pusey (1869; Brussells, rpt. 1966), pp. 780–81.

21. Trame, *Arévalo*, p. 67; Ulrich Horst, "Papst und Konzil nach Raphael de Pornaxio," *Freiburger Zeitschrift für Philosophie und Theologie* 15 (1968): 389–93.

22. John Hine Mundy, "The Conciliar Movement and the Council of Constance," in Louise Ropes Loomis, *The Council of Constance*, ed. John Hine Mundy and Kennerly M. Woody (New York, 1961), p. 44.

23. Hubert Jedin, *A History of the Council of Trent*, trans. Ernest Graf (London, 1957), 1:32–75, 101–38, 245–67; idem, "Concilio e reforma nel pensiero del cardinale Bartolomeo Guidiccioni," *Rivista di storia della Chiesa in Italia* 2 (1948): 33–66; Josef Klotzner, *Kardinal Dominikus Jacobazzi und sein Konzilwerk* (Rome, 1948).

24. Thomas de Vio (Caietanus), *De comparatione pape, et concilii*, in Rocaberti 19:446–525. Mukerin, "Fifth Council of the Lateran," p. 49; Olivier de la Brosse, *Le pape et le concile* (Paris, 1965), p. 302.

25. JdT, *Responsio in blasphemam*, col. 102.

26. Ibid, *"Flores sententiarum de auctoritate summi pontificis,"* Vat. lat. 2580 fols. 84v–93v at 92r; "ubi sic veritas dubii imeniri non possit, tunc convocandus est conventus spaientium ex orbe terrarum et non ante," idem, *Super petitione domini regis Franciae, ut aliud tertium celebraretur universale concilium*, Mansi 35.43–56 at 53; idem, *oratio synodalis*, p. 86.

27. "Non enim videtur possibile quod possit pericula talia in ecclesia contingere quibus provideri non posset nisi per concilium generale, sive universali . . . nullus casus posset contingere in ecclesia cui per Romanae ecclesiae diligentiam providere non posset," SE 3.8.281r.v.

28. *SE* 3.9 .283v–284r, 3.10 .285r–286r. Joseph Fenton, "The Theology of the General Council," in *The General Council*, ed. William Joseph McDonald (Washington, D.C., 1962), pp. 159–60; Binder, *Konzilsgedanken*, p. 149.

29. *SE* 46 .332v.

30. *SE* 3.8 .282v–283r, 3.30.319r, 3.38.320r. Jedin, *Trent*, pp.

28–29, 95–96. Late in life Arévalo moderated his opposition to the convocation of a council, see Trame, *Arévalo*, pp. 193–94.

31. "Concilium universale est congregatio praelatorum maiorum ecclesiae authoritate Romani Pontificis speciali convocata ad aliquid communi intentione solemniter tractendum in religione Christiana. Papa in concilio praesidente, vel aliquo loco sui," CSD D17 ante c1.q1 (1:147).

32. CSD D17 ante c1.q1 (1:147). Binder, *Konzilsgedanken*, pp. 81–85, 190–92.

33. JdT, *Super petitione domini regis Franciae* cols.48, 52–54; idem, *Apparatus*, pp. 21, 66. Binder, *Konzilsgedanken*, pp. 71–79.

34. *SE* 2.34 .276r–277r, 3.6 1.78v–280r, 3.10 .285v.286v, 3.18 .295r; CSD D15.c1, pt. 1 (1:1124). Fenton, "Theology of the General Council," 158–59. Nicholas of Cusa said that there were also councils of the Roman patriarchate whose decisions bound only the Latin Church, see Sigmund, *Cusa*, p. 181.

35. "Est autem hic advertendum quod gl. in c. Convenientibus 1. q.7 omnes synodos reducens ad duas species dicit quod synodorum aliquae sunt universales quibus interest Romanus pontifex vel eius legatus. aliae sunt locales quas congregunt primates, vel metropolitani obsque praesidentia papae vel eius legati . . . quia auctoritas illorum conciliorum localium certis limitibus artatur ultra quos non extenditur. Non sic autem de universalibus cum auctoritate illius fulciantur qui totius orbis Christiani caput et antistes est," SE 3.3.227r.

36. "Concilia universale videntur habere origine ex institutione humana et non a Christo immediate. ergo falsum est quod concilia habeant immediate a Christo potestatem iurisdictionis supra omnes fideles . . . licet bene legatur quod fuerint aliqua per apostolos celebrata . . . sed hoc non arguit institutionem eorum immediatum fuisse a Deo," SE 3.28.204v. For Peter's role in the first councils, see SE 2.5 .274–276r. MC 158.

37. Jean Fleury, "Le conciliarisme des canonistes au concile de Bâle d'après le Panormitain," in *Mélanges Roger Secretan* (Montreux, 1964), p. 58.

38. *SE* 3.28 .304v–305r (Turrecremata referred his readers to his doctrine of jurisdiction).

39. Knut Wolfgang Nörr, *Kirche und Konzil bei Nicholaus de Tudeschis (Panormitanus)* (Cologne, 1964), pp. 92–93, 97–101, 134; Uta Fromherz, *Johannes von Segovia als Geschichtesschreiber des Konzils von Basel* (Basel, 1960), p. 135.

40. Sigmund, *Cusa*, pp. 78–118. This doctrine facilitated Cusa's change of allegiance. He decided that Basel's internal dissensions and its attack on Eugenius IV indicated the absence of the Holy Spirit, see idem, *Cusa*, pp. 166–68, 263–65. This concern with the presence of the Spirit should not be neglected in the discussion of Cusa's "modern" theory of representation, see Antony Black, "The Political Ideas of Conciliarism and Papalism, 1430–1450," *Journal of Ecclesiastical History* 20 (1969): 47.

41. JdT, *Responsio in blasphemam*, col. 74.

42. "Licet universale concilium ecclesiam universalem repraesentare dicatur non tamen est ipsa ecclesia universalis," SE 2.64.354r; "Si concilium universale dicatur habere potestatem a Christo immediate quia universali ecclesiae quam repraesentet data sit . . . necessarium esset ut ad concilium convocarentur omnes fideles qui intra universitatem ecclesiae continentur si concilium debeat exire in actum sive exercitum potestatis suae. sed hoc est inconveniens nec inquam in ecclesia fuit practicatum," SE 3.28.305v.

43. SE 3.28 .304r, 3.44 .325.r.

44. "Licet plenarium concilium non sit materialiter tota universalis ecclesia, est tamen tota auctoritate," SE 3.60.347r, 3.18 .295r, 3.28 .204r.

45. "Dicimus enim quod a hoc quod concilium repraesentet universalem ecclesiam non requiritur praesentia omnium fidelium, hoc enim est impossibile nec aliquo tempore factum levitur sed sufficit quod in ecclesia in eo sint maiores sive potiores Reip. Christianae cujusmodi sunt praelati maiores," SE 3.14.290v. See CSD D17 ante c1.q1 (1:147). Jedin, Trent, 1:27.

46. Valois, Le pape et le concile, 2:56–60; Piccolomini, De gestis, pp. 97–133, 177–81; Loy Bilderback, "Proctorial Representation and Conciliar Support at the Council of Basel," Annuarium historiae conciliarum 1 (1969): 140–52; Nörr, Panormitanus, pp. 165–68. These debates preclude the contention of Black (MC 36) that all conciliarists believed that the majority's will should prevail.

47. "Illi soli veniunt necessario convocandi ad universalia concilia cum quibus tractando veniunt, que universitatem Christiani populi respiciunt qui constituti singulariter leguntur Christiani populi principes, et recotores, patet hoc quia statuere corrigere, et reformare cum sint actus iurisdictionis . . . sed episcopi soli sunt huiusmodi," SE 3.12.287v; "Alii praelati ex quibus congregatur concilium convocandi sunt in partem sollicitudinis . . . ergo sequitur quod papa sit superior auctoritate universali concilio," SE 3.44.324v. The cardinals' role in a council was derived from their close relationship with the pope, see SE 3.26 .301v. Binder, Konzilsgedanken, pp. 123–27; Johannes Baptista Bičiunas, Doctrina ecclesiologica S. Roberti Bellarmini cum illa Joannis Card. de Turrecremata comparata (Rome, 1963), p. 62; Sigmund, Cusa, pp. 161–62.

48. CSD D17 ante c1.q4 (1:150); SE 3.12 .288r, 3.14 .289v. See Nörr, Panormitanus, p. 169.

49. Lay jurists could also participate as experts, see SE 3.15.291v.

50. SE 3.15 .292–293r. Turrecremata denied the applicability to a council of the legal maxim quod omnes tangit, see SE 3.14.290v; CSD D17 ante c1.q4 (1:150). There was agreement among jurists and conciliarists on this point, see Gaines Post, Studies in Medieval Legal Thought (Princeton, 1964), pp. 168–70; Sigmund, Cusa, pp. 163–64; Ernest Fraser Jacob, "Panormitanus and the Council of Basel," in Proceedings of the Third International Congress of Medieval Canon Law, ed. Stephan Kuttner (Vatican City, 1971), p. 210; Paul Ourliac, "L'eglise et les laïques à fin du Moyen Age: Etude de

droit canonique," in *Mélanges offerts au Professeur Louis Falletti* (Paris, 1971), pp. 480–81, 485.

51. Nörr, *Panormitanus*, pp. 120–21; Tierney, "Problem of *Haec Sancta*," p. 367.

52. "Potestas tocius concilii comprehenderetur in eo, a quo dependet et emanat. Dicimus enim quod omnium membrorum virtus continetur in capite, et omnium inferiorum potestas in principe," JdT, *Oratio synodalis*, p. 86. See *SE* 3.22 .292r. Bičiunas, *Doctrina ecclesiologica*, pp. 62–63. See also Trame, *Arévalo*, pp. 39–42; Ulrich Horst, "Papst, Bischofe, und Konzil nach Antonin von Florenz," *Recherches de theologie ancienne et medievale* 31 (1965): 101–2.

53. CSD D17 ante c1.q3 (1:148); *SE* 3.6 .279r–v, 3.44 .324r–v. See Binder, *Konzilsgedanken*, pp. 80–112, 121–23, 137–43. See also Sigmund, *Cusa*, pp. 264–65; Nörr, *Panormitanus*, p. 120. The theory of Black (MC 48–49) that conciliarists thought papal convocation a mere formality overemphasizes their belief that a council could, if necessary, meet without papal approval.

54. "Papa convocando concilium universale incorporet illi auctoritatem suam non tamen conceditur quod incorporet illi omnem eius plenitudinem potestatis sed tantum quantum necesse est ad providendum super illis ad quae illud convocat: unde si patres illius concilii ad alia se extendat quam ad ea quae a Romano pontefice receperint potestatem, et errant usurpando sibi quod non convenit et etiam facta sic per eos extra potestatus datae terminos viribus vacua sunt," SE 3.40.321r. See *SE* 3.32 .311r, 3.46 .328v, 334, 3.47 .333v, 3.52 .337r–v.

55. *SE* 3.22 .297v, 3.24 .299r–300r; CSD D17 ante c1.q5 (1:150–51). Valois, *Le pape et le concile*, 1:311–31; Fromherz, *Segovia*, p. 144.

56. JdT, *Apparatus*, pp.18–19; *SE* 3.66 .254v–355r. Bičiunas, *Doctrina ecclesiologica*, p. 63.

57. "In tali casu [heresy] papa non sic dissolveret sine consensu concilii, nihilominus ubi papa de certo talem dissolutionem non faceret in fraude sed manifeste cognosceret quod pro dicta haeresi extirpanda alio tempore, et alio loco convenienter celebraretur universale concilium posset ipse sua potestate quae a nullo quam a Deo dependet nec ligari potest, illud concilium dissolvere, et aliud pro eadem causa instituere celebrandum . . . cum arguitur de concilio congregati ratione haeresis de qua papa esset infamatus etc. respondetur quod in hac casu ut nobis apparet papa maxime si in fraudem fueret non posset sine consensu concilii in illa parte iudex est, dissolvere concilium," SE 3.69.356v. For a specific reference to *Frequens*, see SE 3.66 .355r. See also Thomson, "Roselli's *Monarchia*," p. 455.

58. *SE* 3.58 .345v. Sigmund, *Cusa*, pp. 145, 171–74, 264–65; Horst, "Antonin," p. 108; Tierney, "Problem of *Haec Sancta*," pp. 368–69.

59. MC 35–36; Fromherz, *Segovia*, p. 138; Nörr, *Panormitanus*, p. 35–36; Brian Tierney, *Foundations of the Conciliar Theory* (Cam-

bridge, 1955), pp. 108–17; Léo Moulin, "*Sanior et Maior Paris:* Note sur l'evolution des techniques lectorelles dans les ordres religieux du VIe au XIIIe siècle," *Revue historique de droit français et étranger,* ser. 4, vol. 36 (1958): 368–97, 491–529.

60. "Omnis papa principaliter auctoritate faciat, licet alii patres consulendo, et consentiendo concurrant," SE 3.32.309v; "Concilium suadet," JdT, *Apparatus,* p. 35.

61. *SE* 3.64 .353r–v; JdT, *Oratio synodalis,* p. 82. Turrecremata followed the doctrine of Alanus, see Brian Tjerney, "Pope and Council: Some New Decretist Texts," *Medieval Studies* 19 (1957): 208–9.

62. "Magis regulariter standum foret iudicio patrum totius concilii quam iudicio Romani pontificis . . . tunc synodus maior est papa quod intelligendum est maioritate discretivi iudicii secundum quod non dubium quia regulariter concilium sit maius Romano pontifici," SE 3.64.352v–353r; see 3.46.332r; JdT, *Oratio synodalis,* pp. 57–58. Fenton, "Theology of the General Council," p. 171. Papalists believed that ordinarily the pope would need good advice, see, e.g., Johannes de Carvajal, *Contra apelantes al futuro concilio,* in Lino Gomez Canedo, *Don Juan de Carvajal* (Madrid, 1947), pp. 343–44.

63. "Ubi autem ita evaniret, quod talibus, quae ad finem pertinere tota synodus per apertissima testimonia s. Scripturae aut s. Patrum doctrinam unanimiter declararet, Papa acquiescere, obediret stare nollet, sed contumaces contradiceret talibus aperte ad fidem catholicam pertinere declaratis, jam utpote haereticus subjectus veniret Concilia, sicut et quilibet alius a fide devius," JdT, *Oratio synodolis,* pp. 58–59. For Turrecremata's discussion of Huguccio's doctrine, see CSD C9.q3.c17 (2:369). Turrecremata thought papally approved councils unlikely to disagree. However, he stated a preference for the decisions of an earlier council in matters of faith; of a later council in matters of positive law, see *SE* 3.63 .351v–352r. Tierney, "Pope and Council," pp. 203–10; idem, " 'Only the Truth Has Authority': the Problem of 'Reception' in the Decretists and in Johannes de Turrecremata," in *Law, Church, and Society: Essays in Honor of Stephan Kuttner,* ed. Kenneth Pennington and Robert Somerville (Philadelphia, 1977), pp. 87–88. Fenton's view ("Theology of the General Council," p. 173) that Turrecremata thought a collision between pope and council over a matter of faith was impossible is clearly erroneous; see Sigmund, *Cusa* pp. 174–77.

64. *De summi pontificis infallibilitate personali* (Naples, 1870), p. 7; Paul de Vooght, "Esquisse d'un enquête sur le mot infaillabilité durant la période scholastique," in *L'Infaillabilité de l'Eglise* (Chevetogne, 1963), p. 139.

65. "Dico autem regulariter quia posset esse quod etiam in facto fidei movetur melioribus rationibus et authoritatibus; quam concilium. unde tunc standum esset diffinitione pape," CSD D19.c8 (1:174). On erring councils, see CSD D18.c9 (1:160); *SE* 3.65 .354r. Binder, *Konzilsgedanken,* p. 184; Tierney, " 'Only the Truth

Has Authority,' " pp. 69–70, 79–80, 82; see Nörr, *Panormitanus,*
pp. 94–96, 105.

66. CSD D4 ante c3.q1 (1:62); *SE* 3.46 .333r.

67. "Plane si concilia universale habent illam supremam auctoritatem immediate a Deo constituendi, diffiniendi, sententiandi,
puniendi, et etiam supra papam sancte universalis ille synodi non
tam regulariter tam devote et humiliter a Romano pontifice gesta
sua poterat confirmari. planum est quod ista stare non possunt
simul quod concilium habeat immediate potestatem a Christo, cui
etiam papa obedire teneatur, et quod concilii sententiae et gesta
nulla sint roboris nisi Romani pontificis auctoritate firmentur superioris est enim roborare actu inferiorum et non enconverso,"
SE 3.34.313v, 3.44 .324v. This was the doctrine of Aquinas, according to Fenton ("Theology of the General Council," pp.
169–70). In recent years Paul de Vooght has fallen into this trap,
trying to prove that Martin V and Eugenius IV sanctioned *Haec
sancta,* see *Les pouvoirs,* pp. 55–80.

68. *SE* 3.41 .322v–323r.

69. JdT, *Contra decretum irritans,* col. 589; CSD D15,c2.q2
(1:137), D16 ante c8.q2 (1:144). Bičiunas, *Doctrina ecclesiologica,*
p. 63. Panormitanus thought this papal power subject to review
by a general council, see Nörr, *Panormitanus,* pp. 111–12, 131,
134–36. Tierney, " 'Only the Truth Has Authority,' " pp. 80–82.

70. JdT, *Contra advisamentum quod non liceat appellare,* cols.
1078–79; *SE* 3.47 .333r–334r, 3.49 .335r, 3.50 .344v–345r. Fenton, "Theology of the General Council," p. 170.

71. "Universale concilium stante unico, et indubitato Romano
pontifice in sede Petri, et contradicente non posset ad alia trac-
tanda diffinenda ac iudicanda debit se extendere quam ad illa
quae per Romanum pontificem fuerit convocatum," SE 3.40.321r.

72. Fenton, "Theology of the General Council," pp. 176–78.

Chapter 6

1. John Neville Figgis, *Churches in the Modern State* (London,
1914), p. 183; Gerhart Ladner, "The Concepts of *Ecclesia* and
Christianitas and Their Relation to the Idea of Papal *Plenitudo
Potestatis* from Gregory VII to Boniface VIII," *Miscellanea historiae
pontificis* 18 (1954): 49–77.

2. Gerd Tellenbach, *Church, State, and Christian Society at the
Time of the Investiture Contest,* trans. Ralph Francis Bennett (Oxford, 1966); Gregory VII, *The Correspondence of Pope Gregory VII,*
trans. Ephraim Emerton (New York, 1969), pp. 103, 167–70.

3. Walter Ullmann, "Cardinal Roland and Besançon," *Miscel-
lanea historiae pontificis* 18 (1954): 107–25; Brian Tierney, "The
Continuity of Papal Political Theory in the Thirteenth Century:
Some Methodological Considerations," *Traditio* 27 (1965): 227–45.

4. John Andrew Watt, *The Theory of Papal Monarchy in the Thirteenth Century* (London, 1965), pp. 9–33; Alfonso Maria Stickler,

"Der Schwerterbegriff bei Huguccio," *Ephemerides iuris canonici* 3 (1947): 1–44.

5. Watt, *Theory of Papal Monarchy*, pp. 34–133.

6. Elizabeth Kennan, "The *De consideratione* of St. Bernard of Clairvaux and the Papacy in the Mid-Twelfth Century: A Review of Scholarship," *Traditio* 23 (1967): 73–115; Walter Ullmann, *The Growth of Papal Government in the Middle Ages*, 2nd ed. (London, 1962), pp. 413–46; Ugo Mariani, *Chiesa e stato nei teologi Agostiniani del secolo XIV* (Rome, 1957), pp. 113–98; Aegidius Romanus, *De potestate ecclesiastica* (Stuttgart, 1961), pp. 9–15; William D. Mc-Cready, "The Problem of the Empire in Augustinus Triumphus and Late Medieval Hierocratic Theory," *Traditio* 30 (1974): 325–49.

7. James Muldoon, "Boniface VIII's Forty Years of Experience in the Law," *Jurist* 31 (1971): 449–77; Marie Dominique Chenu, "Dogme et Theólogie dans la bulle *Unam Sanctum*," in *Mélanges Jules Lebreton* (Paris, 1952) 2:307–16.

8. Brian Tierney, *The Crisis of Church, and State 1050–1300* (Englewood Cliffs, N.J., 1964), pp. 74–84, 97–109, 139–49, 200–210; Jean Rivière, *Le problème de l'Eglise et l'Etat au Temps de Philippe le Bel* (Louvain, 1926); Richard Scholz, *Diet Publizistik zur Zeit Philipps des Schönen und Bonifaz VIII* (Stuttgart, 1930); Georges de Lagarde, *La naissance de l'esprit laïque au déclin du moyen age*, rev. ed., 5 vols. (Louvain, 1956–70).

9. Walter Ullmann, *The Medieval Papacy: St. Thomas and Beyond* (London, 1960); idem, *The Relevance of Medieval Ecclesiology* (London, 1966); Petrus de Palude, *Tractatus de potestate pape*, ed. Petrus Thomas Stella (Zürich, 1966), pp. 203–70; Leonard Boyle, "The *De Regno* and the Two Powers," in *Essays in Honor of Anton Charles Pegis*, ed. J. Reginald O'Donnell (Toronto, 1974), pp. 237–47; Marc F. Griesbach, "John of Paris as a Representative of Thomistic Political Philosophy," in *An Etienne Gilson Tribute*, ed. Charles J. O'Neill (Milwaukee, 1959), pp. 33–50. For the role of Roman law in the formulation of the idea of the state, see Gaines Post, *Studies in Medieval Legal Thought* (Princeton, 1964), pp. 241–561.

10. Ullmann, *Growth of Papal Government*, pp. 19–26; idem, *Principles of Government and Politics in the Middle Ages*, 2nd ed. (London, 1966), pp. 447–57; Michael Wilks, *The Problem of Sovereignty in the Later Middle Ages* (Cambridge, 1963).

11. Sergio Mochi Onory, *Fonti canonistiche dell'idea dello stato* (Milan, 1951); Friedrick Kempf, *Papsttum und Kaisertum bei Innocenz III* (Rome, 1954); Alfonso Maria Stickler, "De ecclesiae potestate coactiva materiali apud magistrum Gratianum," *Salesianum* 4 (1942): 2–23; idem, "Concerning the Political Theories of the Medieval Canonists," *Traditio* 7 (1949–51): 450–63.

12. Brian Tierney, "Some Recent Works on the Political Theories of the Medieval Canonists," *Traditio* 10 (1954): 599–612; Joseph Boots, "Kardinal Juan de Troquemada Verdediger de Indirecte Machte der Pausen in Tijdelijke Aanglegenheden," *Historisch Tijdschrift* 14 (1935): 290–96; Gerhart Ladner, "Aspects

of Medieval Thought on Church and State," *The Review of Politics* 9 (1947): 403–22.

13. "Et quia ad hoc multum operatur, ut supra probavimus quod unus in tota politia Christiana rector et magister praesideat: ideo magis est necessarium ut in spiritualibus praesidet unus in republica Christiana quam in temporalibus," SE 2.4.120v; "in generali duo in ipsa fidelium universitate sunt potestates, scilicet secularis, et spiritualis," SE 1.87.97r. Paul Theeuws, "Jean de Turrecremata: Les relations entre l'Eglise et le pouvoir civil d'après un théologien du XV^c siècle," in *L'Organisation corporative du Moyen Age à la Fin de l'Ancien Régime* (Louvain, 1943) 3:139; Edmond Dublanchy, "Turrecremata et le pouvoir du pape dans les questions temprelles," *Revue Thomiste* 28 (1923): 97. The author was unable to consult Antonio Molina Melià, "Juan de Torquemada y la teoría de la potestad indirecta de la iglesia en asuntos temporales," *Anales Valentinos* 2 (1976): 45–78; see Aquinas in Ewart Lewis, *Medieval Political Ideas* (New York, 1954), 2:566–67.

14. Johannes de Turrecremata (JdT), *Opusculum ad honorem Romani imperii et dominorum Romanorum*, in Hubert Jedin, "Juan de Torquemada und das Imperium Romanum," *AFP* 12 (1942): 268–69; "In potestatibus secularibus in quibus finis ad quem tendit regimen praesidentis, et gubernantis est ipsa pax et tranquillitas universitatis sive felicitas politica. cum hoc sit bonum principalem ad quod universum regimen gubernatoris intendere et respicere videtur," SE 2.84.217r. Jaime Vélez-Saénz, *The Doctrine of the Common Good of Civil Society in the Works of St. Thomas Aquinas* (Notre Dame, 1951), pp. 3–33; Allesandro Passerin d'Entrèves, *Dante as Political Thinker* (Oxford, 1952), p. 31.

15. "Per legem dirigitur homo ad actus proprios in ordine ad ultimum finem. Et si quidem homo ordinaretur tantum ad finem. Et si quidem homo ordinaretur tantum ad finem, qui non excederet proportionem naturalis facultatis hominis non oporteret, quod homo haberet aliquid directivam ex parte rationis supra naturalem legem, et legem humanitatis positivum, que en derivatur. Sed quia homo ordinatur ad finem beatitudinis aeterne, que excedit proportionem naturalis facultatis humane . . . lex divina data fuit ostensum est, quod lex naturalis non sufficiebat ad salutem, ergo lex divina necessarius fuit data," CSD D1.c1q1, pt. 4 (1:24). See *SE* 1.90 .101r, 1.92 .104r. The same doctrine was taught by Aquinas and James of Viterbo, see Theeuws, "Les relations," pp. 162–64; Robert Warrand Carlyle and Alexander James Carlyle, *A History of Medieval Political Thought in the West* (Edinburgh, 1928), 5:348–49.

16. *SE* 1.89 .99r, 2.116 .273v.

17. *SE* 1.87 .97r.

18. "Non intelligimus potestatem regalem causalitate in genere causae efficientis sic pendere a spirituali potestate," SE 1.92.103v. William D. McCready, "Papal *Plenitudo Potestatis* and the Source of Temporal Authority in Late Medieval Papal Hierocratic Theory," *Speculum* 48 (1973): 654–74; Mariani, *Chiesa e stato*, pp.

113–98; Richard Trame, *Rodrigo Sánchez de Arévalo* (Washington, D.C., 1958), pp. 148–49, 154–58; Paul Sigmund, *Nicholas of Cusa and Medieval Political Thought* (Cambridge, Mass., 1963), pp. 287–90; Watt, *Theory of Papal Monarchy*, pp. 13, 19–21, 24–25.

19. "Nullum prius dependet in esse a suo posteriori, sed potestas princpum secularium sive regalis, sive Imperialis praecedunt tempore papatum, sive principatum apostolica dependerit potestas iurisdictionis princpum secularium. . . . Tum ex quod prius fuerunt reges et Imperatores antequam Petrus fuisset factus papa," SE 2.113.264r. See CSD D96.c10.q2 (1:644). Dublanchy, "Turrecremata et le pouvoir du pape," pp. 88–89; Theeuws, "Les relations," pp. 140–49; Jedin, "Torquemada und das Imperium Romanum," pp. 248–54.

20. "Potestas secularis sive regalis sive imperialis secundum esse suum materiale. non dependeat a potestate spirituale; sed a deo mediante naturali hominum inclinatione . . . concedimus quod ambe potestates scilicet tam spiritualis quam secularis a christo sicut ab uno fonte emanat," CSD D96.c10.q3 (1:646); "Imperialis principatus quantum ad debitum esse in hominibus est de iure nature, quod dicitur ius gentium. Patet, quia ius naturale dicitur, quod naturale ratione sit introductum. Sed dominium sive regimen imperiale est debitum esse in hominibus secundum rectam rationem," JdT, *Opusculum*, p. 273; see pp. 271–72. Theeuws, "Les relations," pp. 159–60, 171–74; Aquinas 7:178: I^{a}II^{ac} q.95 ar.4.

21. *SE* 1.90 .100v; CSD D22.c2 (1:208); JdT, *Opusculum*, pp. 269–71, 174–75. See Bernice Hamilton, *Political Thought in Sixteenth Century Spain* (Oxford, 1963), pp. 47–48.

22. "Praesidentia in illa temporalibus fuit quae iure divino non tollitur ab infidelibus sicut dictum est," SE 4 (pt. 2) 20.395r. CSD C11.q3.c24 (2:418–19), C11.q3.c94 (2:438), D96.c6 (1:637–43); *SE* 2.114.269r. Thomas M. Izbicki, "An Argument from Authority in the Indies Debate," *The Americas* 34 (1978) 400–406; James Muldoon, "*Extra ecclesiam non est imperium:* The Canonists and the Legitimacy of the Secular Power," *Studia Gratiana* 9 (1963): 553–80; Kenneth Pennington, "Bartolome de las Casas and the Tradition of Medieval Law," *Church History* 29 (1970): 149–61; Ronald E. Modras, "Paul Vladimiri and His *Opinio Hostiensis*," *St. Meinrad's Essays*, vol. 12, no. 3 (1960): 1–34; Vernancio Carro, *La teologie y los teologos-juristas españoles ante la conquista de America* (Madrid, 1944) 1:211, 2:34.

23. Friedberg 2.714–16: X. 4.17.13; Dante Allighieri, *Monarchia*, ed. Pier Giorgio Ricci (Verona, 1965); d'Entrèves, *Dante as Political Thinker*, pp. 26–51; Post, *Studies in Medieval Legal Thought*, pp. 434–93; Watt, *Theory of Papal Monarchy*, pp. 37–45.

24. "Non sit necesse omnes eos convenire in politia communitati, sed possunt secundum diversitatem climatum et linguarum, et conditionum hominum esse diversi modi vivendi et diversae politiae sicut sunt propter quod non est ita necesse mundum regi per unum in temporalibus plenam in omnibus potestatem ha-

bentem sicut in spiritualibus," SE 2.4.120v. See CSD D2 ante pt. 1 (1:51), C7.q1.c41 (2:327), D63.c33 (1:484). Santiago Maria Ramirez, *El derecho des gentes* (Madrid, 1955), pp. 134–35.

25. "Sed optimum regimen multitudinis est secundum quod continetur sub uno principatu. . . . Ergo videtur quod regimen totius orbis sic sit dispositum ab eterna sapientia, et unus etiam in temporalibus praesideat omnibus populis et nationibus . . . Cum autem universus orbis sic quasi unum corpus mixtum ex diversis membris officiis et statibus constitutum . . . sequitur, quod conveniens fuit et debitum est in humanibus unam supremam potestatem, qua, si etiam reges aut regna dissentirent dispensationi causa sopitu conservarentur quieta et in pace," JdT, *Opusculum,* p. 272. For Turrecremata's use of *Per venerabilem,* see idem, *Opusculum,* p. 277. Jedin, "Torquemada und das Imperium Romanum," p. 260. See also Sigmund, *Cusa,* pp. 291–92.

26. JdT, *Opusculum,* p. 277–78.

27. CSD D2 (pt. 1) q1 (1:52), D10.c13 (1:103), D4 ante c2.q1 (1:60), D1.c11.q1 (1:9), D50.c51 (1:424), D50.c61 (1:427–28), D1.c9 (1:7), C23.q1.c4 (3:213); SE 2.113 .265r, 2.65 .188v, 1.42 .49v. MC 85–129.

28. SE 2.65 .188v5189r, 2.84 .217r. Black (MC 66, 79–80) concentrated on these analogies, ignoring other matters.

29. Johannes Parisiensis, *Uber königliche und papstliche Gewalt (De regia potestate et papali),* ed. Fritz Bleienstein (Stuttgart, 1969), pp. 69–72; Petrus de Palude, *Tractatus de potestate papae,* pp. 203–70.

30. Turrecremata did not acknowledge the source of this schema, see CSD D96.c6 (1:637–43). However, he derived his theory of property rights from John of Paris; cf. SE 2.113 .265r with Johannes Parisiensis, *De regia potestate,* pp. 96–97; see Robert Bellarmine, *De summo pontifice,* in *Scritti Politici,* ed. Carlo Giacon (Bologna, 1950), pp. 113–17.

31. Martin Grabmann, "Studien über den Einfluss der aristotelischen Philosophie auf die mittelalterlichen Theorien über der Verhältnis von Kirche und Staat," *Sitzungsberichte der bayerischen Akademie der Wissenschaft,* Phil. Hist. Klasse 2 (1934): 117–27; Jedin, "Torquemada und das Imperium Romanum," p. 261; Sigmund, *Cusa,* pp. 287–88; Howard Kaminsky, *A History of the Hussite Revolution* (Berkeley, 1967), pp. 40–55; Peter Brock, *The Political and Social Doctrines of the Unity of Czech Brethren in the Fifteenth and Early Sixteenth Centuries* (The Hague, 1957), pp. 25–69.

32. CSD D96.c6 (1:642), D21.c1 (1:186–92); SE 2.116 .271v, 2.113 .263r–v. Turrecremata did cite Aquinas's reference to both powers residing in the pope, see CSD D96.c6 (1:638). This appears to be a reference to the papal states, where, according to Turrecremata, the pope succeeded Constantine, see CSD D96.c6 (1:642), D96.c11 (1:648); SE 2.116 .272v. Tierney, *Church and State,* pp. 165–71.

33. "In Christo fuit potestas, et auctoritas iurisdictionis tem-

poralis licet parum usus iurisdictionis temporali," SE 2.116.271v; "Papa non sic est dicendus habere iurisdictionem in temporalibus iure papatus ut sic dicendus sit totius orbis dominus . . . non potest habere iure papatus id quod Petro et omnibus apostolis fuit prohibitum et interdictum . . . in Matt. 20. ubi Christus ait apostolis. Scitis quia principes gentium dominantur eorum et qui maiores sunt potestatem exercent in eos: non ita erit inter vos . . . si Romanus pontifex iure sui principatus fuisset dominus temporalium non fuisset aliqua donatio facta Sylvestro, sed potius restitutio eius quod supra erat, cuius tamen contrarium Romanus pontifex confitetur et Imperator Constantinus, de constantino habetur in cap. Constantinus distinct. 96. de Romano pontifice habetur in cap. Futuram duodecima q.1," SE 2.113.263r–v. See SE 2.116 .273v; JdT, *Opusculum*, pp. 272–73. Turrecremata contradicted Innocent IV, see Tierney *Church and State*, pp. 147–49. Turrecremata's contemporary Dominicus de Dominicis defended the Donation against the criticisms of Lorenzo Valla, see Domenico Maffei, *La donazione di Constantino nei giuristi medievali* (Milan, 1964) 310–12; Hubert Jedin, *Studien über Domenico de' Domenichi* (Wiesbaden, 1957), pp. 90–94.

34. CSD D96.c10.q3 (1:646); *SE* 2.113 .265r. Aegidius Romanus, *De ecclesiastica potestate*, pp. 86–111; Johannes Parisiensis, *De regia potestate*, pp. 96–97.

35. "De ratione cuiuscunque perfecti principatus est habere iurisdictionem coactivam. Sed principatus ecclesiasticus est maximus perfectus. . . . Ergo principatus ecclesiasticus habet iurisdictionem coactivam," SE 2.46.159r; "Christus commisit Petro regimen ecclesie totum quod necessarium erat et expediebat ad regimen totius ecclesiae. Et quia utraque potestas spiritualis, et temporalis est ad hoc necessaria: ideo utranque potestatem contulit Petro," SE 2.116.271v–272r. C.N.S., Woolf, *Bartolus of Saxoferrato: His Position in the History of Medieval Political Thought* (Cambridge, 1913), pp. 70–101; Johannes Polemar, "*De civili dominio clericorum*," Vat. lat. 5609 fols. 329r–361r.

36. *SE* 2.114 .268r–v; CSD D90.c2 (1:589), D96.c11 (1:648). Theeuws, "Les relations," p. 150; Dublanchy, "Turrecremata et le pouvoir du pape," pp. 93–95.

37. "Pluralitas principatum quorum unus non subest alteri. non est bona, sed non sic est in propositio, quoniam inter omnes Christianos principatus potestas principatus secularis aliquomodo subest potestati iurisdictionis spiritualis sive ecclesiasticae," SE 1.89.99r; "quia iurisdictiones temporalis, scilicet et spiritualis licet sint distincte non sunt tamen contrarie; quod patet; quia unum contrarium non ordinatur ad aliud immo corrumpit ipsum iurisdictio autem temporalis ordinatur ad spiritualem," SE 2.116.272v. CSD D96.c6 (1:637–43); *SE* 1.92 .109r. Watt, *Theory of Papal Monarchy*, pp. 1–8.

38. JdT, *Questiones evangeliorum de tempore et de sanctis* (Basel, 1484), in festo beati Ambrosii q. 3. Theeuws, "Les relations," p. 141; Tierney, *Church and State*, pp. 13–15; Ullmann, *Growth of*

Papal Government, pp. 14–31.

39. "Quemadmodum se habet potestas spiritualis ad secularem, sed omnis praesidet corpori, non econverso, ergo spiritualis potestas est superior terrenam, et ecclesiastica super secularem," CSD D10.c3 (1:96); see D10.c5 (1:97); *SE* 1.90.101v. Theeuws, "Les relations," p. 141; Joseph A. Hergenröther, *Katholische Kirche und Christlicher Staat in ihres geschichtlichen Entwicklung und in Beziehung auf die Fragen der Gegenwart* (1872; rpt. Stuttgart, 1968), 1:391, n. 3; Lewis, *Medieval Political Ideas,* 2:532–33, 580–85.

40. "Ergo potestatis spiritualis et maxime papae qui est universalis dux et rector populi Christiani est dirigere et regulare praecipere atque leges dare potestati seculari quibus in administratione sui officii dirigatur in finem ultimum felicitatis aeterne. Et secundum hoc Romanus pontifex se habet ad reges principes tanquam architectonicus ad artifices, ille enim propter quid et regulas iudicandi scit, isti autem scilicet artifices mechanici tanquam experti in multis ipsum quia sciunt propter quid autem ignorat, propter quod debet illa papa leges dare secundum quas debent iurisdictionem suam exequi ac populam suum regere in ordine ad beatitudinem supernaturalem," SE 2.114.265v. On the achivment of man's temporal end, see CSD D96.c10 (1:646). Theeuws, "Les relations," pp. 167, 171; Dublanchy, "Turrecremata et le pouvoir du pape," pp. 91–92.

41. "Principaliter sua potestas iudicandi ad spirituales causas se extendit. Tamen secundarii et ex consequenti etiam suum iudicium . . . se extendit ad questiones seculares," CSD D10.c8 (1:100); see CSD D96.c6 (1:637–43); *SE* 2.114 .272v. Theeuws, "Les relations," pp. 146–49; Dublanchy, "Turrecremata et le pouvoir du pape," pp. 89–90.

42. CSD D96.c6 (1:637–43); *SE* 2.114 .266v, 268v, 273r–v. The *ratione peccati* argument was much used by Innocent III, see Watt, *Theory of Papal Monarchy,* pp. 34–58.

43. "Est autem authoritas iubendi occidere maleficos penes imperatores sive seculares principes divine legi obediant, exhortatio. unde Bernardus in IIII lib. de consideratione ad Eugenium ostendit qualiter uterque gladius est ecclesiae materialis et spiritualis. et dicit quod ad ipsum pertinet gladius materialis non quantum ad iussum sed quantum ad nutum," CSD D50.c5.q1 (1:400); see D96.c6 (1:637–43); *SE* 2.114 .269v; JdT, *"Tractatus contra principales errores perfidi Machometti et Turcorum sive Sarracenorum,"* Vat. lat. 974 fols. 18ra–55ra at 54va–55ra. Alfonso Maria Stickler, "Il *gladius* negli atti dei concilii et dei RR. Pontefici, sino a Graziano e Bernardo di Clairvaux," *Salesianum* 13 (1951): 441–44; James Brundage, *Medieval Canon Law and the Crusader* (Madison, Wis., 1969), pp. 19–29, 192–94.

44. *SE* 2.114 .267r. Edward M. Peters, *The Shadow King* (New Haven, 1970), pp. 30–80, 116–34, 210–45.

45. CSD D96.c6 (1:637–43).

46. *SE* 2.113 .264r, 2.114 .266v–267v; CSD D10.c8 (1:100), D96.c6 (1:637–43), C15.q6c3q3 (3:71). Friedberg 2.243–44: X.

3.1.13; Watt, *Theory of Papal Monarchy*, pp. 40–41.

47.　CSD D10.c4.q2 (1:97), D10.c1 (1:95); *SE* 2.114 .266v. However, prelates could assign cases involving clerics to lay courts; and clerics who sued in a lay court accepted its jurisdiction, see CSD D96.c1.q2 (1:635), D96.c5 (1:637), D96.c11 (1:648). Brian Tierney, "*Tria quippe distinguit iudicia:* A Note on Innocent III's Decretal *Per venerabilem*," *Speculum* 37 (1962): 48–59.

48.　"Romanus pontifex iure divino habere videtur iurisdictionem temporalem aliquo modo videlicet nobiliori et excellentiori quam potestates secularies: quoniam ad eum iure summi sacerdotii spectat declarare diffinire, et iudicare dubia et ambigua circa quascunque actiones hominum personales quae inter iudices inferiores sive clericos, sive seculares variantur," SE 2.114.268r. See CSD D96.c6 (1:637–43). Watt, *Theory of Papal Monarchy*, pp. 92–105.

49.　"Quia vacante imperio ipse habet iurisdictionem in temporalibus ut in c. licet de foro competenti," SE 2.114.269r. Friedberg 2.250: X.2.2.10; Watt, *Theory of Papal Monarchy*, pp. 41–43.

50.　*SE* 2.46 .158r–159v; CSD D18.c7 (1:159). Carlyle et al., *Medieval Political Thought*, 5:245–49.

51.　"Non modo escommunicare potest. seculares principes sed etiam ipsis in contumacia perserverantibus subditor eorum a sacramento absolvere ne eis fidelitatem observant," SE 2.114.267v. Turrecremata followed Petrus de Palude's doctrine on deposition, see SE 2.114.267r; CSD C15.q6.c3.q2 (3:71). Petrus de Palude, *Tractatus de potestate papae*, pp. 130, 139. Theeuws, "Les relations," p. 146. Turrecremata noted that excommunication of a ruler could entail his deposition, see *SE* 2.114.269v. A penitent prince could recover his throne, however, see CSD C15.q6.c4.q1 (3:71–72). The relationship of excommunication to deposition had a tangled history in canon law, see Peters, *The Shadow King*, pp. 34–35, 44–45, 116–24.

52.　"Quia negligentibus imperatoribus constantinopolitanis subvenire et patrocinari ecclesiae romane: que graviter opprimebatis ab astulpho rege longobardorum: papa Stephanus secundus transtulit imperium romanum a grecis in germanos: et potestatem ac ius eligendi regem imperatorem certis principibus alemanie contulit . . . c. venerabilem," CSD D96.c6 (1:640), see D93.c24 (1:625–26). Friedberg 2.79–82: X. 1.6.34; P. A. van den Baar, *Die kirchliche Lehre der Translatio Imperii Romani* (Rome, 1956), pp. 99–111; Watt, *Theory of Papal Monarchy*, pp. 35–36. Imperial apologists described the papal role as that of a coronation functionary, see Lewis, *Medieval Political Ideas*, 1:310–12, 2:460–62.

53.　"Ostendimus rationabili causa et necessitate maium urgente: posset hanc translationem de imperio aut de aliis regnis facere nihilominus non sequitur propter hoc: quod imperium aut alia regula secundum institutionem suam dependeant a papa," CSD D96.c10.q3 (1:646).

54.　Rivière, *Le probleme*, p. 373–74; Stephan Lederer, *De spanische Cardinal Johann von Torquemada: Sein Leben und seine Schriften*

(Frieburg, 1879), pp. 204–5. This was, on the contrary, an attenuated papalist theory, according to Francis Oakley, *The Political Thought of Pierre d'Ailly* (New Haven, 1964), pp. 40–41; MC 127.

55. Grabmann, "Studien über den Einfluss," pp. 130–32.

56. Dublanchy, "Turrecramata et le pouvoir du pape," pp. 74–82.

57. Michele Maccarone, *Vicarius Christi* (Rome, 1952), pp. 269–75, 279: Theeuws, "Les relations," p. 177; Giovanni Pilati, *Chiesa e stato nei primi quindici secoli* (Rome, 1961), pp. 357–59, 368.

58. John Clement Rager, *Political Philosophy of Blessed Cardinal Bellarmine* (Washington, D.C., 1926), pp. 71–73; Johannes A. Cantini, *De autonomia judicis secularis et de Romani pontificis plenitudine potestatis in temporalibus secundum Innocentium IV* (Turin, 1962); Watt, *Theory of Papal Monarchy*, pp. 49–56; Jacques Maritain, *The Things That Are Not Caesar's* (London, 1930), pp. 127–31; Joseph Lecler, *The Two Sovereignties* (New York, 1952), pp. 75–78.

59. Thomas Sherrer Rose Boase, *Boniface VIII* (London, 1933), pp. 297–301; Guillaume Mollatt, *The Popes at Avignon*, trans. Janet Love (New York, 1952), pp. 190–256.

60. Albert Frederick Pollard, *Factors in Modern History* (London, 1907), pp. 52–78; Jack H. Hexter, *Reappraisals in History* (New York, 1961), pp. 26–44.

61. Sidney Z. Ehler and John B. Morrall, *Church and State Through the Centuries* (London, 1954), pp. 112–21, 125–31; Noel Valois, *Histoire de la Pragmatique Sanction de Bourges sous Charles VII* (Paris, 1906).

62. "Quia non solum praejudicaret primatui apostolicae sedis, sed etiam liberate totius ecclesiae, quia cum clerici et praelati pro majori parte propter peccata nostra nichil faciant in conciliis, nisi iuxta mandata suorum principium," JdT, *Super petitione domini regis Franciae, ut aliud tertium celebraretur universale concilium*, Mansi 35.43–56 at 47. See Aeneas Silvius Piccolomini (Pius II), *De gestis concilii Basiliensis*, ed. Denys Hay and W. K. Smith (Oxford, 1967), pp. 173–75, who described Panormitanus as reluctantly following Aragonese instructions to oppose the deposition of Eugenius IV.

63. "Potestas autem regalis cum ordinata est nunquam desideat a potestate sacerdotali sed ipsi congruit et concordat," CSD D96.c10.q1 (1:644). Most canonists thought the two powers were coordinate, see Watt, *Theory of Papal Monarchy*, pp. 136–37.

64. "De ista questione est glo. notabilis in c. latores de clerico excommunicato ministrante, et in c.1. de tempo. ordina. et ibi ponit glo. versum. Ob populum multum crimen pertransit inultum. Sequitur alia conclusio. quod idem dicendum sit de principe: quem sequitur multitudo. Tolerandum est enim peccatum eius: si sine scandalo multitudinis puniri non posset: nisi forte esset tale peccatum principis: quod magis noceret multitudini spiritualiter, vel corporaliter quam scandalum: quod exinde timeretur. unde al. super illud Mat. XI. de zinzanis. dicit multitudo non est excommunicanda nec princeps populi," CSD D50.c25.q1 (1:414), see C11.q3.c94 (2:438).

65. CSD D10.c5 (1:97). Turrecremata used the same argument to prove that the spiritual (sun) did not produce the temporal (moon), see CSD D96.c10.q3 (1:646). Watt, *Theory of Papal Monarchy*, p. 117.

66. "Si Imperator catholicus est filius papae non potest esse iudex ordinarius patris sui, filius enim patrem non corrigit, sed econtra . . . papa non est de foro Imperatoris nec ratione papatus quem non tenet ab Imperio, sed a solo Deo . . . si Imperator donationem fecit de temporalibus ipsa tamen donationem liberam eam fecit, nec fecit papam feudatorium aut emphyteolatum, aut vassalum," SE 2.95.230r–v; CSD D63.c33 (1:484). See Knut Wolfgang Nörr, *Kirche und Konzil bei Nicolaus de Tudeschis (Panormitanus)* (Cologne, 1964), pp. 66–68. However, Cusa described the emperor as the pope's feudal lord, see Sigmund, *Cusa*, pp. 198–99.

67. CSD D10.c2 (1:96), D10.c7 (1:99), D19.c3.q4 (1:166), D79.c8 (1:526).

68. "Patrone aliqua beneficia conferant, ex gratis, eis data a praelatis ecclesie hoc habent," CSD D10.c5 (1:98).

69. CSD D18.c13 (1:161), D50.c11 (1:406–7), D63.c1 (1:470–71), D63.c15 (1:475). Even the Gregorian reformers did not challenge local rights of patronage, see Tellenbach, *Church, State, and Christian Society*, pp. 67–76.

70. "Authoritatem Imperatores, sive Reges dare non possunt cum de disponendis ecclesiasticis rebus non habeant facultatem" CSD D17.c1.q3 (1:149); "Ecclesia non solvit tributum imperatori, aut principibus secularibus in recognitionem dominii, vel subiectionis, sed solum pro pace, et quietate servanda, quam ipse Imperator, et principes seculares tueri," SE 1.92.104r. Turrecremata cited the payment of the temple tax (Matt. 7:24–27), the injunction "Render unto Caesar, etc." (Mark 12:13–16), and the text "Be subject to the king" (1 Pet. 2:13–15), see *SE* 2.96 .231r–v; CSD C25.q1.c10 (3:316). These taxes applied only to lay gifts of lands and monies, not to tithes and other purely ecclesiastical revenues, see *SE* 1.92 .104r. Tierney, *Church and State*, pp. 178–79.

71. JdT, *Questiones evangeliorum*, in festo sancti Gregorii q. 3; idem, "*Reprobationes trigintaocto articulorum quos tenent Usiti de Maldevis*," Vat. lat. 974 fols. 71r–94v at 79v; *SE* 2.89 .220v; CSD D70.c1.q4 (1:499).

72. "Intelligitur de illis, qui habent regalia a principe. Isti. enim. possunt se excusare [from a synod] quia tenetur reddere Caesari quae sunt Cesaris, et quae sunt Dei Deo. Si. enim. Episcopus in regalibus subsit principi, et principes primo praecipit ei, ut vadat secum in expeditione, tenetur ei obedire, ratione regalium. Et si tali causa ad concilium non iverit ad vocationem Metropolitani non punientem. . . . Sed numquid ita erit si a Papa vocetur. Respondetur, quod non, quia advocationem papae semper veniret primo, etiam si ante sit citatus a principe," CSD D18.c13 (1:161). For a reaffirmation of the condemnation of lay investiture, see CSD D63.c7 (1:472). Sigmund, *Cusa*, pp. 208–9; Robert Benson, *The Bishop-Elect* (Princeton, 1968), pp. 203–372.

73. Franciscus de Zabarella, *"De schismatibus authoritate impera-toris tollendis,"* in Simon Schard, ed., *De iurisdictione, authoritate, et praeeminentia imperiale, ac potestate ecclesiastica* (Basel, 1956), pp. 691–93; Hermann Heimpel, *Dietrich von Niem* (Münster, 1932), pp. 122–23; Georg Erler, *Dietrich von Niheim* (Leipzig, 1887), pp. 345–67; Sigmund, *Cusa,* pp. 108–9; Joseph von Aschbach, *Ges-chichte Kaiser Sigismund* (1838–46; rpt. Stuttgart, 1964) vols. 2, 4; Odilo Engels, "Der Reichsdanke auf dem Konstanzer Konzil," *Historische Jahrbuch* 76 (1966): 80–106.

74. "Ceterum etiam quod etsi aliquando Imperatorum iussa legatur convenisse episcopos non tamen talium episcoporum con-ventu concilio universalia venient dicenda nisi fulta essent auc-toritate Romani pontificis," SE 3.8.281r. "Imperator enim non potest convocare Episcopos ad concilium nisi de auctoritate Pa-pae," CSD D17 post c6 (1:155). On Constantine, see CSD D15.c1, pt. 2 (1:134).

75. *Comm.* ad D.17 ante c.1 q.3 (I 149), "Si vero Cardinales nollent hoc facere. Imperator, et principes christiani, quibus ec-clesie tutela commissa est, possent hoc facere," CSD D17 ante c1q3 (1:149). See Sigmund, *Cusa,* p. 173.

76. "Ubi vero ipsi [cardinales] nollent aut negligentes fuerunt, ipsi praelati ecclesiae habentes zelum dei possent se congregare ad incendum ecclesiae extinguendum, aut ipse Imperator cuius interest ut pax sit in urbe, et fortius in toto orbe, quae esse non potest stante contentione super summi pontificato dicent Christo Matt. Undecimo. Omne regnum in se divisum desolabitur," SE 1.8.283r; "Peccatum scismatis in rebus humanis est perniciossis-simum, quia dissolvit totum regimen humanae societatis," CSD C24.q1.c21 (3:276).

77. CSD D96.c4 (1:636–37); *SE* 3.25 .300v. The emperor had precedence in the pope's absence, see SE 4, pt. 1, 10.367v–368r, 3.14 .290v, 3.15 .291v, 3.25 .300r–301r. See also Sigmund, *Cusa,* pp. 202–8.

78. *SE* 4, pt. 1, 9 .365r–367v, 4, pt. 1, 10 .368v–369r, 2.103 .244r, 2.106 .247r–v. See Nörr, *Panormitanus,* pp. 92, 128.

79. MC 127.

80. Claire Cross, *The Royal Supremacy in the Elizabethan Church* (London, 1969), p. 120; Kenneth Pickthorn, *Early Tudor Govern-ment: Henry VII* (Cambridge, 1934), pp. 174–82; Helmut Georg Königsberger, *The Government of Sicily Under Philip II of Spain* (London, 1951), pp. 144–49; Ehler et al., *Church and State,* pp. 134–44.

Conclusion

1. Charles M. Daley, *Dominican Incunabula in the Library of Con-gress* (Washington, D.C., 1932), p. 78; Leopold David Ettlinger, *The Sistine Chapel before Michelangelo* (Oxford, 1965), p. 111, n. 4. Palmericus owned Vat. lat. 2701, the *Summa de ecclesia.* For the Vatican's holding of Turrecremata manuscripts in the sixteenth

century, see Vat. lat. 3957 fols. 68v–71v; Vat. lat. 3965 fols. 8v–9v. This book employs the edition of the Summa mentioned above (Venice, 1561).

2. Edward A. Ryan, "Three Early Treatises on the Church," *Theological Studies* 5 (1944): 113–40; WE 1–5; Johannes de Ragusio, *Tractatus de ecclesia*, Basel Univ. Bibl. A.I.25 fols. 303v–431r.

3. WE 34; Antonio Perez Goyena, "La primera *Summa de ecclesia*," *Estudios ecclesiasticos* 2 (1923): 260–61.

4. Anton Hermann Chroust and James A. Corbett, "The Fifteenth Century 'Review of Politics' of Laurentius de Arezzo," *Medieval Studies* 11 (1949): 75; Ulrich Horst, "Grenzen der päpstlichen Autoritat: Konziliare Elemente in der Ekklesiologie des Johannes Torquemada," *Freiburger Zeitschrift für Philosophie und Theologie* 19 (1972): 362; Hubert Jedin, *A History of the Council of Trent*, trans. Ernest Graf (London, 1949–57), 1:86; Heribert Smolinsky, *Domenico de' Domenichi und seine Schrift "De potestate pape et termino eius"* (Münster, 1976), pp. 134, 268, 339, 366–90, 393–95, 402, 405. Black (MC 102) erroneously describes Turrecremata as the creator of a novel ideology of papal absolutism.

5. Karl Binder, *Konzilsgedanken bei Kardinal Juan de Torquemada O.P.* (Vienna, 1976), pp. 212–13; Hubert Jedin, "Giovanni Gozzandini, ein Konziliarist am Hofe Julius II," *Römisches Quartalschrift* 47 (1939): 193–267; Joseph Klotzner, *Kardinal Dominikus Jacobazzi und sein Konzilswerk* (Rome, 1948), pp. 72–77; Jedin, *Trent* 1:32–100; WE 196–97; Remigius Bäumer, *Nachwirkungen des Konziliaren Gedankens in der Theologie und Kanonistik "des" frühen 16. Jahrhunderts* (Münster, 1971).

6. Remigius Bäumer, "Zum Kirchenverstädnis Albert Pigges: Ein Beitrag zur Ekklesiologie der vortridentischen Kontroverstheologie," in *Volk Gottes: Festgabe für Joseph Höfer*, ed. idem and Heimo Dolch (Freiburg, 1967), pp. 308–9; Jedin, *Trent*, 1:87–88. Turrecremata's authority was cited both to attack and to defend the marriage bond of Henry VIII and Catherine of Aragon, see Sigismundus Loffredus et al., *"Consilium in causa Reginae Britanniae,"* Barb. Lat. 1492 fols. 236rb–250vb at 240vb; Henry Ansgar Kelly, *The Matrimonial Trials of Henry VIII* (Stanford, 1976), pp. 11–13, 15, 26, 225, 235, 285; Edward Surtz, *The Works and Days of John Fisher* (Cambridge, Mass., 1967), pp. 169–70, 353, 357–61, 370.

7. Johannes Eck, *Explanatio psalmi vigesimi (1538)*, ed. Bernhard Walde (Münster, 1928), pp. 43–48; Sylvester Prierias, *De irrefragibili veritate Romanae ecclesiae*, in Rocaberti 19:227–367; Ambrosius Catherinus Politus, *Apologia pro veritate fidei ac valde pestifera Martini Luteri dogma (1520)*, ed. Joseph S. Schweitzer (Münster, 1955); Thomas de Vio (Caietanus), *De divina institutione pontificatus Romani pontificis (1521)*, ed. Friedrich Lauchert (Münster, 1925); Anton Bodem, *Das Wesen der Kirche nach Kardinal Cajetan* (Trier, 1971); Linus Hofmann, "Die Zügehörigkeit zur Kirche nach dem Lehre des Kardinals Thomas de Vio Cajetan," in *Ekklesia: Festschrift für Bischof Dr. Matthias Wehr*, ed. Theologische Fakultät, Trier

(Trier, 1962), pp. 221–33; Binder, *Konzilsgedanken*, pp. 217–19; *"Tractatus de potestate papae et concilli,"* Vat. lat. 3527 fols. 51r–74v at 62v. Benedictus de Castro Sangri, *De heresibus et heresiarchis alias rite et recte damnatis et reprobatis* (Venice, 1520?) is composed of excerpts from *SE* bk. 4, pt. 2.

8. Bartolommeo Guidiccioni, *"Tractatus de beneficiis,"* Barb. lat. 1160 fols. 2v, 9v–10v, 15r; Barb. lat. 1161 fols. 723r; Hubert Jedin, "Concilio e riforma nel pensiero del Cardinal Bartolomeo Guidiccioni," *Rivista di storia della chiesa in Italia* 2 (1948): 38–44.

9. Paulino Castañeda Delgado, *La teocracia pontifical y la conquista de America* (Vitoria, 1968), pp. 234–41; Venancio Carro, *La teologia y los teologos-juristas españoles ante la conquista de America* (Madrid, 1944), 1:319–45; Bernice Hamilton, *Political Thought in Sixteenth Century Spain* (Oxford, 1963), pp. 171–76; Francisco de Vitoria, *Comentarios a la Secunda Secundae de S. Tomas,* ed. Vicente Beltran de Heredia (Salamanca, 1935), 5:99; Ulrich Horst, "Die Ekklesiologie des Cursus Theologicus Salamanticensis," *Römische Quartalschrift* 69 (1974) 55, n. 35, 61, n. 57; Bartolomé de las Casas, *In Defense of the American Indians,* trans. Stafford Poole (De Kalb, Ind., 1974), p. 253; idem, *De exemptione, cum monitione,* in Helen Rand Parish and Harold Weidmann, *Las Casas in Mexico* (Madrid, 1981); Alonso de la Vera Cruz, *Defense of the Indians: Their Rights,* ed. Ernest Burrus (Rome, 1968), pp. 292–93, 300–301, 403; Binder, *Konzilsgedanken,* pp. 220–23; Alonso de la Vera Cruz, *Speculum coniugiorum* (Milan, 1599), pp. 86–87, 161, 165, 242, 265, 390. Vitoria felt free to disagree with Turrecremata, see Juan F. Radrizzani Goñi, *Papa y obispos en la potestad de jurisdiction segun el pensamiento de Francisco de Vitoria O.P.* (Rome, 1967), pp.278–79. Turrecremata was cited, probably second hand, in Hugo Grotius, *The Freedom of the Seas,* trans. Ralph Van Deman Magoffin (New York, 1916), p. 16, n. 3.

10. Francisco Elias de Tejada "El, concepto del derecho natural en los commentaristas hispanos de Graciano," *Studia Gratiana* 2 (1954): 85–93.

11. Mario Midali, *Corpus Christi Mysticum apud Dominicum Bañez Eiuque Fontes* (Rome, 1962), pp. 30–32, 58, 69, 119, 191; Francisco Suarez, *De legibus* (Madrid, 1971–77), 1:53, 203, 292, 304; 2:30; 3:13, 277, 293, 306; 4:57, 233; 5:195–96; 6:50, 72, 129, 132, 832; Binder, *Konzilsgedanken,* p. 225; Carro, *La teologia,* 2:67.

12. Angelus Walz, *I Domenicani al Concilio di Trento* (Rome, 1961), pp. 153, 184, 221, 301, 308; Jedin, *Trent* 1:40–42, 45, 267, 347; 2:45, 267, 347; Hamilton, *Political Thought,* pp. 176–80; Perez, "La primera *Summa,*" pp. 262–65; Diego Lainez, *Disputationes Tridentinae,* ed. Hartmann Grisar (Innsbruck, 1886), 1:139, 199, 249, 250; 2:470.

13. Binder, *Konzilsgedanken,* pp. 223–29; Johannes Baptista Bičiunas, *Doctrina ecclesiologica S. Roberti Bellarmini cum illa Joannis Card. de Turrecremata comparata* (Rome, 1963); Joseph Fenton, "The Theology of the General Council," in *The General Council,* ed. William Joseph McDonald (Washington, D.C., 1962), pp. 152–57.

14. Jean de Launoy, *Opera omnia* (Geneva, 1731), vol. 3, pt. 2, p. 570; Perez, "La primera *Summa*," pp. 267–68; Victor Martin, *Les origines du Gallicanisme* (Paris, 1939), 2:125–49.

15. *De summi pontificis infallibilitate personali* (Naples, 1870); Johannes de Turrecremata (JdT), *De inerrantia Romani pontificis (ex cura illius opere Summa de potestate papali)* (Turin, 1870); Johannes Thomas Chilardi, *De plenitudine potestatis Romani pontificis in ecclesia (opusculum ex operibus I. de Turrecremata)* (Turin, 1870); Stephan Lederer, *Der spanische Cardinal Johann von Torquemada: Sein Leben und seine Schriften* (Freiburg, 1879), pp. v–vi.

16. JdT, *Tractatus de veritate conceptionis beatissime virginis,* ed. Edward Bouverie Pusey (Brussels, 1966); Edward Bouverie Pusey, *First letter to the Very Rev. J.H. Newman D.D. in Explanation Chiefly in Regard to the Reverential Love Due to the Ever-blessed Theotokos and the Doctrine of her Immaculate Conception with an Analysis of Cardinal de Turrecremata's Work on the Immaculate Conception* (London, 1869). For others' use of Turrecremata's authority before the First Vatican Council, see Hans Schneider, *Der Konziliarismus als Problem der neueren katholischen Theologie* (Berlin, 1976), pp. 124, 131.

17. Angelus Walz, "Von Dominikaner Stammbäumer," *AFP* 34 (1964): 234–39.

18. *The Documents of Vatican II,* ed. Walter M. Abbott (New York, 1966), pp. 41–42, 398–9; Pacifico Massi, *Il magistero infallibile de papa nella teologia di Giovanni da Torquemada* (Turin, 1957), p. 76; Brian Tierney, *Origins of Papal Infallibility 1150–1300* (Leiden, 1972), p. 271; Binder, *Konzilsgedanken,* pp. 229–40.

BIBLIOGRAPHY

Selected Bibliography

Primary Sources—Manuscripts

Dominicus de Dominicis. *"Consilium in materia creationis cardinalium ad petitionem summi domini Pii secundi."* Barb. lat. 1487 fols. 301r–312v.

Johannes de Ragusio. *"Tractatus de ecclesia."* Basel Univ. Bibl. A.I.29 fols. 303v–431r.

Johannes de Turrecremata. *"De paupertate et perfectione."* Vat. lat. 974 fols. 63r–65r.

———. *"Expositio regulae Sancti Benedicti."* Chigi lat. D.VI.91; D.VI.92; D.VI.93; D.VI.94.

———. *"Flores sententiarum de auctoritate summi pontificis."* Vat. lat. 2580 fols. 87v–93v.

———. *"Impugnationes quorundam propositionum quas quidam Alphonsus de Matricali possuit et asseruit."* Vat. lat. 976 fols. 118r–131v.

———. *"Libellus de nuptis spiritualibus."* Vat. lat. 974 fols. 68r–74r.

———. *"Libellus velociter compositus et editus contra certos hereticos noviter impugnantes paupertatem Christi et suorum apostolorum."* Vat. lat. 974 fols. 55v–62r.

———. *"Novus tractatus super paupertatem Christi."* Vat. lat. 974 fols. 62v–63r.

———. *"Reprobationes trigintaocto articulorum quos tenent heretici Usiti de Maldevis."* Vat. lat. 974 fols. 71r–94v.

———. *"Sermo de Sancto Ambrogio."* Palat. lat. 976 fols. 24v–30r.

———. *"Tractatus contra principales errores perfidi Machometti et Turcorum sive Sarracenorum."* Vat. lat. 974 fols. 18r–55r.

———. *"Tractatus de aqua benedicta."* Vat. lat. 976 fols. 97r–101r.

———. *"Tractatus de sacramento eucharistie."* Vat. lat. 976 fols. 131v–162r.

Rodrigo Sánchez de Arévalo. *"Contra tres propositiones concilii Basiliensis."* Vat. lat. 4154.

———. *"Dialogus de remediis schismatis."* Vat. lat. 4002.

Primary Sources—Printed Works

Antoninus de Florentia. *Summa theologica.* 4 vols. 1740. Reprint. Graz, 1959.
Bremond, Antoninus, ed. *Bullarium Ordinis Fratrum Praedicatorum.* 8 vols. Rome, 1729–40.
Deutsche Reichstagsakten. Vol. 13, edited by Gustav Beckmann (Stuttgart, 1925). Vol. 14, edited by Helmut Weigel. Stuttgart, 1933.
Friedberg, Aemilius, ed. *Corpus iuris canonici.* 2 vols. Leipzig, 1879.
Guido Terreni.*Quaestio de magisterio infallibili Romani pontificis.* Edited by Bartolomé Maria Xiberta. Münster, 1926.
Guilelmus ab Ockham. *Dialogus de potestate papae et imperatoris.* 1614. Reprint. Turin, 1966.
Haller, Johannes; Beckmann, Gustav; Wackernagel, Rudolf; Coggiola, Giulio; Herre, Hermann; Dannenbauer, Heinrich; Hartmann, Alfred; Wackernagel, Hans Georg; and Pérouse, Gabriel, eds. *Concilium Basiliense.* 8 vols. Basel, 1896–1936.
Herveus Natalis. *De iurisdictione.* Edited by Ludwig Hödl. Munich, 1959.
Jean Gerson. *"De potestate ecclesiastica."* In *Oeuvres complètes,* edited by Palémon Glorieux, vol. 7. Paris, 1965.
Johannes Hus. *Tractatus de ecclesia.* Edited by Samuel Harrison Thomson. Cambridge, 1956.
Johannes De Segovia. *Historia gestorum generalis synodi Basiliensis.* Edited by Wiener Akademie. 2 vols. Vienna, 1878–1935.
Johannes de Turrecremata. *Apparatus super decretum unionis Grecorum.* Edited by Emmanuel Candal. Rome, 1942.
———. *Commentaria super Decreto.* 5 vols. Venice, 1579.
———. *Expositio brevis et utilis super toto psalterio.* Mainz, 1474.
———. *Gratiani Decretorum libri quinque secundum Gregorianos Decretalium libros titulosque distincti.* 2 vols. Rome, 1726.
———. *Meditationes.* Edited by Heinz Zirnbauer. Wiesbaden, 1968.
———. *Oratio synodalis de primatu.* Edited by Emmanuel Candal. Rome, 1954.
———. *Questiones evangeliorum de tempore et de sanctis et Flos theologie.* Basel, 1484.
———. *Summa de ecclesia una cum eiusdem Apparatu super decreto Papae Eugenii IV in Concilio Florentino de unione Graecorum emanato.* Venice, 1561.
———. *Symbolum pro informatione Manichaeorum.* Edited by Nicolas Lopez Martinez and Vicente Proaño Gil. Burgos, 1958.
———. *Tractatus contra Madianitas et Ismaelitas.* Edited by Nicolas Lopez Martinez and Vicente Proaño Gil. Burgos, 1957.
———. *Tractatus de veritate conceptionis beatissime virginis.* Edited by Edward Bouverie Pusey. 1869. Reprint. Brussels, 1966.
Loomis, Louise Ropes. *The Council of Constance.* Edited by John Hine Mundy and Kennerly M. Woody. New York, 1961.
Mansi, Johannes Dominicus, ed. *Sacrorum conciliorum nova et amplissima collectio.* 53 vols. in 58. Paris, 1901–27.

Marsilius of Padua. *The Defender of Peace.* Translated by Alan Gewirth. New York, 1956.

Nicholas de Lyre. *Postilla litteralis super totam bibliam.* 7 vols. Lyons, 1545.

Obermann, Heiko; Zerfoss, Daniel E.; and Courtenay, William J. *Defensorium obedientiae apostolicae et alia documenta.* Cambridge, Mass., 1968.

Petrus de Palude. *Tractatus de potestate papae.* Edited by Petrus Thomas Stella. Zürich, 1966.

Piccolomini, Aeneas Silvius (Pius II). *The Commentaries of Pius II.* Edited by Leona Gabel. 5 vols. Northampton, Mass., 1936–47.

―――. *De gestis concilii Basiliensis.* Edited by Denys Hay and W.K. Smith. Oxford, 1967.

Rocaberti de Pereleda, Johannes Thomas, ed. *Bibliotheca maxima pontificia.* 21 vols. 1698–99. Reprint. Graz, 1969–70.

Sancti Thomae Aquinatis Doctoris Angelici opera omnia iussu impensaque Leonis XIII P.M. edita. Edited by Fratres Praedicatores. 40 vols. Rome, 1882–.

Secondary Sources

Alberigo, Giuseppe. *Cardinalato e collegialità.* Florence, 1969.

―――. "Le origini della dottrina sullo *ius divinum* del cardinalato, 1053–1087." In *Reformata reformanda: Festgabe für Hubert Jedin,* edited by Erwin Iserloh and Konrad Repgen, pp. 39–58. Münster, 1965.

Asis, Agustin de. *Ideas sociopoliticas de Alonso Polo (El Tostado).* Seville, 1955.

Bäumer, Remigius. "Zum Kirchenverstädnis Albert Pigges: Ein Beitrag zur Ekklesiologie der vortridentischen Kontroverstheologie." In *Volk Gottes: Festgabe für Joseph Höfer,* edited by Remigius Bäumer and Heimo Dolch, pp. 306–32. Freiburg, 1967.

―――. "Luthers Ansichten über die Irrtumfähigkeit des Konzils und ihre theologischen Grundlagen." In *Wahrheit und Verkündigung: Michael Schmaus zum 70. Geburtstag,* edited by Leo Scheffczyk, Werner Dettloff, and Richard Heinzmann, pp. 987–1003. Munich, 1967.

Beltran de Heredia, Vicente. "Colección de documentos para illustrar la vida del Cardenal Juan de Torquemada O.P." *Archivum Fratrum Praedicatorum* 7 (1937): 210–45.

―――. *Historia de la Reforma de la Provincia de España (1450–1550).* Rome, 1939.

―――. "Noticias y documentos para la biografía de Cardenal Juan de Torquemada." *Archivum Fratrum Praedicatorum* 30 (1960): 53–148.

Benson, Robert. *The Bishop-Elect.* Princeton, 1968.

Bičiunas, Johannes Baptista. *Doctrina ecclesiologica S. Roberti Bellarmini cum illa Joannis Card. de Turrecremata comparata.* Rome, 1963.

Binder, Karl. "El cardenal Juan de Torquemada y el movimiento de reforma ecclesiastica en el siglo XV." *Revista de teologia* 3 (1953): 42–65.

———. "Kardinal Juan de Torquemada Verfasser der *Nova Ordinatio Decreti Gratiani.*" *Archivum Fratrum Praedicatorum* 22 (1952): 268–93.

———. *Konzilsgedanken bei Kardinal Juan de Torquemada O.P.* Vienna, 1976.

———. "El magistero del sacro palazzo apostolica del Cardinale di Torquemada." *Memorie Domenicane* 71 (1954): 3–24.

———. *Wesen und Eigenschaften der Kirche bei Kardinal Juan de Torquemada O.P.* Innsbruck, 1954.

———. "Zum Schriftheweis in der Kirchentheologie des Kardinals Juan de Torquemada O.P." In *Wahrheit und Verkündigung: Michael Schmaus zum 70. Geburtstag,* edited by Leo Scheffczyk, Werner Dettloff, and Richard Heinzmann, pp. 511–50. Munich, 1967.

Black, Antony. *Monarchy and Community.* Cambridge, 1970.

———. "The Political Ideas of Conciliarism and Papalism." *Journal of Ecclesiastical History* 20 (1964): 45–65.

———. "The Universities and the Council of Basel: Ecclesiology and Tactics." *Annuarium historiae conciliorum* 6 (1974): 341–51.

Ciolini, Gino. *Agostino da Roma (Favaroni d. 1443) e la sua Cristologia.* Florence, 1944.

Congar, Yves. "Aspects ecclésiologiques de la querelle entre mendiants et séculiers dans la seconde moité du xiiie et le début du xive." *Archives d'histoire doctrinale et littéraire* 38 (1961): 35–151.

———. *L'église de Saint Agustin à l'époque moderne.* Paris, 1970.

———. "Status Eccesiae," *Studia Gratiana* 15 (1972): 1–31.

Cook, William R. "John Wycliff and Hussite Theology, 1415–1436." *Church History* 42 (1973): 335–49.

De summi pontificis infallibilitate personali. Naples, 1870.

Dublanchy, Edmond. "Turrecremata et le pouvoir du pape dans le questions temporelles." *Revue Thomiste* 28 (1923): 74–101.

Eckermann, Karla. *Studien zur Geschichte der monarchischen Gedankens im 15. Jahrhunderts.* Berlin, 1933.

Fenton, Joseph. "The Theology of the General Council." In *The General Council,* edited by William Joseph McDonald, pp. 149–82. Washington, D.C., 1962.

Franzen, August. "The Council of Constance: Present State of the Problem." *Concilium* 7:(1965) 29–68.

Fromherz, Uta. *Johannes von Segovia als Geschichtsschreiber des Konzils von Basel.* Basel, 1960.

Garrataschu, Jacinto. "Los manuscritos del Cardenal Juan de Torquemada en la Biblioteca Vaticana." *La Ciencia Tomista* 41 (1930): 188–217, 291–322.

Gill, Joseph. *The Council of Florence.* Cambridge, 1959.

———. *Eugenius IV, Pope of Christian Unity.* Westminster, Md., 1961.

Gomez Canedo, Lino. *Don Juan de Carvajal.* Madrid, 1947.

Grabowski, Stanislaus J. *The Church: An Introduction to the Theology of Saint Augustine*. St. Louis, 1957.

Gremper, Chrysostomus. "Des Kardinals Johann von Torquemada Kommentur zur Regel des heiligen Benedikt." *Studien und Mittelungen zur Geschichte des Benediktinerordens* 45 (1927): ‧ 223–82.

Heinz-Mohr, Gerd. *Unitas Christiana*. Trier, 1958.

Hendrix, Scott H. *Ecclesia in Via*. Leiden, 1974.

———. "In Quest of the *Vera Ecclesia*: The Crises of Late Medieval Ecclesiology." *Viator* 7 (1976): 347–78.

Hödl, Ludwig. *Die Geschichte der Scholastischen Litteratur und der Theologie der Schlüsselgewalt*. Vol. 1. Münster, 1960.

Hofmann, Georg. *Papato, conciliarismo, patriarchato (1438–1439)*. Rome, 1940.

Horst, Ulrich. "Grenzen der päpstlichen Autoritat: Konziliare Elemente in der Ekklesiologie des Johannes Torquemada." *Freiburger Zeitschrift für Philosophie und Theologie* 19 (1972): 361–88.

———. "Papst, Bischofe, und Konzil nach Antonin von Florenz." *Recherches de théologie ancienne et médievale* 32 (1965): 76–111.

———. "Papst und Konzil nach Raphael de Pornaxio." *Freiburger Zeitschrift für Philosophie und Theologie* 15 (1968): 367–402.

Hurley, Michael. "*Scriptura sola*: Wycliff and his Critics." *Traditio* 16 (1960): 275–352.

Izbicki, Thomas M. "Infallibility and the Erring Pope: Guido Terreni and Johannes de Turrecremata." In *Law, Church, and Society: Essays in Honor of Stephan Kuttner*, edited by Kenneth Pennington and Robert Somerville, pp. 97–111. Philadelphia, 1977.

———. "Johannes de Turrecremata: Two Questions on Law." *Tidjschrift voor Rechtsgeschiedenis* 43 (1975): 91–94.

Jacob, Ernest Fraser. "The Bohemians at the Council of Basel, 1433." In *Prague Essays,* edited by Richard William Seton-Watson, pp. 81–123. Oxford, 1949.

Jedin, Hubert. "Juan de Torquemada und das Imperium Romanum." *Archivum Fratrum Praedicatorum* 12 (1942): 274–78.

———. *Studien über Domenico de' Domenichi (1416–1478)*. Wiesbaden, 1957.

Kaminsky, Howard. *A History of the Hussite Revolution*. Berkeley, 1973.

Kuttner, Stephan. "*Cardinalis*: The History of a Canonical Concept." *Traditio* 3 (1945) 129–214.

———. "Pope Lucius III and the Bigamous Archbishop of Palermo." In *Medieval Studies Presented to Aubrey Gwynn S.J.*, edited by John Andrew Watt, John B. Morrall and Francis X. Martin, pp. 409–53. Dublin, 1961.

Lederer, Stephan. *Der spanische Cardinal Johann von Torquemada: Sein Leben und seine Schriften*. Freiburg, 1879.

Lefebvre, Charles. "L'enseignement de Nicolas de Tudeschis et l'autorité pontificale." *Ephemerides Iuris Canonici* 14 (1958):

312–39.

Lopez Martinez, Nicolas. "El cardenal Torquemada y la unidad de la Iglesia." *Burgense* 1 (1960): 45–71.

Maccarone, Michele. *Vicarius Christi.* Rome, 1952.

McCready, William D. "The Papal Sovereign in the Ecclesiology of Augustinus Triumphus." *Medieval Studies* 39 (1977): 177–205.

Maguire, William Edward. *John of Torquemada O.P.: The Antiquity of the Church.* Washington, D.C., 1957.

Massi, Pacifico. *Il magistero infallibile de papa nella teologia di Giovanni Torquemada.* Turin, 1957.

Meersseman, Gilles. *Giovanni da Montenero O.P.: Difensore dei Mendicanti.* Rome, 1936.

Miralles, Manuel Garcia. "El cardenalato de institucion divino y el episcopado en el problema de la succession apostolica según Juan de Torquemada," *XVI semaña española de teologia,* pp. 249–74. Madrid, 1957.

Mirus, Jeffrey A. "On the Deposition of the Pope for Heresy." *Archivum historiae pontificiae* 13 (1975): 231–48.

Mortier, Daniel Antonin. *Histoire des maîtres généraux de l'ordre des Frères Prêcheurs.* 7 vols. Paris, 1903–14.

Moynihan, James M. *Papal Immunity and Liability in the Writings of the Medieval Canonists.* Rome, 1961.

Muldoon, James. *"Extra ecclesiam non est imperium:* The Canonists and the Legitimacy of the Secular Power." *Studia Gratiana* 9 (1963): 553–80.

Nörr, Knut Wolfgang. *Kirche und Konzil bei Nicolaus de Tudeschis (Panormitanus).* Cologne, 1964.

Oakley, Francis. *Council Over Pope?* New York, 1969.

———. *The Political Thought of Pierre d'Ailly.* New Haven, 1954.

Obermann, Heiko. *The Harvest of Medieval Theology.* Cambridge, Mass., 1963.

Pascoe, Louis B. *Jean Gerson: Principles of Church Reform.* Leiden, 1973.

Petry, Roy C. "Unitive Reform Principles of the Late Medieval Conciliarists." *Church History* 31 (1962): 164–81.

Post, Gaines. "Copyists' Errors and the Problem of Papal Dispensations *contra statutum generale ecclesiae* or *contra statum generale ecclesiae* According to the Decretists and Decretalists ca. 1150–1234." *Studia Gratiana* 9 (1966): 359–405.

———. *Studies in Medieval Legal Thought.* Princeton, 1964.

Proaño Gil, Vicente. "Doctrina de Juan de Torquemada sobre el concilio." *Burgense* 1 (1960): 73–96.

Quétif, Jacques and Echard, Jacques. *Scriptores Ordinis Praedicatorum.* 2 vols. in 4. Paris, 1719.

Ryan, Edward A. "Three Early Treatises on the Church." *Theological Studies* 5 (1944): 113–40.

Sigmund, Paul. *Nicholas of Cusa and Medieval Political Thought.* Cambridge, Mass., 1963.

Spinelli, Lorenzo. *La Vacanza della Sede Apostolica dalle origini al Concilio Tridentino.* Milan, 1955.

Spinka, Matthew. *John Hus' Concept of the Church*. Princeton, 1966.

Stockmann, Johannes Franciscus Robertus. *Joannes de Turrecremata O.P.: vita eiusque doctrina de corpore Christi mystico*. Bologna, 1951.

Stieber, Joachim W. *Pope Eugenius IV, the Council of Basel, and the Secular and Ecclesiastical Authorities in the Empire*. Leiden, 1978.

Suarez Fernandez, Luis. *Castilla el cisma y la crisis conciliar*. Madrid, 1970.

Tavard, Georges Henri. *Holy Writ or Holy Church?* London, 1959.

Theeuws, Paul. "Jean de Turrecremata: Les relations entre l'Eglise et le pouvoir civil d'après un théologien du XVe siècle." *L'organisation corporative du Moyen Age à la fin de l'Ancien Régime*, pp. 137–78. Louvain, 1943.

Thomson, John A.F. "Papalism and Conciliarism in Antonio Roselli's *Monarchia*." *Medieval Studies* 37 (1975):445–58.

Tierney, Brian. *Foundations of the Conciliar Theory*. Cambridge, 1955.

———. "Ockham, the Conciliar Theory and the Canonists." *Journal of the History of Ideas* 15 (1954):40–70.

———. " 'Only the Truth Has Authority': The Problem of 'Reception' in the Decretists and in Johannes de Turrecremata." In *Law, Church, and Society: Essays in Honor of Stephan Kuttner* edited by Kenneth Pennington and Robert Somerville, pp. 60–86. Philadelphia, 1977.

———. *Origins of Papal Infallibility, 1150–1350*. Leiden, 1972.

———. "Pope and Council: Some New Decretist Texts." *Medieval Studies* 19 (1957): 197–218.

Trame, Richard. *Rodrigo Sánchez de Arévalo, 1404–1470*. Washington, D.C., 1958.

Turley, Thomas Peter. "Infallibilists in the Curia of Pope John XXII." *Journal of Medieval History* 1 (1975):71–101.

Ullmann, Walter. *The Growth of Papal Government in the Middle Ages*. 2nd ed. London, 1962.

———. *Principles of Government and Politics in the Middle Ages*. 2nd ed. London, 1966.

Valois, Noel. *Fra Angelico et le Cardinal Jean de Torquemada*. Paris, 1904.

———. *La France et la Grand Schisme d'Occident*. 4 vols. Paris, 1896–1902.

———. *Le pape et le concile, 1418–1450*. 2 vols. Paris, 1909.

Vooght, Paul de. "Esquisse d'un enquêt sur le mot infaillabilité durant la période scholastique." In *L'infaillabilité de l'Eglise*, pp. 99–146. Chevetogne, 1963.

———. *L'hérésie de Jean Hus*. Louvain, 1960.

———. *Hussiana*. Louvain, 1960.

———. *Les pouvoirs du concile et l'autorité du pape*. Paris, 1965.

Watt, John Andrew. "The Constitutional Law of the College of Cardinals: Hostiensis to Johannes Andreae." *Medieval Studies* 33 (1971): 121–51.

———. "The Early Medieval Canonists and the Formation of Con-

ciliar Theory." *Irish Theological Quarterly* 24 (1957):13–31.
———. *The Theory of Papal Monarchy in the Thirteenth Century.* London, 1965.
Wilks, Michael. *"Papa est nomen iurisdictionis:* Augustinus Triumphus and the Papal Vicariate of Christ." *The Journal of Theological Studies,* n.s., 8 (1957): 71–91, 256–71.
———. *The Problem of Sovereignty in the Later Middle Ages.* Cambridge, 1963.
Zuckermann, Charles Abraham. "The Relationship of Universals to Theories of Church Government." *Journal of the History of Ideas* 35 (1975): 579–94.

INDEX